PAUL THE APOSTLE

His Life and Legacy in Their Roman Context

This controversial new biography of the apostle Paul argues for his inclusion in the pantheon of key figures of classical antiquity, along with the likes of Socrates, Alexander the Great, Cleopatra, and Augustus. It first provides a critical reassessment of the apostle's life in its historical context that focuses on Paul's discourse of authority, which was both representative of its Roman context and provocative to his rivals within the Christian movement. It then considers the legend that developed around Paul as the history of his life was elaborated and embellished by later interpreters, creating legends that characterized the apostle variously as a model citizen, an imperial hero, a sexual role model, an object of derision, and an authority to quote from. It is precisely this rewriting of Paul's history into legend that makes the apostle a key transformative figure of classical antiquity.

J. Albert Harrill is Professor of Classics at The Ohio State University. A New Testament scholar, he is the author of *Slaves in the New Testament: Literary, Social, and Moral Dimensions* (2006) and *The Manumission of Slaves in Early Christianity* (1995). He has contributed to numerous reference works on the Bible and Christianity, and his articles have appeared in such journals as *New Testament Studies*, *Journal of Biblical Literature*, *Studia Patristica*, and *Religion and American Culture*.

PAUL THE APOSTLE

HIS LIFE AND LEGACY IN THEIR ROMAN CONTEXT

J. Albert Harrill

The Ohio State University

CAMBRIDGE
UNIVERSITY PRESS

CAMBRIDGE UNIVERSITY PRESS
Cambridge, New York, Melbourne, Madrid, Cape Town,
Singapore, São Paulo, Delhi, Mexico City

Cambridge University Press
32 Avenue of the Americas, New York, NY 10013-2473, USA

www.cambridge.org
Information on this title: www.cambridge.org/9780521757805

First published 2012

Printed in the United States of America

A catalog record for this publication is available from the British Library.

Library of Congress Cataloging in Publication Data

Harrill, James Albert, 1963–
Paul the Apostle : his life and legacy in their Roman context / J. Albert Harrill.
    p. cm.
Includes bibliographical references and index.
ISBN 978-0-521-76764-4 (hardback) – ISBN 978-0-521-75780-5 (paperback)
1. Paul, the Apostle, Saint.   I. Title.
BS2506.3.H37   2012
225.9′2–dc23   2012016337
[B]

ISBN 978-0-521-76764-4 Hardback
ISBN 978-0-521-75780-5 Paperback

for Steven Goldman

"That Saint Paul. . . . He's the one who makes all the trouble."
– Rinaldi in Ernest Hemingway, *A Farewell to Arms*

CONTENTS

FIGURES AND BOXES

FIGURES

BOXES

PREFACE

Writing this book has made me rethink what a historical biography of the apostle Paul should be for students and general readers. That intellectual labor has also gone into teaching the course Paul and His Influence in Early Christianity in its multiple versions to hundreds of undergraduates at Indiana, DePaul, and Creighton Universities for nearly twenty years. The fresh, vigorous dialogue in class with such curious minds, at times astonishingly brilliant, has kept my teaching a challenging and lively experience. Rethinking the historical figure of Paul in his context of the Roman Empire continues to sustain my enthusiasm for New Testament studies.

Let me explain briefly what this book is. I aim to bridge the divide between the findings of professional academics and the expectations of a nonacademic audience. I have written strictly as a historian, drawing conclusions about what we can know from the available evidence rather than accepting the truth claims of a religious faith. When reading this book, I suggest keeping at hand a copy of the New Testament so that you can look up the various biblical passages as they arise in the book's analysis. For nonbiblical writings about Paul, Meeks and Fitzgerald (2007) provides an excellent sourcebook and a potential companion volume.

Books on Paul have an astonishing abundance; hundreds have appeared in the last two decades alone. There are bibliographies and reviews of research, comprehensive theological treatments of his life and thought, chronologies and biographies, accessible introductions, anthologies, and reference works. Why another book on Paul? In a word, frustration. I had grown frustrated with the rush of popular books that depict Paul as *the* most important early church leader of his day, even the "second founder" of Christianity (or "Anti-Christ," after Friedrich Nietzsche's famous declaration). That romantic notion, which dates to the nineteenth century, lacks historical support. I also find problematic the academic studies known as "Paul and empire" books, which claim to set Paul over against his own culture of the ancient Roman world. In their view, Paul outright opposed or otherwise negotiated his way around Roman imperialism in order to subvert and so destroy it. In contrast to such studies, the issue for this book will be to ask different questions: How did Roman culture shape Paul's thinking? What did the rhetoric and theology of his writings mean in their Roman context? How did this context create the apostle's various legacies after his death? I seek to understand the participation and deep implication of Paul's letters in their wider culture, in order to investigate the figure's *Roman* identities in life and legend. This book is, therefore, a critical response to what I find to be seriously misleading claims in recent books on Paul and his historical context.

I also challenge contemporary conceptions of Paul's legend, which continue to have enormous influence on Western culture. *A Farewell to Arms*, the World War I novel by Ernest Hemingway (1929), set in Italy, offers a literary example of this influence. Early in the novel, a notorious grand narrative about Paul arises – the doctrine of Original Sin. (*Original Sin* characterizes the state of every human being to have an inescapable predisposition to moral depravity as a result of Adam's fall.) In a moment of confession to his army chaplain, the American protagonist Frederic Henry expresses his exasperation over his immoral behavior while on leave by paraphrasing a famous line of Paul: "I had drunk much wine and afterward coffee and Strega and I explained, winefully, how we did not do the things we wanted to do; we never did such things" (Hemingway 1929, 13; see Rom. 7:19). Later, his macho alter ego Rinaldi, a carousing Italian army physician, paraphrases another line attributed to Saint Paul (1 Tim. 5:23) to bait this same chaplain into an argument over whether Scripture supports the soldierly habit of drinking. Failing to catch the priest's ire, Rinaldi grouses about the hypocrisy of Paul. Here is the scene:

> "Drink some wine, priest," Rinaldi said. "Take a little wine for your stomach's sake. That's Saint Paul, you know."
> "Yes I know," said the priest politely. Rinaldi filled his glass.
> "That Saint Paul," Rinaldi said. "He's the one who makes all the trouble." The priest looked at me and smiled. I could see that the baiting did not touch him now.
> "That Saint Paul," Rinaldi said. "He was a rounder and a chaser and then when he was no longer hot he said it was no good. When he was finished, he made the rules for us who are still hot. Isn't that true, Federico?"
> (Hemingway 1929, 173)

Paul the Saint, Rinaldi complains, was formerly Paul the Sinner whose words now preach the end of the fun for the rest of us. Through the characters of Frederic and Rinaldi, Hemingway thus evokes the most enduring master narrative in the West about Paul – the prototypical religious convert. Such a depiction of Paul endures throughout modern literature, philosophy, and history; it is not unique to Hemingway's novel.

The following pages will challenge the idea of Original Sin and other grand narratives of the apostle as fictions invented after Paul's death. The popular portrayal of Paul's "life story" – from sinning to sainthood, from the Jewish "Saul" to the Christian "Paul" – represents more the legend than history. I thus offer a critical reassessment of Paul and his legacy in Western culture. In the end, I hope that the reader will see that Paul is not the only one making "all the trouble." The second half of this book surveys the difficulties that ancient interpreters made for one another in the name of Saint Paul.

Many people and institutions have helped me bring this project to fruition, and I offer my humble thanks to them all. The project came at the kind invitation of the classics editor in the New York office of Cambridge University Press. The Alexander von Humboldt Foundation granted a research fellowship at the University of Münster, during which my academic host, Hermut Löhr, introduced me to the unforgettable experience of giving a public lecture in German. Further support came from Indiana University in the forms of a sabbatical, a research supplement leave, and overseas conference grants. As well, a number of academic audiences listened to the ideas presented here; their questions and responses helped me improve and sharpen my arguments in meetings of the Society of Biblical Literature and in lectures and colloquia at The Ohio State University, Indiana University, Uppsala University, Humboldt University in Berlin, and University of Münster. Multiple conversations with Karl Galinsky have been particularly helpful for the articulation of my thesis about Paul's Roman language of authority. Scholars can find in Harrill (2011) more detailed arguments for the points made in Chapter 3; I thank Mohr Siebeck Verlag in Tübingen for permission to reprint and adapt portions of that earlier article. Translations of classical works generally follow those in the Loeb Classical Library, and translations of the Bible from the New Revised Standard Version are altered when not sufficiently literal for my purposes. References cited in Notes and Further Reading give credit to the sources of material borrowed, summarized, or paraphrased in each chapter.

My spouse and historian of ancient Christianity, David Brakke, inspired me to venture beyond my field of Pauline studies into the wider terrain of patristics and late antiquity. Jason BeDuhn offered expert advice on the Manichaeans, as did Stephen J. Shoemaker on the Muslim Paul.

Bart Ehrman kindly shared a section of his forthcoming monograph on forgery in early Christianity, which informs my discussion of the topic. Paula Fredriksen, my former colleague at Boston University, provided a number of helpful bibliographic suggestions; her historical reconstruction of Paul's apocalyptic hope for Gentiles guides my presentation here. Dale Martin read the entire manuscript in its penultimate stage and offered sage criticism. Susan Gubar and Donald J. Gray, fabulous colleagues in English literature, each read the full work and gave detailed comments on how to reshape it for nonspecialists. I also owe a great debt to Mary Jo Weaver; her generous comments at all stages of my writing encouraged me to realize the project. Last but not least, four Indiana University under-graduates provided feedback on a draft of the manuscript used in class as a trial textbook: Erik Hoffer, Amy Kiray, Russell White, and Samuel Wirt. Shortcomings that remain are, of course, my own.

I dedicate this book to Steven Goldman for his long-standing friendship and wonderful love of learning. Indeed, as he writes in his most recent book, "Learning is one of the best things about being human – that nearly magical ability to collect and use information, to create new knowledge building on old, to receive the abstracted wisdom of people who have gone before us whom we will never meet" (Goldman 2011, 62).

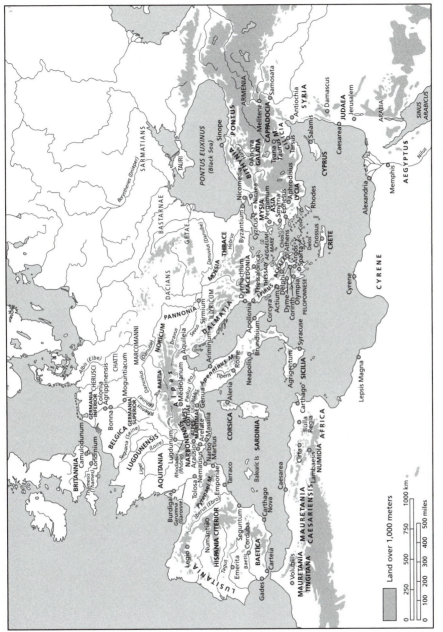

Figure 1. The Roman World. Paul's early career centered in Damascus and Antioch (Antiochia), both in Roman Syria.

INTRODUCTION

Socrates, Alexander the Great, Cleopatra, Augustus – no one would deny that these are key figures of classical antiquity. But does Saint Paul belong in this company? This book shows that Paul may not have been famous during his lifetime, but that Roman culture shaped his writings and, in the centuries following his death, he was just as transformative as Alexander. Situating Paul in his ancient Roman context finds continuity between the Jewish "Saul" and the Christian "Paul." Rather than providing a traditional biography of the West's prototypical religious convert, this book reassesses the apostle's life by focusing on his particularly Roman discourse of authority, which provoked the challenge of rivals. Included here as part of the figure's "life story" are the often hilarious legends that remade the figure into many different Pauls. In the thinking and sensibilities of his later interpreters, Paul became the imperial hero, the sexual role model, and the object of derision, as well as a book to quote from. Paul is, therefore, a key figure of classical antiquity because of the legend he became in the eyes of his later interpreters.

This book thus covers Paul's life and his legend (literary afterlife). I start with a survey of the available primary sources, an introduction to what counts as historical evidence. Important to understand will be the commonplace usage of a pseudonym in ancient writing, which will show that not every work bearing Paul's name is authentic. After this introduction, the procedure is first to situate Paul's life in its ancient context (Chapters 1–3), then to trace the development of his legacy ultimately to the prototypical religious convert and the alleged discoverer of a human being's introspective conscience (Chapters 4–6).

Understanding that Paul's multiple identities have changed over time makes intelligible why he has alternatively attracted and repelled readers, both ancient and modern. This problem brings me to make a number of methodological points on the important differences between this book and traditional biographies of Paul that are available elsewhere.

1. This Book Is Not a Traditional Biography

The current popularity of biography among general readers suggests that it is ideal for bridging the unfortunate divide between professional historians and nonacademic audiences. In particular, "unauthorized" biographies, written without the endorsement of the subject, allegedly dig up the glamorous dirt and tell the "real" (untold) story of their famous figures. My account of Paul is unquestionably unauthorized, for it appears without an endorsement of church authorities and without a Christian faith that takes the Bible's authority for granted. The academic standards of professional history and its competing interpretations about the past dictate the need for an independent judgment about Paul that is skeptical of any assertion of divinely revealed knowledge and of absolute certainty.

Yet the project of traditional biography brings with it contradictory assumptions. On the one hand, in popular imagination, a biographer is supposed to be objective and so document the coherent unity, striking personality, and expressive selfhood of the subject. Transparent language ought to unveil the "real" meaning of a subject's life, which is already present in the sources, rather than to create new meanings. The assumption is that a biographer can know another person's "essential" (authentic) self, even if the subject (like the apostle Paul) is long dead. For example, concerning his massive biography of the nineteenth-century writer Gustave Flaubert (*The Family Idiot*), Jean-Paul Sartre tells us confidently that he knows his subject completely and perfectly enough to be certain that Flaubert would be a boring dinner companion, if the counterfactual prospect ever were to arise (Sartre 1977, 119, 123). Biographical knowledge is thus believed to be so powerful as to predict "real" and "live" social interaction with a deceased subject. On the other hand, biography is supposed to tell a story in which the character comes alive, as in the psychologically penetrating "realism" of a novel by Jane Austen, William Makepeace Thackeray, or George Eliot. To perform this literary miracle of incarnation, traditional biographers often draw on novelistic techniques of literary fiction such as scene painting, foreshadowing, juxtaposition, and even dialogue. In the contradictory strains of the genre's assumptions, traditional biography is at once supposed to be truth and story, objective documentary and creative writing.

Let me say up front that I shall not attempt to meet such expectations. I agree with current research in literary theory that challenges the previous confidence in traditional biography to recover and reenact a self. Many contemporary circles of academics, including historians like me, thus question earlier beliefs in the transparency of language, the possibility of objectivity, the explanatory power of narrative, and the self as a unified and knowable subject. Moreover, to use nineteenth-century Victorian novels as a model for biography is bad methodology. Their scene-painting techniques and psychoanalysis of the self may create the impression of realism, but they imagine an ancient subject like Paul to be too *modern*.

To write a biography of Paul is, therefore, a perilous undertaking. There simply are not sufficient sources and requisite evidence to write one. Given this predicament, a traditional biographer might aim to enlarge the range of evidence. I, however, will *reduce* the available evidence to a small archive of primary sources (Paul's undisputed letters). I refuse to combine all the available sources into a single synthesis. Readers, therefore, should not expect a composite ("whole") picture of Paul as if one could harmonize all the available sources, biblical and nonbiblical. Such a project would produce a hagiography. Any biographical project necessarily makes judgment calls over what to include and what to exclude, in order to offer reasoned conclusions about the subject. My biography presents a crucial but often overlooked facet of Paul – his *Roman* identification, which, in turn, brings with it a continuity between the Jewish "Saul" and the Christian "Paul." Furthermore, I include the diverse legends in which later interpreters have sought to represent the figure from antiquity to modernity, which stretches the bounds of traditional biography beyond the subject's death.

This book offers one historian's solution to reconcile the tension of these contradictory assumptions by taking up the unconventional and revisionist form of *antibiography*. In contrast to a traditional biography, an antibiography abandons the traditional quest for the essential self (a fixed identity) in a linear chronology (the typical chapter-by-chapter march from birth to death), in favor of decentering the subject into multiple selves and developing more open-ending narrative structures. Consequently, I offer many different Pauls rather than "the" Paul.

In this regard, I shall have occasion to discuss what is called the *historical Paul*, which should not be confused with the "real" Paul who lived in the past. History is not the same thing as the past. It is the reconstruction of the past from careful investigation of and debate over the surviving evidence. Despite a popular misuse of the term in science fiction, *history* is not a place one might go someday (that would be the *past*); one can only *do* (or read) history. The historical Paul thus stands as a modern, debated construct of biblical experts. What constitutes the facts about the apostle in contemporary scholarship is in many instances an open question. This book, accordingly, addresses how historical *facts* about Paul come to be. This leads to a second way that my book differs from many other books on Paul.

2. The Difference between Primary Sources and Secondary Sources

What we know about Paul begins in the primary sources. What are primary sources? They are remnants from the past, also known as evidence – anything that survives archaeologically, such as a coin, a writing, a painting, a posthole, a skeleton, a box of tools. I proceed on a fundamental principle uniting all historians, namely, the distinction between primary and secondary sources. What are secondary sources? They are interpretations of the past that modern scholars produce on the basis of their analysis of the remnants we call primary sources. Examples include academic books, such as the one you are reading now, articles in scholarly journals, school textbooks, and documentary television series. Debates and disagreements occur in secondary sources in large part because the primary evidence is often fragmentary and otherwise difficult to interpret. Because historians can only be as good as their sources, the first task in any historical inquiry is to determine the nature of the available primary source material. For Paul, the problem is formidable.

To be sure, listing all the ancient evidence for Paul – the extant writings bearing his name and the other ancient works containing Pauline traditions (see Appendixes 1 and 3) – brings together an impressive number of sources. We seem to have a lot more evidence for Paul than for many other figures in classical antiquity. But the historical value of this material varies significantly. Paul clearly did not write all the writings attributed to him. For example, *The Correspondence of Paul and Seneca* (ca. fourth century) is an obvious ancient forgery, in Latin no less, which imagined Paul to have converted Seneca (the Roman philosopher and tutor of the emperor Nero) to Christianity. Much of the so-called Pauline writings and traditions turn out, in fact, to be legends born of a period after Paul, reinventing him as a larger-than-life figure more useful to later Christian theologies. These diverse and numerous legends include accounts of Paul's martyrdom in Rome, sermons attributed to Peter that condemn Paul as "Satan's apostle," new Pauline letters to additional churches and individuals, his various tours of heaven and hell, and other apostolic adventures with women and lions, all of which have virtually no historical value for reconstructing the life and thought of Paul. Therefore, we need to apply an important rule of thumb to guide our handling of the sources, so as not to misuse them. Not all primary sources are created equal. Some are original works directly from the man himself; others come only second-hand and are derivative, written decades and even centuries after Paul. Therefore, our fundamental principle of historical inquiry that separates the primary from the secondary applies also to the ancient evidence itself. That is, some ancient works that appear to provide primary evidence for Paul are actually secondary sources.

Given this rule of thumb, a typical proposal is to limit our acceptable primary sources to those appearing in New Testament. For this plan, we might turn first to the canonical Acts of the Apostles, an extended narrative of the early church that includes Paul's conversion and missionary career. We might then "fill in" material from the letters bearing Paul's name, which in canonical order are Romans, 1 and 2 Corinthians, Galatians, Ephesians, Philippians, Colossians, 1 and 2 Thessalonians, 1 and 2 Timothy, Titus, and Philemon. The Epistle to the Hebrews, though often attributed to Paul in church tradition, does not bear his name. Although this proposal has the advantage of including the earliest sources on Paul, it would also be inadequate because modern critical scholars dispute the historical reliability of the book of Acts and whether Paul wrote all the letters attributed to him in the New Testament.

Modern critical scholars conclude that nearly half of the New Testament letters that claim to be from Paul are in fact pseudonymous – that is, written by someone else under his name. Six of the canonical epistles bearing Paul's name have important differences from the other seven – in style, vocabulary, theology, and view of church institutionalization – which have sparked valuable debates about their genuineness since the nineteenth century. For example, a consensus of academic biblical scholarship holds that Paul did not write 1 Timothy, 2 Timothy, and Titus (ca. 95–125), the discrete corpus known as the Pastoral Epistles; those works assume developed institutions of church hierarchy that did not exist in Paul's day (see Chapter 4). Similar reasons persuade a vast majority of critical scholars that Paul did not write Ephesians. The question of whether Paul wrote Colossians and 2 Thessalonians divides critical scholars: a few affirm that Paul wrote both, some that he wrote only one (usually 2 Thessalonians), and most others that both are pseudonymous. The case of 2 Thessalonians is particularly interesting because, either way scholars come down on its authorship, the letter still shows that the circulation of fake Pauline letters concerned early Christian congregations (see Box 1).

It is no surprise that early Christians forged letters in Paul's name. Pseudonymous works of teachers and other figures commonly circulated in the ancient Mediterranean world, a practice that modern scholars

---

Box 1 The Earliest Known Warning about Fake Pauline Letters

The writing in the New Testament known as 2 Thessalonians warns its readers that fake Pauline letters may be circulating in the local congregation. In an irony of history, many modern scholars conclude that 2 Thessalonians itself is pseudonymous – that is, falsely bearing Paul's name. We thus likely have a fake Pauline letter protesting the spread of fake Pauline letters! Such letters ventriloquized Paul *as if* written by him.

> As to the coming of our Lord Jesus Christ and our being gathered together to him, we beg you, brothers and sisters, not to be quickly shaken in mind or alarmed, either by spirit or by word *or by letter, as though from us,* to the effect that the day of the Lord is already here. (2 Thess. 2:1–2; emphasis added)

---

soft-pedal by preferring to call it *pseudepigraphy* ("false writing") rather than forgery. In the case of Paul, following ancient custom, he likely made copies of his letters, as did the communities that received them. Later churches then edited partial collections into a corpus. The editing and copying process of textual transmission by hand – long before the invention of movable type and the printing press in the fifteenth century – encouraged scribes to interpolate the text (to alter or add words and lines). The copies were then exchanged with other congregations, as the Epistle to the Colossians (late first century) attests: "And when this letter has been read among you, have it read also in the church of the Laodiceans; and see that you read also the letter from Laodicea" (Col. 4:16). Such a letter to believers in the Asia Minor city of Laodicea-Lycus does not exist – it is doubtful that Paul ever wrote one, given the likelihood that Colossians itself is pseudonymous – but the reference encouraged the forgery of at least two replacements in late antiquity. The one that survives today (ca. second to fourth century, see Appendix 1) is a banal pastiche written to be the "real" Letter to the Laodiceans possibly in opposition to an even earlier forgery, and is complete with a sister reference to Colossians 4:16: "And see that (this epistle) is read to the Colossians and that of the Colossians to you" (*Letter to the Laodiceans* 20).

Such forgeries were almost always condemned in antiquity. Ancient education inadvertently enabled it, however. For example, students in Greco-Roman schools (Greek *gymnasia*) commonly had to compose a speech or letter imitating the text of a famous past figure – what Socrates or

Cleopatra would have typically said in a stock situation, for example – a set rhetorical exercise known as *declamation* (speech in character). The skills learned in declamation thus made it possible for forgers to have a good sense about how to proceed. But there was nothing in the ancient curriculum that encouraged anyone to publish one's own writing in the name of another. Quite the contrary, using imitative skills in this way was actively discouraged in the environment of ancient literary culture. When such activities were detected, the products were condemned as "lies" and "bastards," and never sanctioned. Nonetheless, many works passed, unbeknownst to ancient readers, as the authentic writing of a famous figure. Examples include the pseudonymous dialogues of Plato, the spurious works of Aristotle, and mathematical theorems attributed to Pythagoras. In this regard, ancient Jews shared those cultural habits of their "pagan" neighbors. Diverse Jewish pseudonymous writings bearing false ascriptions to biblical and other prophetic authorities from Israel's past date from the Hellenistic and Roman periods – the so-called Old Testament Pseudepigrapha.

Why was all this literature produced? A major reason was to gain an audience for the writing. The *wisdom* bearing the name "King Solomon" would command notice and an immediate readership, for example. The widespread practice of authors lying about their identities in order to lend authority to their own views makes intelligible the pseudonymous authorship of Pauline letters. Later Christian authors wanted apostolic authority for their views. Lacking such authority themselves, they created it by forging Paul.

Acts of the Apostles: A Secondary Source for the Historical Paul

The historical problems of the Acts of the Apostles reduce the number of sources confidently going back to Paul even further. Although using Acts as a primary source for Paul may seem understandable, given the importance of Paul as a major character in the book and its coherence as a narrative, it is highly misleading in reconstructing a context for the historical figure. Acts is not a "history" in the modern meaning of the term. Rather, its theological narrative shares affinities with Greco-Roman popular literature. Acts presents Paul schematically, as the greatest hero of a "unified" Church who brings the gospel from its origins in Jerusalem to the imperial capital of Rome, with powerful orations, great miracles, and dramatic travels as God's "chosen instrument" of salvation (Acts 9:15). Modern

---

Box 2 Comparing Acts and Galatians: Paul's First Jerusalem Visit as an Apostle

Acts	Galatians
When he [Paul] had come to Jerusalem, he attempted to join the disciples, and they were all afraid of him, for they did not believe that he was a disciple. But Barnabas took him, brought him to the apostles, and described for them how on the road he had seen the Lord, who had spoken to him, and how in Damascus he had spoken boldly in the name of Jesus. So he went in and out among them in Jerusalem, speaking boldly in the name of the Lord. He spoke and argued with the Hellenists; but they were attempting to kill him. When the believers learned of it, they brought him down to Caesarea and sent him off to Tarsus. (Acts 9:26–30)	Then after three years I did go up to Jerusalem to visit Cephas [Peter] and stayed with him fifteen days; but I did not see any other apostle except James the Lord's brother. In what I am writing to you, before God, I do not lie! Then I went to the regions of Syria and Cilicia, and I was still unknown by sight to the churches of Judea that are in Christ; they only heard it said, "The one who formerly was persecuting us is now proclaiming the faith he once tried to destroy." And they glorified God because of me. (Gal. 1:18–24)

---

critical scholars have found many stories in Acts to be concocted out of the author's theological themes or otherwise adapted from prior sources and existing legends. Accepting the book of Acts literally as straightforward and unproblematic evidence of Paul's life is naive. Historical claims about Paul and Christian origins should be drawn from the book of Acts only with great caution (see Chapter 4).

Such caution means *interrogating* the evidence of Acts in light of what Paul says in his own letters, a method called synoptic reading. Let's do that now. Both Acts and Galatians claim to report the same event – Paul's first visit to Jerusalem following Christ's revelation to him – but there are clear contradictions between them (see Box 2).

The book of Acts depicts the event as a public visit, in which Paul developed intimate and long associations with the Jerusalem apostles. In contrast, Paul in Galatians describes it as a private meeting only with Peter, an encounter with no other apostle except James the brother of Jesus. Acts states that Paul preached openly among the Judean believers and entered into debates with nonbelievers – observable activities that made him so personally well known in the city that a plot arose against his life. But in Galatians, Paul himself states that his brief visit was uneventful, leaving him still unknown by sight to the churches of Judea well after he departed the city, without a hint of a death plot. Reading the two sources synoptically, therefore, makes their contradictions clear. Acts narrates what Paul himself swears, before God, never occurred (Gal. 1:20). To force the two different accounts of Acts and Galatians together will not work, because such an attempt at harmonization would create a narrative unlike what we find in either source – in other words, bad methodology.

At this point a reader might ask, Wasn't Luke a companion of Paul and so an eyewitness of the events he narrates in the book of Acts? In reply, I would of course agree that the author of Acts also wrote the Gospel of Luke. We know this to be the case from the evidence in the sources themselves: the first line of Acts (1:1) explicitly mentions the preface of Luke (1:1–4). Acts is the second part of a two-volume work, the first part being the Gospel of Luke, with Luke's preface being intended to cover the work of Luke–Acts as a whole. But this does not prove that Luke, a Pauline associate mentioned only in other writings (Philem. 24; Col. 4:14; 2 Tim. 4:11) and otherwise unknown, wrote Luke–Acts. Indeed, the name *Luke* occurs in neither Acts nor the Gospel, and in fact the author never tells his name. The work is therefore anonymous. The title "The Gospel according to Luke" is not original but secondary (an *inscriptio*), which Christian scribes copying the manuscript later added to the text to indicate the work's place in a canon of Scripture. We know this in part because the title presupposes (the Gospel *according to Luke*) a later collation of multiple Gospels into a single literary corpus. (Scholars, including myself, continue to call the author "Luke," but for convenience.) Our main source of the legend that Luke, "the beloved physician," traveled with Paul and supposedly recorded the apostle's preaching in a "book" (the canonical book of Acts) is the church father Irenaeus of Lyons (see Appendix 3). That legend, however, contradicts the evidence in Luke's prologue, in which the author admits not being an eyewitness to the events that he narrates (see Box 3).

Box 3 Luke–Acts Describes Itself as a Secondary Source: The Prologue

Since many have undertaken to set down an orderly account of the events that have been fulfilled among us, just as they were handed on to us by those who from the beginning were eyewitnesses and servants of the word, I too decided, after investigating everything carefully from the first, to write an orderly account for you, most excellent Theophilus, so that you may know the truth about which you have been instructed. (Luke 1:1–4)

The author of Luke–Acts asserts "the truth" of his writing in part because he also acknowledges his work not to be contemporary with the events to which it refers. In our terms, Luke admits to writing a secondary source: the stories come secondhand (Luke 1:2, "handed on to *us* by *those* who from the beginning were eyewitnesses"). The author depends upon earlier written sources currently in circulation (Luke 1:1, "many have undertaken to set down an orderly account") and exercises critical judgment over his sources (Luke 1:3, "after investigating everything carefully") on the belief that reliance upon those prior sources alone prevents the truth to be told (Luke 1:4, "so that you may know the truth concerning the things about which you have been instructed"). The evidence of the prologue, which describes the entire two-volume work as a secondary source, thus undermines the later church legends about the author being a companion of Paul.

Nonetheless, dissenting interpreters often point to an outworn claim that four passages of Acts (16:10–17; 20:5–15; 21:1–18; 27:1–28:16) switch to the first person ("we") as alleged evidence of the historical reliability of Acts, from its nature as a eyewitness source (a personal diary in which the author personally participated in the events narrated). But this objection fails to consider carefully the evidence and any alternative explanations. The abruptness with which the "we" passages begin and end in the narrative read more like fragments of a prior source, a stock travelogue of sorts, around which the author of Acts built those sections of his work. The "we" is not necessarily "Paul and Luke"; even if that were the case, the first person could be pseudonymous.

Leaving aside the eyewitness claim as unfounded, we move to another potential objection: Doesn't the fact that the author of Luke–Acts used prior written sources, "investigating them carefully," guarantee the work's overall historical reliability? Not really. When we compare Luke and one of the sources we know he used, the Gospel of Mark, it becomes clear that "Luke" felt free both to edit Mark and to depart from it entirely. The author of Luke changed stories in Mark dramatically to fit his own theological portrait of Jesus as a prophetic hero. Likewise in Acts, the same author changed Paul to match his own theological portrait of a hero, as I will show in Chapter 4. We know Mark to be one of the written sources used in the Gospel of Luke because the narrative of Luke incorporates the entire plot of Mark in a verbatim parallel of passages (what we call plagiarism). To see how the author of Luke freely shaped his sources to fit particular theological themes and meanings rather than to ensure what we would call historical accuracy, let's repeat our method of synoptic reading. The synoptic parallel this time comes from the episode of Jesus in the garden of Gethsemane on the night of his arrest. Pay close attention to the depiction of Jesus' emotional state and demeanor facing death (see Box 4).

The parallel confronts us with several clear contradictions. Mark depicts Jesus to be in gut-wrenching agony over his impending arrest and execution; the Markan Jesus cries and pleads repeatedly on the ground (three times, no less) in desperation, begging God for his life. In contrast, Luke has edited down Mark's version in order to depict Jesus in no agony at all; rather than groveling on the ground, the Lukan Jesus is on bended knee offering up a calm prayer, only once, displaying his fortitude and strength. (The passage in Luke 22:43–44, on Jesus sweating blood, is a textual interpolation not appearing in our earliest manuscripts; later Christian scribes apparently attempted to resolve the contradiction of Mark and Luke on the Gethsemane scene.) The synoptic exercise helps us see the literary freedom that the author took with his sources.

In sum: just as modern critical scholars do not use the Gospel of Luke primarily as a source for reconstructing the historical Jesus – such would be bad methodology – so too are they unlikely to use the Acts of the Apostles as a source primarily for reconstructing the historical figure of Paul. The book of Acts and the pseudonymous epistles attributed to Paul in the New Testament are secondary to the events they describe and present serious difficulties as sources. The process of elimination, then, should make clear which sources are the sound ones to use first and foremost in a historical biography (or antibiography) of Paul: the Pauline letters whose authenticity is beyond reasonable dispute. In roughly chronological order, they are 1 Thessalonians, 1 Corinthians, Galatians, 2 Corinthians, Philippians, Philemon, and Romans. My book reconstructs the historical Paul primarily on this evidence, a third difference from a traditional biography of the apostle (which often simply follows the book of Acts).

Box 4 Gospel Parallel: The Difference between Mark and Luke

Mark	Luke
They went to a place called Gethsemane; and he [Jesus] said to his disciples, "Sit here while I pray." He took with him Peter and James and John, and began to be distressed and agitated. And he said to them, "I am deeply grieved, even to death; remain here, and keep awake." And going a little farther, he threw himself on the ground and prayed that, if it were possible, the hour might pass from him. He said, "Abba, Father, for you all things are possible; remove this cup from me; yet, not what I want, but what you want." He came and found them sleeping; and he said to Peter, "Simon, are you asleep? Could you not keep awake one hour? Keep awake and pray that you may not come into the time of trial; the spirit indeed is willing, but the flesh is weak." And again he went away, and prayed, saying the same words. And once more he came and found them sleeping, for their eyes were very heavy; and they did not know what to say to him. He came a third time and said to them, "Are you still sleeping and taking your rest? Enough! The hour has come; the Son of Man is betrayed into the hands of sinners. Get up, let us be going. See, my betrayer is at hand." (Mark 14:32–42)	When he [Jesus] reached the place, he said to them, "Pray that you may not come into the time of trial." Then he withdrew from them about a stone's throw, knelt down, and prayed, "Father, if you are willing, remove this cup from me; yet, not my will but yours be done." . . . When he got up from prayer, he came to the disciples and found them sleeping because of grief, and he said to them, "Why are you sleeping? Get up and pray that you may not come into the time of trial." (Luke 22:40–46; minus vv. 43–44, a later interpolation)

See Ehrman 2012, 146–49.

3. PAUL'S AUTHENTIC LETTERS

The authentic letters are primary (and valuable) sources because they come from Paul, but present their own problems. They are not just texts, but *events* having specific occasions in Paul's activity with his communities. We often do not know their exact contexts; several letters appear edited or composite. Even as primary sources, therefore, Paul's letters are incomplete and sometimes muddled. To an extent, this is to be expected. Paul's letters were "in-house" private correspondence that dealt with the everyday business and social situations of his followers. Paul did not address a general public, outside the small circles of converted Gentiles, in any of his authentic letters. The letters thus contain only one half of a dialogue – bits and pieces of what apparently were ongoing conversations, visits, and other personal exchanges between Paul, his converts, and other contemporaries in his small group of Jesus followers. When reading Paul's letters, we are in one sense eavesdropping on the (mostly lost) conversations of other people in the past. In another sense, however, this analogy to eavesdropping can also mislead us into a false confidence in the objectivity of letters. Letters are a delayed form of communication, without the immediate reactions and interruptions of the listener. Lacking the spontaneity of a live conversation, letters are strategies of self-presentation that subordinate the participation of the audience to generic conventions and tropes. Letters also do not offer us access to the modes of bodily language that help convey meaning in a face-to-face exchange, such as a speaker's facial expressions, gestures, and intonation. Although ancient writers typically compared an exchange of letters to a face-to-face conversation, we need to recognize the consequential differences between reading letters and eavesdropping on a live conversation. Paul's letters are deliberate, literary compositions.

To introduce the textbook basics of what a university student would learn in an introductory course on the New Testament, I give in the sections below a précis of each of Paul's seven letters.

1 Thessalonians (ca. 51)

Paul's first letter to the Thessalonians deals with specific difficulties that his nascent congregation experienced only a few months following his initial departure from their city. Thessalonica, in Macedonia, was an important station on the major Roman military highway that ran from Byzantium (modern Istanbul) to the Adriatic Sea, the Ignatian Way (Latin Via Egnatia). Paul visited the city as he traveled on this road from Philippi (1 Thess. 2:2), before turning south to Athens (1 Thess. 3:1) and finally to Corinth.

The letter, therefore, was an occasional one, arising from a specific circumstance and addressing a particular audience. The recipients were all Gentiles (former pagans, non-Jews), which we know because Paul writes that they had all "turned from idols" (1 Thess. 1:9) – hardly a description of Jews. Paul wrote the letter probably from Corinth in Greece soon after his associates had returned from Thessalonica with distressing news of a serious crisis. Grieving the unexpected deaths of some fellow believers, the Thessalonians were enduring harassment from their local Gentile families and pagan neighbors, who wanted them to come back to the family idols of their traditional ancestor worship. The Thessalonian believers had begun to question their new social identity and religious convictions.

The letter thus holds great historical value for reconstructing the process by which Paul evangelized converts. Evidence of Paul's missionary method appears in a key passage: "You remember our labor and toil, brothers and sisters; we worked night and day, so that we might not burden any of you *while we proclaimed to you the gospel of God*" (1 Thess. 2:9, emphasis added). This passage attests that Paul evangelized while working to support himself in a craft. In other words, Paul brought up his religious message to customers and other visitors whom he met while doing manual labor in a local workshop. This evidence corrects a common misconception that Paul gained his converts from powerful orations to crowds in the city and eloquent sermons to Jews in the synagogue. Paul was neither a great orator nor what we might call a street preacher (see 1 Cor. 2:1–5; 2 Cor. 10:10). Historically, the letter shows also how Paul dealt with the problem of new converts. Paul exhorted the congregation to bind their little group together and aspire to live quietly, "so that you may behave properly toward outsiders and be dependent on no one" (1 Thess. 4:12). Paul depicted the community as a new family of "brothers (and sisters)" in Messiah Jesus, an association that replaced formerly pagan family ties.

Paul wrote this letter after several decades of working as an apostle and reflecting on the purpose of his mission (see Chapter 1). Paul's first surviving letter, therefore, represents the writer as an experienced and seasoned pastor.

Galatians (ca. 54)

Paul's letter to the Christians in Galatia, a region in Central Asia Minor (modern day Turkey), offers good historical evidence that the apostle's main competitors and opponents were fellow missionaries of Messiah Jesus. This primary source undermines the "harmonious" portrait of Christian origins in the Acts of the Apostles. The historical Paul disagreed sharply with the Christian leaders in Jerusalem and those who claimed to be their envoys.

Paul wrote his letter to the Galatians for an occasion quite different from that of 1 Thessalonians. Several years after he had left Galatia, Paul became furious when rival Christian missionaries arrived in the area with different teachings about Messiah Jesus. The opponents were, apparently, much like Paul: they were Jewish missionaries traveling around Asia Minor and the Aegean for the purpose of converting and teaching Gentiles about Messiah Jesus. But their gospel was clearly different from what Paul proclaimed, for Paul began the letter as follows: "I am astonished that you are so quickly deserting the one who called you in the grace of Christ and are turning to a different gospel" (Gal. 1:6). Directly challenging Paul's authority to preach Messiah Jesus, the rival missionaries insisted on the need for circumcision in order for male Gentiles to "finish" their conversion. Paul explained the situation as dire: "It is those who want to make a good showing in the flesh that try to compel you to be circumcised" (Gal. 6:12). Those rival teachers also accused Paul of religious fraud, of being a demonic messenger who played down the importance of the Jewish Law merely for gain and popularity, a charge that Paul denied angrily in the letter. As a parent in ancient culture would have rebuked a misbehaving child who should have known better, Paul thus wrote to chastise his male Gentile converts for accepting the idea of circumcision from those rival teachers. In the course of the rebuke, Paul defended himself against rumors about his past, his teaching, and his legitimacy as an apostle.

1 Corinthians (ca. 53/54)

The First Letter to the Corinthians provides the most important evidence for the social history of a Pauline congregation. This church stood on the brink of a collapse, and the problems were various. Paul addressed the Corinthians explicitly as Gentiles – "You know that when you were pagans [Greek *ethnē*, literally "Gentiles"], you were enticed and led astray to idols that could not speak" (1 Cor. 12:2). We learn from this evidence that the congregation was ethnically Gentile (like all of Paul's other converts of record), not Jewish, and that the converts came from diverse socioeconomic backgrounds (1 Cor. 1:26). In such a mix, each group apparently had different expectations of obligation and authority. The event of the letter thus was the sort of conflict that would have naturally emerged as a radically apocalyptic sect encountered the ordinary structures of a Roman urban household: obsession with order, gender hierarchy, patron–client relations, mastery of slaves, and articulations of status and honor.

To elevate their status over those of fellow believers, some members had attempted to preserve the long-standing conventions of Rome's fundamentally hierarchical society within the radically apocalyptic social world that the whole congregation was constructing. As we shall see in Chapter 2, Paul's main goal in the letter was to urge the congregation to *reconcile* their internal discord caused by such conflicts of status.

This letter that we know as 1 Corinthians belongs to an extended and complex history of correspondence between Paul and his troubled congregation at Corinth. The chronology of the correspondence is difficult to figure out because some letters apparently do not survive and others exist only in fragments. The canonical First Corinthians is not, historically, Paul's "first" letter to Corinthians: it mentions a prior letter (5:9), not extant, whose moral exhortation Paul has to clarify in our 1 Corinthians.

2 Corinthians (ca. 54–56)

The Second Letter to the Corinthians, despite its appearance in the canon as a single epistle, contains fragments of as many as five different letters of Paul – plus an interpolated scrap (6:14–7:1) of another letter apparently penned by opponents who advocated a position opposite to that in Paul's teaching. The key piece of 2 Corinthians' jigsaw puzzle is the angry appeal of chapters 10–13, whose tone shifts abruptly from the peace and thankfulness of the previous section. The angry rebuke of chapters 10–13 belongs to a letter fragment likely written before chapters 1–7, which is another fragment of yet another letter. In other words, the sequence of writing the two main sections of 2 Corinthians is more or less the reverse of their transmitted order. An additional literary problem presents itself. One other section (2 Cor. 8–9) deals with raising money for the collection that Paul intends to take to the Jerusalem church. But, curiously, Paul introduces the collection a second time (2 Cor. 9) as if it were a *new* topic, which suggests that 2 Corinthians 8 and 9 each belonged originally to a separate letter on fund raising. My working hypothesis for reconstructing the full history of Paul's Corinthian correspondence appears in Appendix 2, and its chronological arrangement will be discussed in detail in Chapter 2.

In contrast to the internal conflicts of 1 Corinthians, the problems that Paul addressed in the letter collection we call 2 Corinthians were mostly *external* conflicts. The letter fragment preserved in 2 Corinthians 10–13 attacks the arrival and teaching of rival missionaries who preach a "different gospel" about Messiah Jesus (2 Cor. 11:4–5). These traveling missionaries at Corinth were, like Paul, "Hebrews" (2 Cor. 11:22) but, unlike him, took stock in powerful orations, apparently had credentials from the Jerusalem church leaders, and scoffed at Paul's weakness in body and speech (2 Cor. 10:10). The letter offers no clues as to their identity beyond Paul's hate speech toward them: Paul mocked them as "super apostles," claimed to expose their demonic origin as "servants of Satan," and warned the congregation of their Satanic masquerade as "apostles of Christ" (2 Cor. 11:5–15). Although they might recall Paul's opponents in Galatia, the opponents at Corinth seem to have been a different group of teachers because the issues are different. The fragment of the letter preserved in 2 Corinthians 10–13 makes no mention of circumcision and the Jewish Law – the main issue of Galatians.

In any case, the historical evidence of 2 Corinthians thus confirms that Paul and his associates were but one small group among many different circles of traveling Christian apostles to Gentiles in the cities of the Roman East, whose missions sometimes complemented and sometimes clashed with one another.

Philippians (ca. 56)

Further evidence of early Christian diversity and conflict appears in the Letter to the Philippians, which Paul wrote from an imprisonment for his missionary activities, most likely in Ephesus in Asia Minor (on the Aegean coast of modern day Turkey) (Phil. 1:7). The Philippian congregation had sent a delegate named Epaphroditus with financial assistance for Paul while in prison. Thanking the Philippians for their generosity, Paul wrote that he was sending his associate Timothy back to them with Epaphroditus, and that the Philippians should beware of rival Christian missionaries who urged circumcision (and who may have gotten Paul arrested in Ephesus). Paul's invective casts his fellow Christian opponents as raving animals – "Beware of the dogs, beware of the evil workers, beware of those who mutilate the flesh" (Phil. 3:2) – so intense was his hatred of them that he refused to see them as people. Paul's language thus constructed a web of friendship with the Philippians so as to make clear how terrible and dangerous the opponents were to his mission.

Philemon (ca. 56)

As in the case of Philippians, Paul wrote the Letter to Philemon while he was imprisoned. The shortest writing in the New Testament (only a page in printed Bibles), the letter contains deferential and circumspect language unusual for Paul; it reads like a carefully crafted petition for something he wanted. Paul wrote that he was sending the slave Onesimus back to Onesimus's master Philemon (an associate of Paul). Some recent scholars have reasonably argued that Onesimus was not a "runaway" slave, because the letter lacks an explicit reference to flight, or any mention of a slave's remorse that we would expect from a letter dealing with the return of a fugitive. Whether the letter's ultimate purpose was to petition Philemon to free Onesimus from slavery is uncertain. But the letter's subtle pleas offer unmistakable signs of Paul manipulating Philemon rhetorically. As a historical source, the letter provides important evidence not only for slavery in early Christianity but also for the particularity of Paul's correspondence. The particularity of Philemon proved indeed problematic for later interpreters to circulate it and use it as "Scripture," because the letter did not so much proclaim Messiah Jesus as discuss a private business transaction about a slave.

Romans (ca. 57)

Later interpreters found more useful than Philemon the Letter to the Romans, Paul's longest and last extant writing. Unlike the other letters, this one addressed believers whom Paul did not convert and over whom he had no authority. Paul wrote the letter during a final stay at Corinth to introduce himself to the congregations at Rome in advance of his intended stopover in the imperial capital on his way to a new mission in Spain (Rom. 15:23–24). Paul's delegate Phoebe, one of his patrons at Corinth and a female leader (Greek *diakonos*) of a local house church (Rom. 16:1–2), was the letter's carrier and envoy. Paul composed it at a decisive turning point in his career. Having accomplished what he saw as a full mission in the eastern Mediterranean, from Jerusalem to the northern shores of the Aegean Sea (Rom. 15:19), he now looked to the western half of his Roman world. Rome epitomized the universality and Spain the extremity of his mission to "all the Gentiles" (Rom. 1:5). The letter introduced Paul's basic teachings and "gospel," which makes intelligible the letter's unusually elongated style and content. Nearly all the Roman Christians likely knew Paul only by reputation and with some suspicion, though some people knew him personally (see Rom. 16:3–15).

In the work, Paul asked rhetorical questions, quoted popular maxims and proverbs, parodied rival positions, personified the speech of fictitious characters, and used the rhetoric of antitheses and reductio ad absurdum (carrying a proposition to its absurd extreme in order to refute it). Greco-Roman moral philosophers deployed this schoolroom style of speech, called *diatribe*, to introduce their distinctive tenets to an audience of potential students. Introductory and with an ad hoc construction of themes, Romans is not the total compendium of Paul's thinking that early modern interpreters like Luther took it for (see Chapter 6). The ad hoc themes include Paul's free melding of Jewish scripture with his own reflection on his past controversies in Corinth and especially Galatia. His thematic exposition in chapters 1–11 turns about the single question of the relationship between Jew and Gentile, revisiting the problem of the Jewish law that had dominated his letter to the Galatians – the contrast between "works" of the law and the "grace" of faith. The hortatory themes of chapters 12–15 deal with moral and social issues familiar from his Corinthian correspondence, such as internal factionalism. Modern scholars debate whether historical events in Rome, such as the emperor Claudius's expulsion of Jews (ca. 49), influenced Paul's choice of themes. But there are no clues strong enough to deduce from Paul's admonitions the actual problems that might have existed in the Roman congregations. In any case, the letter provides good historical evidence that Paul's thinking drew from the themes and experience of his own proselyting.

Paul's response to these problems argued, in part, that believing Gentiles must stop their arrogant behavior toward unbelieving Jews. Jewish unbelief in Messiah Jesus allowed time for the "full number" of Gentiles to come into the faith and was thus an essential part of God's plan for the salvation of "all Israel" (Rom. 11:25–26; see Chapter 2). In Chapter 5, we shall meet one ancient interpreter who got this point – Origen of Alexandria (ca. 185–251). He thus understood what a consensus of modern scholars today reconstructs as the historical meaning of Romans.

In summation, not all ancient works are equally valid kinds of evidence. Some are not contemporary with Paul's life, being outright fakes or based on hearsay. Examples include the apocryphal Pauline acts and letters produced in the second to the fourth centuries. Those works have no historical value in the context of Paul's life, though of course they contribute to our understanding of how his legend evolved in later contexts (see Chapter 4). In this regard, ancient works can be secondary in one context (the life of Paul) but primary in another (the legend of Paul), which means that the clear-cut distinction between primary and secondary sources established in this chapter will be complicated in the latter part of this book.

In the historical reconstruction of Paul's life, some biblical writings (like the Acts of the Apostles and the disputed Pauline letters of Colossians, Ephesians, the Pastoral Epistles) are not primary sources. To use them to reconstruct the events in Paul's career would abuse a basic principle of all historical research. We must rely primarily on the seven authentic letters, which cover only a concentrated time in his life, about a decade, when he founded his own congregations (the approximate years 50 to 57). It humbles a biographer of Paul to stand back and realize how tiny an archive we have to reconstruct the life of the man. The primary sources add up to little more than fifty printed pages. Modern scholars debate the historical Paul so intensely in large part because our evidence is so sparse; a few conservative scholars even appeal to this paucity of evidence to argue for the necessity of supplementing the letters with the book of Acts (which I refuse to do, for reasons specified previously).

Yet the nature of our primary sources should press us into caution, not despair. In that spirit, we move now to the first half of our investigation – the life of Paul.

PART

I

THE LIFE

1

FROM PHARISEE TO APOSTLE

Many people today, if they are familiar with the figure, believe that Paul lived a life full of paradoxes. Born and raised Jewish, and proud of it, he traveled in a "pagan" world with its different sensibilities. He felt compelled to adopt and then proselytize a faith he had formerly persecuted. He claimed to be an apostle of Jesus Christ, yet had neither met the Galilean peasant Jesus nor been one of his chosen Twelve Disciples. He did not think of himself as "Christian," but he later became known as the key figure that established Christianity. He bore a Roman name (Greek *Paulos*, from the Latin *Paulus*) and apparently also a Jewish one (Saul, but it is only mentioned in the Acts of the Apostles). Attempts to heighten these paradoxes shape the most popular theme in Paul's biography; as scholars tell his story, they often try to resolve these paradoxes by saying that the Jewish "Saul" converted to become the Christian "Paul" and also repudiated his past life in Judaism. A closer examination of the evidence, however, shows a cultural continuity between Saul's early life in Judaism and Paul's later Christian mission. Paul and Saul cannot be bifurcated or divorced. Instead of underscoring the paradoxes between Paul's Jewish past and his later Gentile mission, I argue for continuity.

The sections in this chapter show this continuity in Paul's birth and education, his "conversion" at the city of Damascus in Roman Syria, and his contentiousness with Jesus' original apostles.

1. BIRTH AND EDUCATION

The first problem we have to face in any biography (or antibiography) of Paul is that the primary evidence imposes severe limitations on what we can know, as the Introduction explained. We do not even know that the name "Paul" came from his conversion to Christianity. Such an explanation does not appear in any of the earliest sources. In the Acts of the Apostles, the switch of his name from Saul to Paul occurs not at his conversion (Acts 9:1–18) but in the narrating of his missionary activity abroad (Acts 13:1–13); the switch of names is incidental. And Paul never uses the name "Saul" in his letters, which may be merely a function of his communicating with Gentiles. He possibly grew up with the two names of Paul/Saul. Such double names were common in ancient Judaism's multilingual environment. Another example is the case of the apostle Peter, whom Paul calls by both a Greek name (*Petros*, "stone") and its Jewish-Aramaic equivalent (Cephas). Peter, according to the Gospels, also went by a more traditional Hebrew name (Simon), but this is unmentioned in Paul's letters.

We are especially ignorant about Paul's early life. He was probably born around the turn of the first century (ca. 10 C.E.), making him about the same age as Jesus or a bit younger. The book of Acts names Tarsus in the Roman province of Cilicia (on what is today the southern coast of Turkey) as the birthplace of Paul (Acts 22:3), but we cannot be sure that this is true. In any case, this Greek-speaking coastal metropolis was a prosperous center of textile production, commercial trade, and great philosophical learning. "The people of Tarsus," writes a contemporaneous Greek observer named Strabo, "have devoted themselves so eagerly not only to philosophy but also to the whole round of education in general, that they have surpassed Athens, Alexandria, or any other place that can be named where there have been schools and lectures of philosophers" (Strabo, *Geography* 14.5.13; trans. Jones 1929, 347, altered). This cosmopolitan city, so famous for trade and philosophy, would have immersed the young Paul in Greco-Roman culture. But the youth would have received cultural immersion also in any other major city of the Roman East.

Paul was Greco-Roman. From his writings, we learn a little about Paul's rhetorical style, his probable education, and the social status of his family. He was literate, a native Greek speaker. His letters deployed moral exhortation, rhetorical clichés, and a conversational form of lecture known as the *diatribe* familiar from the Greco-Roman schoolroom and popular orations. Paul made his arguments with attention to grammar and to the sports of foot racing, boxing, and exercise training, all part of Hellenistic schooling (Greek *gymnasium*). He mentioned the Greco-Roman figure of a *paidagōgos* ("pedagogue," child-minder), the household slave responsible for escorting the freeborn child to teachers and for overseeing the child's education generally (Gal. 3:24). He even quoted at least once a pagan proverb – "bad company ruins good morals" (1 Cor. 15:33) – from one of the leading authors used in ancient education, the

Athenian playwright Menander (fourth century B.C.E.). Generations of Greek and Roman youths had to memorize and formally recite Menander's plays before their teachers. Paul's writing thus reflects participation in a Greco-Roman curriculum from the primary level (grammar) to some higher education (rhetoric and philosophy). Because education was a private expense – only a small percentage of the ancient Mediterranean population could read and write – Paul's parents must have had some social standing and financial means to provide this good education to their son. Paul's education surpassed the majority of the ancient Mediterranean population, but it was below that of Rome's aristocratic elite.

His education combined Jewish and Greco-Roman identities with apparent ease. In this regard, we should not place Judaism and Hellenism into separate containers as if they were mutually exclusive cultures. To be sure, Paul drew heavily on the Jewish scriptures, citing them more than ninety times in his letters and showing an impressive facility with memorized texts comparable to what we find in the sayings of the Talmudic rabbinic sages. But the citations were his own paraphrases of the Greek version of the Hebrew Bible, known as the Septuagint (abbreviated LXX), which was *Hellenistic* literature. Paul also knew how to make particular arguments about the proper way to read Scripture, which combined miscellaneous passages (regardless of their original contexts) into a single text to explicate its so-called underlying significance (see Rom. 10:5–21). This dynamic form of biblical exegesis resembles in fairly general terms what became later known as rabbinic *midrash*.

Paul analyzed Scripture with an interpretative eye to explicate the "real" meaning of the text (as he saw it) from people and events in his own contemporary situation. He preached apocalyptic eschatology – prophetic forecasts about the imminent destruction of the world and the inauguration of a heavenly realm on earth – and outright changed the biblical texts he cited to make the words say what they were *supposed* to mean in support of his worldview, a method whose idea (but not every detail) shows continuity with biblical interpretations in other Jewish writings of his day. For example, Paul's style of biblical exposition has some affinities to what we find in the Dead Sea Scrolls (where it is called *pesher*, Hebrew for "interpretation"), a source roughly contemporaneous with his letters. The Dead Sea Scrolls, rediscovered in 1945 in the Judean desert region of Khirbet Qumran, advanced the rules and theology of Jewish sectarians, known from other writings as the Essenes. Like Paul, the Essenes espoused an apocalyptic eschatology. And for them, too, the "original" (Hebrew) meaning and context of a particular passage did not control how they understood and used the Bible. The Pesher from Cave Four of the Dead Sea Scrolls combined texts from 2 Samuel and the Psalms, with other scriptural passages, to depict the Qumran community itself as the eschatological interim Temple ("House of the Lord"), and as living in the final days when the Messiah ("the Branch of David") will come (see Box 5).

Paul also avoided the literalism of flat (surface) reading, which follows Greek and Roman literary techniques. When a literal text appeared to work against his argument, for example, he tended to neutralize it through symbolic figures of speech. One such figure was *allegory*, a well-known device of Hellenistic literary criticism that ancient philosophers used to explain away unwanted, undignified tales of the gods and goddesses found in Homeric epic and classical mythology – such as the embarrassing tales of the divine Olympians engaged in all sorts of adulterous and other erotic exploits (see Box 6). Paul thus displayed a revisionist reading of Scripture that shifted his interpretative methodology – pesher, midrash, Greco-Roman methods of interpretation – along the full spectrum of his plural identities as both Jewish and Greco-Roman.

Paul affirmed pride in being Jewish and associated his past life with the faith he later came to embrace (see Box 7). Importantly, Paul had little guilt or remorse over his past. *He never called himself a "sinner"* (this is important to remember when we come to Chapter 6). Paul never rejected his identity as a "Hebrew," an "Israelite," and a member of "the tribe of Benjamin" – even when he claimed a clean break on at least one level with what he had earlier considered most dear (see Phil. 3:8, a likely reference to his former Pharisaic self and position of power in the neighborhood synagogue, and not to his Jewishness in general). In place of a rejection, we find that intense religious zeal characterized every phase of his career, from his schooling in Jewish ancestral tradition and his persecuting the church to his Christian evangelizing. Paul's personality remained the same after he became an apostle, without repudiating his ancestral tradition of Judaism. Paul thus did not change from Judaism to "Christianity," in the sense of a faith apart from the religion of Israel. Indeed, the terms "Christian" and "Christianity" were not invented yet; they only appeared decades after Paul's death. (I shall, however, occasionally continue to use the anachronistic term *Christian* for Paul and his religious contemporaries, but only for convenience considering they themselves would have neither recognized nor used it.) In short, Paul always considered himself a Jew, and a very good one – even once a "Pharisee."

Box 5 Midrash on the Last Days (Dead Sea Scroll Known as 4Q174)

...*(I will appoint a place for my people Israel and will plant them that they may dwell there and be troubled no more by their) enemies. No son of iniquity (shall afflict again) as formerly, from the day (that I set judges) over my people Israel [2 Sam. 7:10].* This is the House which (He will build for them in the) last days, as it is written in the book of Moses, *In the sanctuary which Thy hands have established, O Lord, the Lord shall reign for ever and ever* [Exod. 15:17–18]. This is the House into which (the unclean shall) never (enter, nor the uncircumcised,) nor the Ammonite, nor the Moabite, nor the half-breed, nor the foreigner, nor the stranger, ever; for there shall My Holy Ones be. (Its glory shall endure) for ever; it shall appear above it perpetually. And strangers shall lay waste no more, as they formerly laid waste the Sanctuary of Israel because of its sin. He has commanded that a Sanctuary of men be built for Himself, that there they may send up, like the smoke of incense, the works of the Law.

The Lord declares to you that He will build you a House [2 Sam. 7:11]. *I will raise up your seed after you* [2 Sam. 7:12]. *I will establish the throne of his kingdom (forever)* [2 Sam. 7:13]. *(I will be) his father and he shall be my son* [2 Sam. 7:14]. He is the Branch of David who shall arise with the Interpreter of the Law (to rule) in Zion (at the end) of time. As it is written, *I will raise up the tent of David that is fallen* [Amos 9:11]. That is to say, the fallen *tent of David* is who shall arise to save Israel.

Explanation [Hebrew *midrash*] of *How blessed is the man who does not walk in the counsel of the wicked* [Ps. 1:1]. Interpreted [Hebrew *pesher*], this saying (concerns) those who turn aside from the way (of the people) as it is written in the book of Isaiah the Prophet concerning the last days, *it came to pass that (the Lord turned me aside, as with a mighty hand, from walking in the way of) his people* [Isa. 8:11]. They are those of whom it is written in the book of Ezekiel the Prophet, *The Levites (strayed from me, following) their idols* [Ezek. 44:10]. They are the sons of Zadok who (seek their own) counsel and follow (their own inclination) apart from the Council of the Community.

(Why) do the nations (rage) and the people meditate (vanity, the kings of the earth) rise up, (and the) princes take counsel together against the Lord and against (His Messiah)? [Ps. 2:1]. Interpreted, this saying concerns (the kings of the nations) who shall (rage against) the elect of Israel in the last days. (Trans. in Vermes 2004, 525–56, italics indicate biblical verses. See, in general, Lim 2002 and Brooke 2000)

Box 6 Allegorical Interpretation and Classical Mythology

Homer's doctrine on the gods is usually concentrated on what is useless, or even improper, as the myths he tells about the gods are unseemly. In order to counter this sort of accusation, some people invoke the manner of speaking; they feel that all was said in an allegorical mode and has to do with the nature of the elements, for instance, as in the case of conflict between the gods. Thus, according to them, dryness struggles against humidity, heat against cold, light against heavy; water extinguishes fire, but fire dries out air; this applies as well to all the elements making up the universe; there is a fundamental opposition between them; they incorporate once and for all corruption at the level of individual beings, but they last eternally as a whole. These are the struggles that Homer depicted by giving to fire the names of Apollo, Helios, and Hephaistos, to water those of Poseidon and Scamander, to the moon that of Artemis, to air that of Hera, etc. In the same way, he sometimes gave names of gods to dispositions of the soul, to thinking that of Athena, to madness that of Ares, to desire that of Aphrodite, to beautiful speaking that of Hermes, all faculties to which these gods are linked. This mode of defense is quite ancient and goes back to Theagenes of Rhegium, who was the first to write about Homer; its nature is thus to take into account the manner of speaking. (Porphyry, third century C.E.; trans. in Brisson 2004, 35–36)

The Pharisees

Although the ancient Pharisees got bad press in the New Testament Gospels for blind, punctilious observance of the Jewish law as "hypocrites," Paul showed no familiarity with this later Christian stereotype. Rather, he assumed that both his Gentile and Jewish contemporaries respected the Pharisees for their learning and knowledge. The Pharisaic sages urged the use of ancestral oral tradition to interpret the written Torah (a term expanded beyond the Pentateuch to cover the whole Hebrew Bible, or "Old Testament," at this time not yet a closed canon of Scripture). Their religious sect was also a political party. The Pharisees had a history of seeking political influence in the Judean state, briefly coming to power under the reign of the Hasmonean queen Salome Alexandra (76–67 B.C.E.), but they enjoyed little actual sway in the society or government in the Roman era of Paul's lifetime. The adherents were relatively few (about

---

Box 7 Paul's Pride in Being Jewish

What little Paul says about his upbringing is made in passing. These passages show Paul to have been astonishingly candid about his past persecutions of Jesus followers, and to have made explicit connections between his past and present life in Judaism.

> I myself am an Israelite, a descendant of Abraham, a member of the tribe of Benjamin. (Rom. 11:1)

> If anyone has reason to be confident in the flesh, I have more: circumcised on the eighth day, a member of the people of Israel, of the tribe of Benjamin, a Hebrew born of Hebrews; as to the law, a Pharisee; as to zeal, a persecutor of the church; as to righteousness under the law, blameless. (Phil. 3:4–6)

> You have heard no doubt of my earlier life in Judaism. I was violently persecuting the church of God and was trying to destroy it. I advanced in Judaism beyond many among my own people of the same age, for I was far more zealous for the traditions of my ancestors. (Gal. 1:13–14)

---

six thousand members) and tended to represent social levels lower than the Jewish aristocratic elite that formed the basis of its rival party, the Sadducees. The non-elite position of the Pharisees matches Paul's own socioeconomic status.

As one option among the many other sects in the variety that was ancient Judaism, the Pharisaic party worked to adapt Torah regulations so as to make Jewish religious life possible in a Gentile world. Unfortunately, few primary sources survive from the Pharisees themselves. Besides Paul, the only other extant first-century writer claiming a Pharisaic education is the Jewish historian Flavius Josephus (ca. 37–100 C.E.), another key figure in ancient Judaism whom I mention often in this chapter. Critical use of Josephus for a historical reconstruction of the Pharisees helpfully corrects the polemical caricatures of them in the later New Testament Gospels. Josephus explains that the Pharisees expounded biblical laws "expertly" (often mistranslated as "strictly"), that is, according to the additional ordinances passed down in the oral teachings of the Pharisaic sages (the "traditions of the fathers"). These traditions expanded Torah observance beyond its normal applicability within the sacred sphere of the Jerusalem temple and its priesthood, into the "profane" world of everyday Jewish life among the Gentiles (see Box 8). The Pharisees' teachings are important for our

---

Box 8   The Pharisees among the Jewish Schools of Thought

Now at this time were three schools among the Jews, which thought differently about human actions; the first of these were called Pharisees, the second Sadducees, and the third Essenes. The Pharisees, for their part, say that certain events, but not all, are the work of fate; with others it depends on ourselves whether they shall take place or not. . . . the Pharisees passed on to the people certain ordinances from a succession of fathers, which are not written down in the laws of Moses. For this reason the party of the Sadducees dismissed these ordinances, averring that one need only recognize the written ordinances, whereas those from the tradition of the fathers need not be observed. Conflicts and major differences developed between the two groups over these matters. The Sadducees persuade only the wealthy, however, and have no popular following, whereas the Pharisees have the support of the populace. (Josephus, *Antiquities of the Jews* 13.171–172, 297–298; trans. in Mason 1991, 196, 217–18)

---

study of Paul because they included beliefs in life after death, the resurrection, divine providence, and an apocalyptic eschatology, all of which Paul also espoused. More conservative Jewish circles criticized the Pharisees for being too "relaxed" in biblical interpretation because they extended Torah into ordinary life outside the Temple and its priesthood, accusing them of being "pro-Gentile" – a further connection to Paul.

This information gleaned from Josephus coheres with a reexamination of the Dead Sea Scrolls in recent Jewish studies research. The sectarian Essenes withdrew into the desert wilderness to await the imminent coming of the End Times. They reimagined their own community as God's Elect in a "new covenant" and aimed to replicate the Jerusalem temple in the organization and ritual of their sectarian life. Self-styled "Covenanters," the Essenes denounced other Jews as apostates from "true Israel," specifically condemning an organized group of enemies they derisively called the "Seekers after Smooth Things" and the "Builders of the Wall." It is almost certain that these enemies were Pharisees.

Evoking the biblical rebuke against Hebrew prophets who speak "smooth things" yet prophesy only "illusions," the first epithet (Seekers after Smooth Things) attacks the seeking out of convenient yet "false" evasions of Jewish Law. The target of the condemnation corresponds to the so-called relaxed interpretations by which the Pharisees rendered Torah applicable in a Gentile world. The second epithet (Builders of the Wall) condemns the attempt to "fence off" the Torah with additional legal and interpretative ordinances, that is, the authoritative oral tradition on how to follow the Law that the Pharisees claimed had been handed down from Jewish ancestors. A sobriquet similar to "Builders of the Wall" but with positive meaning appears also in the Mishnah, a compilation of legal traditions of celebrated rabbis (sages) that was codified around 200 C.E. and later became the basic part of the Jerusalem and Babylonian Talmuds. (A consensus of modern scholars connects the rabbinic sages to the earlier Pharisees based on similarities in beliefs about the observance of Torah, the temple cult, and other teachings). The Dead Sea Scroll community thus denounced the Pharisees for being too lax in their interpretations of Torah, for claiming Torah to be applicable everywhere, and for accommodating the holy covenants to unholy Gentile society. The apocalyptic scenarios of the Dead Sea Scrolls even pictured the Pharisees orchestrating a satanic war in league with unholy Gentiles against Israel and Torah.

All this evidence suggests that the apostle Paul may not have been idiosyncratic in his religious convictions. His preoccupation with Gentiles seems to have been lifelong and to have focused on their eschatological participation in God's plan for Israel's salvation. We know this because much of Pauline theology corresponds to recent reconstructions of what ancient Pharisees also taught: too lax an approach to Jewish law (in the eyes of opponents), an expanded notion of temple holiness from the priesthood and its sacrifices into ordinary life among the Gentiles, and apocalyptic beliefs in a final judgment and the resurrection of the dead. Indeed, the specifically Pharisaic belief in the resurrection may have encouraged Paul to interpret his revelatory experience at Damascus as an encounter with the risen Messiah Jesus.

Paul's lifelong preoccupation with Gentiles and his participation in wider Greco-Roman culture are the major points of continuity between his past life in Judaism as a Pharisee and his present life in Judaism as an apostle of his divine lord Jesus. This continuity appears most clearly in his use of the Greek language, extends to his rhetoric, and reaches to contemporaneous Jewish sources about the Pharisees. The portrait of a Jewish Saul changing into a Christian Paul who completely repudiated his past Jewishness is, therefore, misleading and erroneous. This finding requires us to reexamine the pivotal event of Paul's life, his so-called conversion to Christianity.

2. THE EVENT AT DAMASCUS

In his late twenties or early thirties, Paul first encountered at Damascus worshippers of a crucified Galilean criminal, Jesus of Nazareth, and grew hostile to them (ca. 34–35). A traveling artisan and a neighborhood Pharisaic party boss, Paul campaigned vigorously to root out these small assemblies of Jesus followers from the neighborhood synagogues and the Jewish households in which they were based. He persecuted the Jewish offenders "to the utmost" (Gal. 1:13, often mistranslated "violently"), referring to the harshest juridical punishment available in synagogue discipline – the "forty lashes minus one" (see Deut. 25:3; cf. 2 Cor. 11:24). What caught Paul's ire probably revolved around his fellow Jews allowing the presence of uncircumcised Gentiles in the nascent synagogues and house congregations of Jesus worshippers. Understanding the historical context of synagogues among the dispersed Jewish communities beyond Palestine will help explain otherwise puzzling features of this controversy.

Diaspora Synagogues, Godfearers, and Jesus Followers

The Romans crucified Jesus of Nazareth (ca. 30) as a Jewish messianic pretender and bandit. To Roman authorities and important Judean leaders, the obscure Galilean peasant deserved a public execution because he preached a powerful "kingdom," which verged on political sedition against the Roman Empire (see Mark 15:26–32; John 19:19–20). With its ringleader executed, the Jesus movement appeared dead as well, at least in the eyes of Rome's provincial authorities. Yet the movement's missionaries soon spread abroad with enthusiastic stories of a divine (or at least a postmortem) Jesus, raised from the dead. Believers passed on the miraculous tales in two main rituals, an initiatory washing (baptism) and a common meal (the Lord's supper, or Eucharist). The storytelling about miracles found many receptive audiences. Within only a few years, tiny assemblies (congregations) of Jesus worshippers flourished within Jewish communities even beyond Judea.

Jewish populations outside the Judean homeland of Israel are known as the Diaspora. For the ancient Diaspora, the most important Jewish institution was the synagogue, which functioned as a community center for Jewish education, Torah reading, and worship of the God of Israel. Importantly, the attendees were not only local Jews but also Gentile neighbors sympathetic to Judaism. Such Gentile sympathizers were of many kinds, but most were so-called Godfearers who nonetheless remained "pagans" – practicing multiple religious commitments and having allegiance to Judaism in varying degrees. Such Godfearers differed from their fellow Gentiles who completely abandoned "paganism" and converted to Judaism outright as Jewish proselytes. Predictably, in antiquity's patriarchal culture, the ritual removal of the male foreskin (circumcision) was *the* distinguishing mark of membership in the common ancestry and kinship of Jews as a distinct people (Greek *ethnos*). Most male Gentile sympathizers to Judaism did not accept this mark (in other words, did not "convert") because adult circumcision was a painful operation, had a foreign heritage, and received ridicule and scorn in Greco-Roman culture for mutilating the ideal male form. Moreover, conversion would have meant giving up participation in cultic activities directed at any other deities, requiring Gentile proselytes to withdraw from a wide swath of traditional culture.

From Persecutor to Apostle

Increasingly numbered among the Jesus followers were these Godfearing but uncircumcised Gentiles who likely heard the proclamation in the shared cultural space that the Diaspora synagogue provided. The growing mix of uncircumcised Gentiles threatened to reopen long-standing rifts not only among Jews (about the right way to worship the God of Israel and which laws of Torah were most important) but also between Jews and their pagan neighbors. The Jews and their pagan neighbors in a large metropolis like Damascus lived within walls containing a checkerboard pattern of crowded districts, in which tensions and outright ethnic violence between Gentiles and Jews were frequent. Synagogue leaders solicited the patronage of Roman imperial authorities and tried to foster good social relations with local Greeks and Syrians as a whole, to reduce the likelihood of anti-Jewish violence.

Josephus records a particularly gruesome episode of anti-Jewish violence in Damascus, which occurred ca. 66 during the First Jewish War against Rome. He blames the anti-Jewish violence on the relative ease by which Gentile wives (who did not have to undergo circumcision) became Jewish proselytes and the subsequent division of their families as the major causes of the anti-Jewish hostility. Breaking ties of family blood incited the urban riot:

> Meanwhile, the people of Damascus, learning of the disaster that had befallen the Romans, were fired with a determination to kill the Jews who resided among them. As they had for a long time past kept them shut up in

the gymnasium – a precaution prompted by suspicion – they thought that they should have no difficulty with the job. Their only fear was that of their own wives who, with few exceptions, had all become converts to the Jewish religion, and so their efforts were mainly directed to keeping the secret from them. In the end, they came upon the Jews, cooped up as they were and unarmed, and in one hour's time slaughtered them all with impunity, to the number of ten thousand five hundred. (Josephus, *Jewish War* 2.559–561; trans. Thackeray 1989, 539, altered)

This episode offers an analogue for making intelligible Paul's harassment of Jesus's followers in the local synagogues. Why did Paul persecute the church? He likely was cracking down on his fellow Jews who invited uncircumcised Gentiles to worship Jesus in local synagogues without making them proselytes, which threatened to fuel prejudicial fear among pagans that the Jews were secretly trying to recruit to increase their numbers. That is to say, Paul condemned the new faith not only for preaching a crucified criminal as the Messiah but also for dividing pagan families too easily. To proclaim the crucified criminal Jesus as a divine lord to uncircumcised Gentiles turned them away from their pagan families and neighbors without the need for the formal conversion of becoming proselytes that normally required circumcision. The relative ease of such male "conversions" (on par with the conversions of women, described by Josephus) endangered the fragile concord between the Jewish minority and Gentile majority in neighborhoods throughout the city. It also flouted Torah conventions. This hypothesis suggests that, immediately prior to his change to become an apostle of the faith, Paul already had an intense religious engagement with the Jesus movement at Damascus. Paul, therefore, did not adopt the new faith out of the blue. Rather, the faith of these odd believers had already occupied his religious zeal, even if disapprovingly, before he became its apostle.

Paul's own letters confirm this historical contextualization. The key text has already been quoted, but now I provide its second half:

If anyone else has reason to be confident in the flesh, I have more; circumcised on the eighth day, a member of the people of Israel, of the tribe of Benjamin, a Hebrew born of Hebrews; as to the law, a Pharisee; as to zeal, a persecutor of the church; as to righteousness under the law, blameless.

Yet whatever gains I had, these I have come to regard as loss because of Christ. More than that, I regard everything as loss because of Christ. More than that, I regard everything as loss because of the surpassing value of knowing Christ Jesus my Lord. For his sake, I have suffered the loss of all things, and I regard them as rubbish, in order than I might gain Christ and be found in him, not having a righteousness of my own that comes from the law, but one that comes through the faith of Christ, the righteousness from God based on faith. (Phil. 3:4–10)

The language describes a model of conversion in which an entire value system remains intact but is radically reversed, being turned upside down. In other words, Paul's transformation did not repudiate the content of his former values, but rather reversed the positive and negative poles within the *same* ideological system. The social phenomenon is analogous to prison guards turning to identify with their inmates, political zealots on the extreme left suddenly embracing the extreme right, or persecutors becoming fascinated by what they deplore. Paul therefore did not "convert" in the sense of changing from one religion to another, but rather moved from Pharisaic Judaism to join a rival Jewish sect that had already deeply engrossed his emotional and religious attention, albeit hostilely.

Of course, *conversion* is our term, not Paul's. Paul never described the change that his revelatory experience caused to his career as a "conversion" from one religion to another. Instead, he used the biblical language for the call of a Hebrew prophet: Paul claimed to have been a famous fetus set apart by God "before I was born" (Gal. 1:15), echoing the Lord's words to the Old Testament prophet Jeremiah who was called "to the nations" (Gentiles):

> Now the word of the LORD came to me saying,
> "Before I formed you in the womb I knew you,
> and before you were born I consecrated you;
> I appointed you a prophet to the nations."
>   (Jer. 1:4–5; see also Isa. 49:1–6)

The difference is important because in the Jewish Bible to "call" someone did not mean to "convert" him or her. Rather, the term *calling* and the mission "to the Gentiles" had specific precedents and meanings in Paul's Jewish heritage, echoing the divine calling of Hebrew prophets such as Jeremiah, a prophet "to the nations" (Jer. 1:5). Paul's language thus points to his beliefs, habituated from reading his Bible, in the Lord "calling" an unlikely Hebrew to serve and lead God's people to salvation. Ancient Jews understood such a calling to be not one's own vocation, but rather an absolute subservience to the dominating influence of God, for which the Hebrew Bible used the metaphor of slavery (e.g., Exod. 14:31 and Num. 12:7–8, concerning Moses). The apostle Paul identified himself as a "slave of Jesus Christ" (Rom. 1:1; Gal. 1:10; Phil. 1:1). The slave self-identification expressed total obedience and loss of self to a divine master (Lord) – the one who "made me his own" (Phil. 3:12, "grabbed me").

How did the Lord "grab" him? Paul neither described the revelatory event in detail nor offered it as a model that other believers should experience, too, for it made him not just a believer but also the unique apostle to the Gentiles "sent from God." He made only brief declaratory statements about his Damascus experience, mainly to assert his apostolic authority in response to conflicts with and reprisals from his opponents within the Christian movement, and to declare his freedom from the original apostles in Jerusalem. Paul had in his own eyes the clear right to found and lead new congregations of Gentiles dedicated to the worship of Messiah Jesus (see Chapter 2). He insisted on having seen the divine body of the risen Jesus in an authentic vision, of the same kind witnessed by Peter and "the twelve" original disciples (see Box 9).

Paul's insistence on having actually witnessed a divine lord (in the same way as the other believers had previously reported) would have been a message familiar to ancient audiences. In the context of ancient Mediterranean religions, Paul experienced what his contemporaries would have called an epiphany, the manifestation of a deity's presence before a mortal. An epiphany had specific dramatic conventions for ancient audiences, such as the miraculous displays of life-threatening power that were often staged in ancient theater and described by predictable tropes in Greco-Roman literature. Stock accounts of epiphanies typically depicted witnesses becoming so-called confessors, who declared a personal testimony to the power of the deity and returned the favor by spending some time in temples announcing to all and sundry the "good news" (Greek *euangelion*) of the deity's manifestation in their daily lives. Pagan "confessors" were famous in the ancient Mediterranean world for creating new shrines, cults, and priesthoods in honor of their patron deity, and writing up their experiences in a narrative for deposit in a temple for pilgrims to read. The figure of the confessor was not unambiguously positive, however. Especially when overzealous, the confessor often received scorn in classical antiquity as a talkative beggar, a nuisance to regular (official) priests, and a religious fraud. Such charges hounded Paul's career as an apostle (cf. 2 Cor. 2:17; 4:2). Paul's later interpreters, both friends and foes, used the stock tropes of a pagan confessor's epiphany to "fill in the details" about that revelatory experience at Damascus, even if Paul himself was reticent to talk about it.

Paul wrote that his religious zeal compelled him to harass and then join believers who proclaimed a crucified criminal as a divine lord to

---

Box 9 Paul's Gospel Narrative: Who Saw Jesus First Does Not Matter

Paul's gospel unfolded a serial narrative. It began with Christ's atoning sacrifice "for us" on the cross and his appearances from the dead to certain believers one after another, to Christ's coming again in the very near future to save the eschatologically restored Israel and to destroy the rest of the world (unbelieving idolaters). Complaining about the dubious competition of "I saw him first," Paul wrote himself into a story that had been "handed down" by prior believers.

> Now I would remind you, brothers and sisters, of the good news [Greek *euangelion*, gospel] that I proclaimed to you, which you in turn received, in which also you stand, through which also you are being saved, if you hold firmly to the message that I proclaimed to you – unless you have come to believe in vain.
>
> For I handed on to you as of first importance what I in turn had received: that Christ died for our sins in accordance with the scriptures, and that he was buried, and that he was raised on the third day in accordance with the scriptures, and that he appeared to Cephas, then to the twelve. Then he appeared to the more than five hundred brothers and sisters at one time, most of whom are still alive, though some have died. Then he appeared to James, then to all the apostles. Last of all, as to one untimely born, he appeared also to me. For I am the least of the apostles [a possible pun on his Roman name *Paulos*, Latin "little one"], unfit to be called an apostle because I persecuted the church of God. But by the grace of God I am what I am, and his grace toward me has not been in vain. On the contrary, I worked harder than any of them – though it was not I, but the grace of God that is with me. Whether then it was I or they, so we proclaim and so you have come to believe. (1 Cor. 15:1–11)

---

uncircumcised Gentiles. In modern psychological terms, one might say that Paul had a *stress experience* inducing him to identify with his victims. Paul's religious vision thus led him to reverse his values and to see the inclusion of uncircumcised Gentiles not as threatening to Israel, but as the ultimate and necessary step in God's eschatological salvation of all Israel. What kind of vision led to Paul's gospel? Although some interpreters imagine that Paul conceived his entire message in the moment of his calling, the reality is that Paul spent some time – indeed, several decades – revising his beliefs, thinking through the implications of his calling, and developing it into a mission. Immediately after his Damascus experience (ca. 35/36), for example, Paul did not try to join the original apostles in Jerusalem. Rather, he "went away at once into Arabia" (Gal. 1:17), perhaps staying little over a year. By "Arabia" (a vaguely defined geography in antiquity), Paul probably means the northwest territory of the Arab kingdom of the Nabateans, a client state of Rome, ruled by Aretas IV (9 B.C.E.–40 C.E.), which bordered Damascus. Because the Nabatean Kingdom held a powerful monopoly on the caravan routes connecting Damascus to the eastern trade, its Hellenistic cities were choice destinations for many Romans and other foreign travelers. We know little about the purpose of Paul's journey other than its apparent circuitousness and near disaster. Perhaps Paul went on his first Gentile mission, to the Nabateans, and had failed.

Flight from Damascus

Whatever the case, when Paul returned to Damascus around 36/37, he faced mortal danger. Nabatean troops of the expansionist King Aretas had temporarily seized Damascus in a regional conflict with the current Jewish king of Galilee, Herod Antipas (a son of Herod the Great). Paul needed to escape the city – perhaps his activities in Arabia had aroused the hostility of Nabatean authorities, or the Nabatean governor was simply rounding up local Judeans suspected of siding with King Antipas – and so in the dead of the night supporters aided his flight. According to Paul himself, supporters lowered him down the city walls by means of a basket. Importantly, Paul narrates the flight as an example of his "weakness" (see Box 10). While the episode may illustrate personal ingenuity and survival skills, Paul emphasized its humiliation. A different version of the story, less historically reliable, appears in the canonical Acts of the Apostles (see Box 11).

The failures in Arabia and Damascus led Paul finally to Jerusalem, a trip to introduce himself to the original disciples of Jesus – or, at least, to the leading apostle Peter (Cephas). Yet this introductory meeting instigated greater conflict rather than more missionary cooperation. At Jerusalem, and later at Antioch in Roman Syria (modern Antakya, Turkey), Paul faced growing and eventually irreconcilable differences with a certain group of believers from Jerusalem, which Paul came to blame on its leaders. The conflicts led Paul to launch his own Gentile mission far afield, in Asia Minor and Greece, separate from the Jerusalem apostles (see Chapter 2).

> **Box 10 Paul's Flight from Damascus**
>
> If I must boast, I will boast of the things that show my weakness. The God and Father of the Lord Jesus (blessed be he forever!) knows that I do not lie. In Damascus, the governor under King Aretas guarded the city of Damascus in order to seize me, but I was let down in a basket through an opening in the wall, and escaped from his hands. (2 Cor. 11:30–33)
>
> Paul placed the account of his ambush at Damascus at the end of a list enumerating various conflicts in his mission that the everyday hazards of ancient travel compounded:
>
> Five times I have received from the Jews the forty lashes minus one. Three times I was beaten with rods. Once I received a stoning. Three times I was shipwrecked; for a night and a day I was a drift at sea; on frequent journeys, in danger from rivers, danger from bandits, danger from my own people, danger from Gentiles, danger in the city, danger in the wilderness, danger at sea, danger from false brothers and sisters [i.e., opponents in Christ]; in toil and hardship, through many a sleepless night, hungry and thirsty, often without food, cold and naked. And, besides other things, I am under daily pressure because of my anxiety for all the churches. Who is weak, and I am not weak? Who is made to stumble, and I am not indignant? (2 Cor. 11:24–29)
>
> The passage conforms to a stock "hardship catalog" (Greek *peristasis*) that ancient rhetoric used to distinguish between true and false speech. In contrast to noble hardships, however, Paul chooses *ignominious* ones that display his "weakness" as an apostle. The list specifies, for example, humiliating floggings: "beaten with rods" and "the forty lashes minus one." The latter is likely the very synagogue discipline that Paul previously had inflicted upon Jesus followers in Damascus. Paul thus describes his flight from Damascus as an ignominious episode, a hard lesson in his early career as an apostle.

3. Face-Off in Jerusalem and Antioch

Jerusalem: Paul and the "Circumcision Faction"

Paul's first trip to Jerusalem following Christ's appearance to him was a brief, introductory visit. Around 37, "three years" after his initial revelation, Paul came to see Peter alone, staying in the home of Peter for

---

Box 11 The Flight from Damascus in the Book of Acts

The story of Paul's ambush in Damascus appears in two ancient sources, which disagree with each other. Unlike Paul's own account, which clearly states that he fled an attempt by the occupying military governor under King Aretas to arrest him (Box 10), the book of Acts makes no mention of the Nabatean authorities but instead blames the attempt to capture Paul/Saul on a plot by *Jews* in Damascus to kill him:

> After some time had passed, the Jews plotted to kill him, but their plot became known to Saul. They were watching by the gates day and night so that they might kill him; but his disciples took him by night and let him down through an opening in the wall, lowering him in a basket. (Acts 9:23–25)

Local Jewish opposition to the rise of Christianity in the Roman Empire is an important theological leitmotif in Luke's work (see, e.g., Acts 23:12–15). Because the author repeats scenes like this one throughout the narrative, Acts' account of Paul's flight arising from a Jewish plot is likely a stock literary scene and so unhistorical.

On the stock portrayal of Jews as negative characters in Acts, see Wills 1991.

---

just "fifteen days," during which each made the other's acquaintance probably for the first time (Gal. 1:18). We do not know who, if anyone, made the introductions; a later tradition says it was Barnabas (Acts 9:26–27), a figure whom Paul mentioned in his letters as an associate on the second visit to Jerusalem (Gal. 2:1). In any event, Paul kept his visit short because he anticipated hostility from the Jerusalem believers at large, who knew him only by reputation and not by sight (Gal. 1:18–24). After all, Paul, the former persecutor of the church, was now suddenly its self-proclaimed apostle to the Gentiles; Paul probably appeared to his host as a curiosity. During his visit, Paul encountered also James, the "brother of the Lord," a fellow Jerusalem apostle with Peter. This actual brother of Jesus and a rising leader in the nascent Jerusalem church had much in common with Paul – neither belonged to the original Jesus circle of Twelve Disciples, only becoming an apostle through religious visions after Jesus' death – but the two could not get along. Over the next fourteen years, Paul's subsequent relationship with James (and Peter) grew increasingly competitive and strained.

After his first "acquaintance meeting" with Peter (and James), Paul traveled to what he calls "Syria and Cilicia" (Gal. 1:21). The geography is shorthand for the principal cities in the regions, meaning Antioch in Syria and Tarsus in Cilicia; in other words, he went home and afterward to Antioch. Capital of the Roman province of Syria, Antioch on the Orontes River was the third largest city in the Roman Empire and a major commercial center connecting the Mediterranean to the East. Over the next dozen years in Antioch (ca. 37–49), Paul partnered with other self-appointed apostles – most notably, his mentor Barnabas (the same Barnabas mentioned before in Jerusalem) – in the local household (and, perhaps, synagogue) congregations that welcomed both Jews and uncircumcised Gentiles together on a regular basis. The Gentiles whom Paul met at Antioch were likely Godfearers already familiar with Jewish ritual and Scripture, who assembled with like-minded messianic Jews in private rooms for instruction, baptism (a Jewish priestly rite prescribed in the Torah; see Lev. 16:24), and a ritual meal (the Lord's supper, based on the Passover Seder). In this urban Diaspora context, Paul learned a great deal from the local assemblies about the Messiah Jesus and developed his thinking about the gospel. Paul's success as a local apostle in the mix of Jewish-Gentile house churches in Antioch increased his circle of associates. "Fourteen years" later (ca. 49), Paul experienced another revelation, which he said to have prompted him to make a *second* visit to Jerusalem (Gal. 2:1). Unlike the first, this second meeting was to be a showdown. Paul expected a face-off. The conflict centered on the very question beginning to divide believers: whether uncircumcised male Gentiles could continue to be welcomed into the church in their own right, *as Gentiles* (not as converted Jews), without having to accept circumcision (the normal ritual of male conversion into Israel).

Let me provide some historical background about this conflict. From its inception, the mission for Christ had normally included Gentiles without requiring them to convert as Jewish proselytes. Reinforcing this ethnic inclusion were apocalyptic hopes, alive in ancient Judaism, in the eschatological pilgrimage of "the nations" – that is, Gentiles – to Israel at the End of the Ages *as Gentiles*. Scriptural prophecy of this pilgrimage included a host of passages. The prophet Isaiah looks forward to the last days, when "all the nations" (Gentiles) will "stream" into Jerusalem: "Many peoples shall come and say, 'Come, let us go up to the mountain of the LORD, to the house of the God of Jacob; that he may teach us his ways and that we may walk in his paths'" (Isa. 2:2–3). "In those days," concurs the prophet Zechariah, "ten men from nations of every language shall take hold of a Jew, grasping his garment and saying, 'Let us go with you, for we have heard that God is with you'" (Zech. 8:23). And the Book of Tobit, a second-century B.C.E. sacred Jewish writing of the Old Testament Apocrypha, declares: "Then the nations in the whole world will all turn back to worship God in truth. They will abandon their idols, which deceitfully have led them into their error" (Tobit 14:6). From these and other scriptures, it is clear that many ancient Jews believed Gentiles would abandon their idols not as converted "Jews" (proselytes) but as uncircumcised Gentiles coming to worship the "living God of Israel." The appearances of the risen Jesus had convinced his earliest followers that the Final Judgment, which they understood these passages to prophesy, was imminent. Uncircumcised Gentile believers turning to Messiah Jesus and away from idols must have confirmed all the movement's intensely apocalyptic convictions. As the years went by without the expected return of Jesus, however, these apocalyptic hopes began to fade into the disappointment of unfulfilled promises.

By the time Paul made his second visit to Jerusalem to see Peter and James, the original apostles in the Jerusalem church had been preaching the imminent coming of the Kingdom of God for nearly a generation. Yet the Kingdom had not come. The delay of Jesus' second coming caused the church in Jerusalem to reinterpret its core beliefs about conversion. The growing disappointment over the Kingdom's delay led many – Paul called them a "faction" and a belligerent gang of "false believers" – to press for a new membership requirement for Gentiles in the Judean church assemblies: outright conversion through the concrete practices of circumcision and all the other Torah observances (such as keeping kosher). In contrast to this "circumcision faction," Paul was a former persecutor of the faith who now had a call from Messiah Jesus himself to preach to Gentiles *as Gentiles*, and God had not revealed any change of plan to him. The new apostle still had the eschatological hope in the salvation of Israel that included the incoming of the Gentiles with their foreskins intact. Indeed, Paul names his oral proclamation to the Gentiles the very "Gospel for the Foreskin" (Greek *euangelion tēs akrobustias*; Gal. 2:7).

From the Antioch congregations, Paul brought a band of associates that included his mentor Barnabas and an uncircumcised Greek protégé named Titus. To Paul and his growing circle of friends, the faith of Titus displayed the "obvious" fact that Gentiles *do* participate in the salvation of eschatological Israel as uncircumcised Gentiles, not as "Jews" (proselytes). In a *private* meeting with only three apostles, Paul laid his Gospel for the Foreskin before the leadership "pillars" supporting the Judean congregations: Peter, James the brother of the Jesus, and a certain John. Paul intended that this meeting would proceed like his first visit and be kept away from the eyes and ears of the Jerusalem believers at large, who as a whole still mistrusted him. To the Pillars, Paul made his stand absolutely clear: either his way or the highway.

As events unfolded, it would be the highway for Paul, because an uninvited gang of Jerusalem believers ("false brothers," according to Paul) slipped into the private meeting and caused a big ruckus. This third party demanded that Titus be circumcised, and that Paul recant his Gospel for the Foreskin. The battle to defend Gentile foreskins, which Paul would fight for the rest of his life, had begun:

> Then after fourteen years I went up again to Jerusalem with Barnabas, taking Titus along with me. I went up in response to a revelation. Then I laid before them (though only in a private meeting with the acknowledged leaders) the gospel that I proclaim among the Gentiles, in order to make sure that I was not running, or had not run, in vain. But even Titus, who was with me, was not compelled to be circumcised, though he was a Greek. But because of false believers secretly brought in, who slipped in to spy on the freedom we have in Christ Jesus, so that they might enslave us – we did not submit to them even for a moment, so that the truth of the gospel might always remain with you. And from those who were supposed to be acknowledged leaders (what they actually were makes no difference to me; God shows no partiality) – those leaders contributed nothing to me. On the contrary, when they saw that I had been entrusted with the Gospel for the Foreskin [*euangelion tēs akrobustias*], just as Peter had been entrusted with the gospel for the circumcised (for he who worked through Peter making him an apostle to the circumcised also worked through me in sending me to the Gentiles), and when James and Cephas and John, who were acknowledged pillars, recognized the grace that had been given to me, they gave to Barnabas and me the right hand of fellowship, agreeing that we should go to the Gentiles and they to the circumcised. They asked only one thing, that we remember the poor, which was actually what I was eager to do. (Gal. 2:1–10)

Paul's version of events makes it clear that he won that day, at least with the Pillars. Peter, James, and John were persuaded to accept the Gospel for the Foreskin and its ongoing mission at Antioch, with the one stipulation that Paul during that mission raise funds in a collection for the poor among the Jerusalem believers. With this pledge and a handshake, Paul thought he had sealed the deal that the Lord himself told him to make.

But the deal fell apart shortly thereafter. The collapse of the deal suggests that not all the parties understood the agreement in the same way.

Antioch: Paul's Face-Off with Peter

Shortly thereafter, at Antioch, Peter and Paul became embroiled in a major dispute over a communal meal. The details are sketchy but the conflict clear. Peter was visiting from Jerusalem and had, for a while, not kept kosher; he readily had eaten food together with uncircumcised Jesus-believing Gentiles. Envoys soon appeared from the Judean churches – Paul calls them a certain gang "from James" – at which point Peter suddenly became a more orthodox Jew and withdrew ("kept himself separate") from the table fellowship of sharing Gentile (nonkosher) food. (The problem must have involved the ritual status of the food itself, likely in Eucharistic meals, rather than just eating with Gentiles at the same table, because – despite long-standing claims in New Testament scholarship – we have no evidence that ancient Jews understood mere proximity to and association with a Gentile to have been defiling under Torah.) Peter apparently displayed his true loyalty to (and fear of) the rising power of James and the circumcision faction in Jerusalem that bore his authority. Peter's abrupt change of behavior led many of the Jewish believers to side with his separation from table fellowship, questioning the ritual (kosher) status of its food and wine. Opposing them were the Gentile believers who sided with Paul. With the battle lines drawn, Paul and Peter had a face-off. This time Paul lost.

Losing the contest, Paul became an enemy of the circumcision faction in Jerusalem associated with James, the brother of Jesus. He even lost Barnabas, his old mentor, to Peter's side. Paul recounted years later, however, that he won the heated argument by his in-your-face rhetoric to Peter, a comeback more likely conceived in *l'esprit d'escalier* (slow on the repartee) as the French saying goes. Be that as it may, Paul wrote that he called out Peter as a "hypocrite." The charge expressed what Paul saw as a betrayal not only by Peter but also by his adoptive home congregations in Antioch on the divisive question of Gentiles and Jewish Law:

> But when Cephas [Peter] came to Antioch, I opposed him to his face, because he stood self-condemned; for until certain people came from James, he used to eat with Gentiles. But after they came, he drew back and kept himself separate for fear of the circumcision faction. And the other Jews joined him in this hypocrisy, so that even Barnabas was led astray by their hypocrisy. But when I saw that they were not acting consistently with the truth of the gospel, I said to Cephas before them all, "If you, though a Jew, live like a Gentile and not like a Jew, how can you compel the Gentiles to live like Jews?" (Gal. 2:11–14; see also Box 19, Chapter 4)

The face-off between Paul and Peter gave the circumcision faction an enlarged group of followers, increased influence at Antioch, and a new allegiance with the reactionary James. Adherents of that faction, as traveling missionaries, bore a gospel message that emphasized the "works" of the Jewish Law (circumcision, a kosher diet, and proper Sabbath observances). In their view, full conversion alone enabled a share in the resurrection of Messiah Jesus that heralds the eschatological salvation of Israel. These missionary teachers would become rival apostles, whom Paul fiercely opposed as his greatest enemies (see Chapter 2).

What did Paul do next? Forced to leave town after yet another failure, he was determined not to work the territory of his (now) rival apostles from Antioch and Jerusalem. Paul and his close circle of associates would have to go at it alone. Out of this humiliation, however, would come the most productive period of Paul's career.

2

COMMUNITIES IN THE MAKING

Now in his mid or late forties, Paul began a new mission (ca. 50), which involved frequent travels in Asia Minor, Macedonia, and Greece. We do not know Paul's actual missionary routes. In this regard, maps of the "journeys of Saint Paul" mislead about the nature of our sources. To be sure, the book of Acts narrates his three so-called missionary journeys: the first in Cyprus and Asia Minor (Acts 13–14); the second in Asia Minor, Macedonia, and Greece, in which Paul appears before the famous Roman governor Gallio (alias Marcus Annaeus Novatus, the elder brother of the philosopher Seneca and proconsul of Achaea in 52) (Acts 15:40–18:22); the third along a similar route but with a three-year stay at Ephesus, and ending in Jerusalem (Acts 18:23–21:16). Acts narrates also a final (fourth) journey of Paul, from Jerusalem to Rome, as a prisoner for a trial before an unnamed Roman emperor who would have been Nero (Acts 27:1–28:16). But the historical reliability of these legendary grand tours, as we shall see, is doubtful.

1. PAUL'S TRAVELS

Paul's own letters do not describe a pattern of three great "tours." Unlike the accounts in Acts, no trips were "commissioned" by church leaders in Jerusalem, Antioch, or elsewhere. Certainly, Paul was a traveler. We know, for example, that he followed the main Roman East–West road, the Via Egnatia, in southern Macedonia from Philippi down to Thessalonica, and also that he reached Corinth through Athens (1 Thess. 2:2; 3:1). He visited Corinth at least three times (1 Cor. 2:1; 2 Cor. 1:23; 13:1), had an extended stay (and a likely imprisonment) in Ephesus across the Aegean (1 Cor. 15:32; 16:8; cf. 2 Cor. 1:8), and returned at least once to Macedonia via the Asia Minor port of Troas on the Hellespont (2 Cor. 2:12). Paul typically sent associates ahead of him to prepare for his arrival in a city

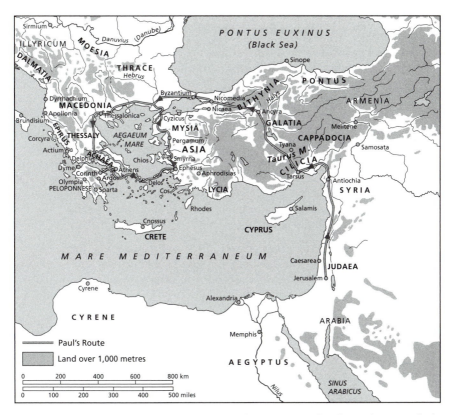

Figure 2 (Map 2). Paul's Missionary Travel: A Geographical Circle around the Aegean.

(Phil. 2:19; Philem. 22), sometimes losing track of their whereabouts when his travel plans changed (1 Cor. 16:10–11). Paul, in retrospect, described his missionary travel as a geographical circle (Greek *kuklō*) around the Aegean, whose gigantic arc stretched "from Jerusalem and as far around as Illyricum" (Rom. 15:19) (see Figure 2). Paul's reference to Illyricum (modern Bosnia and Herzegovina, Serbia and Montenegro, and Albania) is unclear. It may have designated travel westward along the Via Egnatia, but more likely exaggerated the geographical extent of his influence (a modern analogy would be to say, "reaching the whole eastern seaboard").

In sum, Paul made spontaneously decided journeys: he canceled whole trips and vacillated about his travel plans (see Box 12). Paul's eastern circle of success in the Aegean encouraged him to plan a new, westward mission to Spain – not mentioned in the book of Acts – via stopovers at Jerusalem and Rome (Rom. 15:25–28). But he never made it to Spain.

Box 12 Paul's Spontaneously Decided Journeys

For we wanted to come to you – certainly I, Paul, wanted to again and again – but Satan blocked our way. (1 Thess. 2:18–19)

And when I arrive, I will send any whom you approve with letters to take your gift to Jerusalem. If it seems advisable that I should go also, they will accompany me. (1 Cor. 16:3–4)

Since I was sure of this, I wanted to come to you first, so that you might have a double favor; I wanted to visit you on my way to Macedonia, and to come back to you from Macedonia and have you send me on to Judea. Was I vacillating when I wanted to do this? Do I make my plans according to ordinary human standards, ready to "Yes, yes" and "No, no" at the same time? (2 Cor. 1:15–17)

But I call on God as witness against me: it was to spare you that I did not come again to Corinth. I did not mean to imply that we lord it over your faith; rather, we are workers with you for joy, because you stand firm in the faith. So I made up my mind not to make you another painful visit. (2 Cor. 1:23–2:1)

When I came to Troas to proclaim the good news of Christ, a door was opened for me in the Lord; but my mind could not rest because I did not find my brother Titus there. So I said farewell to them and went on to Macedonia. (2 Cor. 2:12–13)

This is the reason that I have so often been hindered from coming to you. But now, with no further place for me in these regions, I desire, as I have for many years, to come to you when I go to Spain. For I do hope to see you on my journey and to be sent on by you, once I have enjoyed your company for a little while. At present, however, I am going to Jerusalem in a ministry to the saints; for Macedonia and Achaia have been pleased to share their resources with the poor among the saints at Jerusalem.... So, when I have completed this, and have delivered to them what has been collected, I will set out by way of you to Spain. (Rom. 15:22–28)

Rather than attempting to map out the confusion of Paul's spontaneously planned itineraries, a more productive approach to the question of his travels reconstructs the general method of his mission. This is because Paul frequently sent delegates ahead to the next city, to prepare his way, and back to cities he had already visited, with letters to congregations addressing specific concerns and crises. We know little more than the names of those in his circle and their functions as letter carriers, envoys, and co-workers: Titus (the uncircumcised Greek of Paul's second Jerusalem visit), Timothy, Silvanus and Sosthenes (co-authors of several letters), Phoebe (a female patron), Junia (a prominent, female apostle), Apollos (another apostle), and the couple Prisca and Aquila (co-workers with a church in their house). In fewer than ten years (ca. 50 to 57), Paul and his tiny circle of associates created an impressive urban network of tiny apocalyptic groups dedicated to the imminent final coming of Messiah Jesus. Each was a small household-based congregation (perhaps little more than three dozen adherents) of Gentiles (former pagans) whose males remained uncircumcised. Paul favored Roman colonies and provincial capitals on major Roman roads as his mission field. (Roman colonies had Latin constitutions and magistracies modeled after the city of Rome, which essentially made them extensions of the imperial capital and their leading citizens full Romans in law.) Unlike Jesus of Nazareth who apparently avoided urban centers in his ministry, Paul was at home in the big city.

Ancient travelers normally walked, even for long distances; the average pace was about fifteen to twenty miles a day in the Greco-Roman era. The unified network of Roman roads connected all major cities, with inns located along mile stations. Travel was a hazard, so people packed lightly, went in groups, took their slave attendants, and watched out for robbers, especially at night. For those who could afford it, travel by boat was available on rivers and the sea – actual boat tickets, on papyrus, survive from Hellenistic Egypt – but only during the sailing season from May to October. Paul likely did most of his traveling on foot accompanied by his band of associates, with occasional sea voyages across the Aegean (from Corinth to Ephesus) and into the Mediterranean (from Corinth to Jerusalem). He made no mention of traveling as wealthy people did, that is, on horseback or in carriages.

But the evidence of one wealthy Roman does help us to reconstruct a historical context for ancient travel in this area of the Mediterranean: Cicero's correspondence during his governorship of Cicilia (51–50 B.C.E.). When Cicero sailed from Athens to Ephesus, the voyage took two hundred nautical miles and two weeks (ancient Greek ships hugged coastlines rather than plowed the open sea, making their way slowly through the Aegean Islands). Because the Roman statesman found the sea voyage stomach turning, he chose to continue the journey to his province overland. From Ephesus, Cicero traveled up the Meander Valley to reach the first city of his province (Laodicea-Lycus) in nine days – a distance of approximately 125 miles (200 km). Then he crossed the Taurus Mountains through the only practicable route, the narrow gorge known as the Cilician Gates (today's Gülek Pass), where the ancient Persian "Royal Road" crossed from the

Anatolian plateau into the Cilician plain, to reach its principal city of Tarsus; it was July, and Cicero complained of the hot and dusty roads. Yet the Roman governor and his proconsular entourage of baggage and staff (Latin *cohors*) moved by land many times from one end of the province to the other, for his judicial and administrative duties. Paul likely traveled Asia Minor and the Aegean along many of the same Roman routes.

2. The Workshop Context of Paul's Ministry

When he arrived in a city, Paul supported himself by his trade as a traveling artisan. He typically sent his associates to a city beforehand, to network with sympathetic householders and to find low-level jobs in local workshops. Greco-Roman cities had hundreds of workshops, mostly modest in scale and household based, dedicated to various kinds of craft production (pottery, masonry, tanning, weaving) for both local and distant markets. Paul worked by trade in leather, which in the ancient world included a whole range of jobs like weaving, tanning, and shoemaking. According to Acts (18:3), Paul was a "tentmaker," though that translation may be too specific. Because Greco-Roman artisans routinely met with fellow workers of the same trade in neighborhood voluntary associations (Latin *collegia*) for meals and fellowship, Paul likely sought out such a neighborhood association of leatherworkers to make his initial contacts in a new city.

Paul worked at his trade "night and day," remained unmarried, and claimed the believers he converted as his sole children. Paul addressed these Gentiles with Jewish terms familiar from his Scripture – saints (literally, "holy ones"), the Elect, members of Israel, heirs according to Abraham's promise – because he believed that the divine salvation of Israel was for all. After planting small cells of Gentile converts in a city, Paul kept in contact with them through envoys and the occasional letter. Paul was constantly on the move because he was certain that the end of the world was imminent. His travel plans had an international scope and an apocalyptic urgency (see Rom. 13:11).

The Introduction included a précis on each of Paul's seven authentic letters. Let us now use what we learned to integrate the letters into a history of Paul's apostolic career. As I mentioned, the first Pauline letter that survives is 1 Thessalonians, which provides the best evidence for reconstructing the social context of Paul's missionary activity. Paul evangelized while employed in a local workshop: "You remember our labor and toil, brothers and sisters; we *worked* night and day, so that we might not burden any of you *while we proclaimed* to you the gospel of God

(1 Thess. 2:9, emphasis added). Such a setting would have exposed Paul to a wide socioeconomic mix of people. Ancient workshops were family businesses that connected visitors to the larger network of household relationships in an urban neighborhood. They employed both slave and free labor side by side. Their proprietors were not typically members of the aristocratic elite but rather artisans themselves. The patronage and slave-holding that grew businesses also interconnected the rich and the poor economically, tempering (what we might call) class distinctions. In fact, ancient cities crammed masses of people close together in tight physical spaces, without separate "rich" and "poor" districts, in average population densities matching those of urban slums today. Lacking the sanitation, medicine, and technology to control the infectious agents of diseases, ancient cities (like modern slums) were subject to horribly high mortality rates in aggregate.

In his letters, Paul called the local congregation an "assembly" (Greek *ekklēsia*). This political term came from Greek democracy and denoted the collective body of voting citizens in a city (Greek *polis*). The same term also appears in the Septuagint to refer to all Israel assembled before the Lord. Paul, like the translators of the Septuagint, probably used both meanings without any sense of cultural tension. The meeting space of a Pauline assembly would have likely been a private room of a small, cramped apartment in one of the typical tenement buildings (Latin *insulae*) that lined the urban streets of large Greco-Roman cities. As high as six stories, *insulae* had shops occupying the ground floor, where manufacturing of leather products, pottery, textiles, and other handicrafts took place; living quarters for the owners and other workers constituted the upper rooms. (No purpose-built churches existed before the fourth century.) Paul had founded his congregation in the social context of such a small workshop for handicrafts, which mixed rich and poor, workers and customers, and locals and travelers together.

3. The Social Psychology of Paul's New Converts

As the Introduction mentions, Paul reminded his believers in 1 Thessalonians how in their conversion they had "turned to God from idols" (1 Thess. 1:9), thereby implying that the entire congregation was Gentile (Jews already rejected the worship of idols: figurines and statues of the pagan gods). As former pagans, the Gentile converts nonetheless still had family, friends, and neighbors who continued to participate in the regular civic and domestic worship of the Greco-Roman deities – an important social factor to note. Paul wrote this letter less than a year after founding his small congregation in Thessalonica. Subsequent to Paul's departure, some members of the community had unexpectedly died (1 Thess. 4:13), which had left the living members of the congregation in disorder and doubting Paul's message about the imminent Final Judgment. The apostle dealt with this crisis by empathizing with the problems of new converts. Paul referred to the "afflictions" (often misleadingly translated "persecutions") that his community members were suffering collectively (1 Thess. 3:3). Here, *affliction* (Greek *thlipsis*) likely carries the psychological meaning of distressful disorder, which both conversion and mourning normally occasion.

Understanding the social psychology is important, because new converts in general often experience insecure emotions and identity crises. Not merely a change in an individual's personal beliefs, ancient forms of conversion urged a radical transformation of one's identity that disrupted family ties and former group associations. When Paul left the newly founded congregation to continue his mission, the believers began to have feelings of being "orphaned" (cf. Paul's use of the term in 1 Thess. 2:17), a crisis in their new identity made worse by some of their members dying unexpectedly (1 Thess. 4:13). The crisis was acute, especially because of peer pressure from those whom they now viewed as immoral idolaters – the former friends and family who urged the believers to return to their traditional cults and ancestor worship. Responding to the problems of social loss, psychic distress, and bereavement, Paul urged his believers to form a new sense of "family," away from their previous ones, in the congregation itself. He reminded believers that they suffered *mixed* emotions also at conversion, having receiving the gospel with both "affliction" and "joy" (1 Thess. 1:6). Paul thus emphasized the normalcy of suffering in the conversion experience itself, which he depicted as a foretaste of the apocalyptic wrath that would come soon. And he gave specific advice on how to alleviate the affliction (stress, disorientation): bind yourselves together as a group and so form a new family of "brothers and sisters":

> Now concerning the love of brothers and sisters (Greek *philadelphia*), you do not need to have anyone write to you, for you yourselves have been taught by God to love one another; and indeed you do love all the brothers and sisters throughout Macedonia. But we urge you, beloved, to do so more and more, to aspire to live quietly, to mind your own affairs, and to work with your hands, as we directed you, so that you may behave properly toward outsiders and be dependent on no one. (1 Thess. 4:9–12)

Paul's affective (kinship) language resembles that of other ancient Jews addressing analogous feelings of "affliction" in Gentile proselytes to Judaism. In the apocryphal romance *Joseph and Aseneth*, a work in the Old Testament Pseudepigrapha, the female protagonist is a Gentile who recently has converted to Judaism (in the story, she later marries the patriarch Joseph). A key scene has Aseneth pray to God for help with her distress (affliction) in words similar to those used by Paul to describe the Thessalonians in their distress (see Box 13). Paul's affective language in 1 Thessalonians was, therefore, not unique but came from commonplace Jewish moral exhortations about Gentiles who have abandoned their pagan worship and come to Israel.

The question of how Gentiles properly come to Israel was the subject of Paul's Letter to the Galatians, the apostle's angry rebuke of his congregation for accepting the teachings of rival missionaries (as the Introduction discussed). Paul founded those churches by happenstance. A "physical infirmity" (Gal. 4:13) caused his extended stay in the Anatolian area, where hospitable Greek-speaking Gentiles welcomed him into their homes (Gal. 4:14). Paul apparently evangelized his hosts while recuperating. He and his band of associates were traveling not to found congregations in Galatia, but rather to pass through the region on their way to the Aegean coast. Paul did not identify the Galatian city to which he wrote, but he likely journeyed overland through the interior highlands of north-central Anatolia, which would place him in one or more of the local capitals in the area, such as Ancyra (today's Turkish capital Ankara). This ill-defined territory collectively called "Galatia" had good highways linking an impressive number of Roman colonies and large urbanized settlements.

Paul had founded a new congregation after his recuperation. He then continued on his journey with his associates, following the Ignatian Way into Macedonia before turning south into Achaea (mainland Greece).

4. The Challenge of "Another" Gospel

A few years after Paul's departure from Galatia, rival missionaries representing the "circumcision faction" (with which Paul had a conflict earlier in Antioch) arrived in the area and taught the local Pauline congregation a very different gospel message. Paul's defensive and angry rhetoric against them suggests that they knew Jewish Scripture well, taught the Galatians about Torah and circumcision as necessary for conversion to Christ, and slandered Paul's past. In their view, Paul's expedient laxness about circumcision and other Torah requirements was neither the complete gospel message nor from the Lord. Rival missionaries of the circumcision faction

Box 13   Proselytes in Distress over Their Recent Conversions

The proselyte Aseneth, the daughter of an Egyptian priest and the future wife of the patriarch Joseph (Gen. 41:45, 50–52), received much character development in the Jewish romance *Joseph and Aseneth*. Composed in Greek between the first and second centuries C.E., the work described her desolation and distress from "turning from idols," the deities of her native Egyptian religion, and feelings of being "orphaned" after her family's rejection. Her alienation resembles the distress of Paul's recent Thessalonian converts.

> Rescue me, Lord, before all this (persecution) comes upon me. Rescue me, Lord, the desolate and solitary, because my father and my mother disowned me and said, "Aseneth is not our daughter," because I have destroyed and ground (to pieces) their gods, and have come to hate them. And now I am an orphan and desolate and I have no other hope save in you, Lord, and no other refuge except your mercy, Lord, because you are the father of the orphans, and a protector of the persecuted and a helper of the afflicted [*thlibomenōn*]. Have mercy upon me, Lord, and guard me, a virgin (who is) abandoned and an orphan, because you, Lord, are a sweet and good and gentle father.... Be mindful, Lord, of my humiliation and have mercy upon me. Look at my orphanage and have compassion on the afflicted. For behold, I fled everything and took refuge in you, Lord, the only friend to people. (*Joseph and Aseneth* 12.11; 13.1; trans. Burchard 1985, 222, altered)

Similarly, the philosopher Philo of Alexandria, Paul's older contemporary and fellow Jew, addressed the psychological distress of new proselytes. On the need for Gentile converts to have a "new refuge" and a new "family," Philo writes to his compatriots that God commands all Jews to "love the incomers, not only as friends and kinsfolk but as themselves both in body and soul: in bodily matters, by acting as far as may be for the common interest; in mental by having the same griefs and joys, so that they may seem to be separate parts of a single living being which is compacted and unified by their fellowship in it" (Philo, *On the Virtues* 103; trans. Colson 1939).

For further reading, see Malherbe 1987, 43–46; Malherbe 1998; Lipsett 2011, 86–122.

that had previously trashed Paul's reputation in Jerusalem and Antioch now had reappeared years later, in Galatia.

Paul had to neutralize their slander about his gospel and his early contacts with the original apostles in Jerusalem. "For I want you to know, brothers and sisters," Paul wrote, "that the gospel that was proclaimed by me is not of human origin; for I did not receive it from a human source, nor was I taught it, but I received it through a revelation of Jesus Christ" (Gal. 1:11–12). Paul upbraided his Galatians for their childlike "foolishness" in binding themselves to such obviously false teachers and their crudely magical "evil eye" glances (Gal. 3:1–2). Firing back with ritual cursing of his own, Paul angrily rebuked his Galatians for accepting the teaching of circumcision:

> I am astonished that you are so quickly deserting the one who called you in the grace of Christ and are turning to a different gospel – not that there is another gospel, but there are some who are confusing you and want to pervert the gospel of Christ. But even if we or an angel from heaven should proclaim to you a gospel contrary to what we proclaimed to you, let that one be accursed! As we have said before, so now I repeat, if anyone proclaims to you a gospel contrary to what you received, let that one be accursed! (Gal. 1:6–9)

Why did the Galatian believers accept this "other" gospel that the rival missionaries brought, given the overwhelming scorn of circumcision among Gentiles? An answer can be found in examining parallel evidence for ancient Jewish debates on the importance of circumcision as the requirement of male membership in Israel, found in Josephus's *Antiquities of the Jews* (20.38–40; trans. Feldman 1965. See Gilbert 1991). Josephus tells the story of King Izates of Adiabene (a northern Mesopotamian kingdom on the fringe of the Roman Empire), who as a Gentile sympathizer of Judaism sought advice about the religious value of circumcision from Jews in his court. The account is important because it shows that the conflict between Paul and his opponents at Galatia belonged to a wider debate about the circumcision of Gentile converts, which had divided Jews against themselves in Paul's day.

The story is as follows. Living in exile but later recalled to his native land of Adiabene in Mesopotamia to take the throne, the crown prince Izates and his wives welcomed a certain Jewish merchant named Ananias. Ananias taught the wives and other women in Izates's court to worship God after the manner of Jewish tradition. In the course of his wives' and his own mother's conversions, Izates expressed his desire also to convert as a Jewish proselyte. Unlike the women, however, Izates faced the Torah requirement of circumcision. Zealous for circumcision, he wanted the surgery without delay. But Ananias (now a royal courtier to a new king) persuaded Izates against the operation, telling the king that he could "worship God even without being circumcised if he indeed had fully decided to be a devoted adherent of Judaism, for it was this that counted more than circumcision" (Josephus, *Antiquities of the Jews* 20.41; trans. Feldman 1965, 409).

Being persuaded for a while, Izates in the meantime welcomed into his court another Jewish advisor, a merchant and Pharisee named Eleazar visiting from Galilee and spreading Jewish teachings with his travels. As a Pharisee, Eleazar spoke more authoritatively on Torah and expounded Jewish ancestral laws more expertly than the non-Pharisee Ananias. Eleazar thus urged King Izates to accept circumcision as required by Torah:

> For when he (Eleazar) came to him to pay him (Izates) his respects and found him reading the law of Moses, he said, "In your ignorance, O King, you are guilty of the greatest offense against the law and thereby against God. For you ought not merely to read the law but also, and even more, to do what is commanded in it. How long will you continue to be uncircumcised? If you have not read the law concerning this matter, read it now, so that you may know what an impiety it is that you commit." Upon hearing those words, the king postponed the deed no longer. (Josephus, *Antiquities of the Jews* 20.44–46; trans. Feldman 1965, 411–13)

In the end, Izates found Eleazar more persuasive than Ananias, his initial court teacher on Torah, and without further delay called for his surgeons to perform the operation necessary for his conversion. As a result, Josephus wrote that the Gentile kingdom of Adiabene flourished under its proselyte Jewish king, happily ever after. Josephus, a Pharisee by education, thus offered a morality tale on God's protection of proselytes who worship the living God properly, through circumcision and other Torah requirements. The story thus promoted Pharisaic beliefs over rival interpretations of Torah in the varieties of ancient Judaism.

Our interest in the Izates story lies in its depiction of the particular conflict between the Jewish teachers, Ananias and Eleazar, as rival religious advisors in the proselyte king's court. The narrative provides an important parallel to contextualize the analogous conflict over Torah between Paul and the missionary teachers at Galatia. With its clear condemnation of Torah laxness and watered-down Gentile conversion requirements for the sake of expediency, the position of Eleazar on circumcision parallels that of Paul's opponents. Likewise, the position of Ananias against the necessity of circumcision for Gentiles to join Israel corresponds to Paul's own view. The conflict between Paul and his Galatian opponents thus participated in ongoing, wider debates over proselyte circumcision already under way among ancient Jews of the time.

Understanding Paul's case against circumcision begins with learning its Jewish context in the idea of Israel and covenant (see Box 14). Paul

---

Box 14 Paul on Israel and Covenant

A *covenant* is a solemn promise between two or more parties, made binding with an oath. Paul's case against circumcision insisted on the difference in validity between the two kinds of covenants (the unconditional and the conditional) that God promised to Israel in the Jewish scriptures.

1. *People and the Land (Gen. 17).* An *unconditional* (everlasting) covenant to the uncircumcised Abram (renamed, Abraham) and to his offspring. The Lord adopts Israel as his chosen people forever, with the perpetual right to the land of Canaan, without stipulations. Circumcision, while mentioned afterward, appears as the "sign" of this covenant (cf. the rainbow as the sign of God's covenant with Noah) and not its content. Paul read *and his offspring* as meaning "Messiah Jesus," thus connecting his gospel to the *Akedah*: Abraham's binding of his only son, Isaac, on the altar for an atoning sacrifice demanded by God (Gen. 22; cf. Rom. 8:32).

2. *Nation and Torah (Exod. 19–20).* A *conditional* covenant to Moses receiving the Law on Mount Sinai. The Lord promises that the wandering Hebrews shall become a nation *but only if* it obeys his commandments stipulated in Torah. These include the supplementary requirements for membership into Israel, such as circumcision (Lev. 12:3), which Paul identified as the "works of Torah" that were no longer valid after the faithful death of Jesus on the cross.

3. *King and Royal Dynasty (2 Sam. 7).* An *unconditional* covenant to King David of Israel. The Lord promises to have adopted David as a chosen son (the Son of God) and to establish the Davidic (Messianic) royal house as an everlasting dynasty over Israel, without stipulations. Paul believed this covenant pointed, apocalyptically, to Jesus as the Messiah, the son of David and Son of God.

See Galatians 3–4 and Romans 11. For further reading, see Hays 2002.

---

defended his circumcision-free gospel in a series of complex and convoluted biblical arguments. He argued that, in the Abrahamic covenant, the ancestral father of Israel was reckoned as "righteous" (that is, in the proper covenant relationship with God) *before his circumcision*, by his faithful trust in God and the divine promises of an heir. Arguing that two of the biblical covenants were clearly contradictory (the *unconditional* Abraham promise and the *conditional* Mosaic Law), Paul insisted that the irrevocable promises to Abraham took priority over the revocable law that Moses received "four hundred and thirty years later" (Gal. 3:17). The problem of the law, for Paul, was not just that it came afterward; the "righteousness" of God came not from doing the works of the law, despite what the law said. The Mosaic covenant was incapable of giving the life that it promised. Instead of life and promises, the law gave death and curses: "Cursed is everyone who does not observe and obey all the things written in the book of the law" (Gal. 3:10; cf. Deut. 27:26 and 28:58–68); "Cursed is everyone who hangs on a tree" (Gal. 3:13; cf. Deut. 21:23). Paul reasoned that because Jesus died on a cross (a "tree") but obviously was not "cursed" by God, the conventional ways of reading the Torah must no longer be valid. Paul, therefore, reversed Jewish tradition in a revisionist reading of Scripture (see Box 15).

Paul imagined the faithful death of Jesus on the cross to be an apocalyptic event that effected God's grace of divine redemption from the "curse" of the law, thus establishing a new creation – faithful Gentiles *as Gentiles* (in Paul's rhetoric of synecdoche, "foreskins") inheriting the blessings of Abraham's promise. Paul thus argued that uncircumcised Gentiles can become "righteous" (justified) by God's grace.

But Paul's contrast of grace and works condemned neither the Jewish religion nor "ritual legalism," an important point to note when we come to the later history of Pauline interpretation (see Chapters 5–6). On the question of Jewish unbelief in Messiah Jesus, the historical Paul viewed it as a positive thing for Gentiles – in fact, God's plan. Paul wrote that God had not abandoned the Jews but had intentionally prevented most of them from believing in Jesus so that the Gentiles may enter into the proper covenant relation with God (Rom. 9–11). In the end, Paul believed that *all Israel* will be saved.

Paul recognized that his case against circumcision, which collapsed the ethnic boundary between Jew and Gentile, raised dreadful questions about God's faithfulness to Israel's election. Did God lie to the Jews? Did God play a trick on Israel? Did God mislead the Jews by giving them the law? How can one trust an unpredictable God? Paul's made his answer to these questions clearer in his letter to the Romans than he had in his previous

---

**Box 15 Paul's Revisionist Reading of Scripture: The Allegory
of Sarah and Hagar**

The rival missionary teachers in Galatia preached the importance of
circumcision by emphasizing a traditional interpretation of the Sarah
and Hagar story (Gen. 21). In this tradition, Sarah's freeborn son Isaac,
whom Abraham circumcised on the eighth day, represents Jews (the
chosen people of Israel), and Hagar's slave-born son Ishmael, whom
Abraham cast out of the house, represents Gentiles (the rejected people).
To defend his Gospel for the Foreskin, Paul deployed a remarkably revisionist reading of Scripture. In Paul's revision, Isaac symbolizes uncircumcised Gentiles, and Ishmael symbolizes the circumcised, discarded
offspring of the Mosaic covenant – that is, Paul's opponents and their
circumcision faction in the "present Jerusalem." Paul thus reversed the
story's traditional reading.

> Tell me, you who desire to be subject to the law, will you not listen
> to the law? For it is written that Abraham had two sons, one by a
> slave woman and the other by a free woman. One, the child of the
> slave, was born according to the flesh; the other, the child of the free
> woman, was born through the promise. Now this is an allegory: these
> women are two covenants. One woman, in fact, is Hagar, from Mount
> Sinai, bearing children for slavery. Now Hagar is Mount Sinai in Arabia
> and corresponds to the present Jerusalem, for she is in slavery with her
> children. But the other woman corresponds to the Jerusalem above; she
> is free, and she is our mother.... Now you, my brothers and sisters, are
> children of the promise, like Isaac. (Gal. 4:21–28)

---

letter to the Galatians: faithful Gentiles do not replace the Jews in God's
covenant. Paul, in fact, condemned Gentile arrogance against unbelieving
Jews:

> So that you (Gentiles) may not claim to be wiser than you are, brothers and
> sisters, I want you to understand this mystery: a hardening has come upon
> part of Israel, until the full number of the Gentiles has come in. And so all
> Israel will be saved;
>
> > "Out of Zion will come the Deliverer; he will banish ungodliness from
> > Jacob."
> > "And this is my covenant with them, when I take away their sins."
> > [cf. Isa. 59:20–21; 27:9]

> As regards the gospel they are enemies for your sake; but as regards election they are beloved, for the sake of their ancestors; for the gifts and calling of God are irrevocable. Just as you were once disobedient to God but now have received mercy because of their disobedience, so they have now been disobedient in order that, by the mercy shown to you, they too may now receive mercy. For God has imprisoned all in disobedience so that he may be merciful to all. (Rom. 11:25–32)

The modern Western claim that Pauline theology attacked Judaism (as a "legalistic" religion) mistakes the single biggest difference between the modern and ancient people on the definition of religion. Modern people typically define *religion* in terms of Protestant Christianity, as a "faith" (a distinct, coherent, and unified system of beliefs), whereas ancients (Jews like Paul) saw religion as a practice (ritual behavior, honoring the divine) and, chiefly, the cultic practice of blood sacrifice. We need to place Paul's vocabulary of grace and righteousness ("justification") in its ancient Jewish context, when the temple in Jerusalem was still standing. By *faith* (Greek *pistis*), Paul meant the faithful trust in God and his promises that characterized the covenant relation affirmed daily in the Jewish national sacrifices at the Jerusalem temple. To Paul, faith was not simply cognitive assent to beliefs about God; it was a behavior – "turning from idols," to participate in the exclusive worship of the God of Israel. And, to Paul, *works* (Greek *erga*) referred specifically to supplemental practices of Torah that separated Jews and Gentiles (circumcision, Sabbath observance, kosher dietary restrictions), not religious ritual to "earn" salvation.

Paul preached that Gentiles participated in the crucifixion of Jesus and his apocalyptic victory over death through the ritual immersion of baptism in the *ekklēsia* (assembly, congregation) rather than through the practice of circumcision and other "works of Torah" (practices beyond what Paul believed was Torah's core). Baptism, in his belief, collapsed the long-standing national distinction between Jew and Gentile and telescoped time back to the Garden of Eden and its original divine creation of a single human race (Gal. 3:28; cf. Gen. 1:27). Paul thus substituted *baptism in Christ* (new ritual) for *circumcision* (old ritual) as the sign of covenant between God and Israel.

It is nonsense, historically, to say that Paul's gospel abolished all ritual. Paul insisted that faithful Gentiles must adopt the customs and beliefs of a member of Israel. He required his former pagans to turn away from their ancestral gods, which is the first table of the Jewish law (Exod. 20:3; Deut. 5:7), and to practice moral holiness as a congregation of Israel by reaching out to one another in the love of neighbor (Rom. 13:9), which is the cultic Holiness Code (Lev. 19:18) – these are *ritual* demands. To characterize Paul's teaching as a "Law-free" mission is, therefore, fundamentally misleading. His insistence that Gentiles turn from idolatry to the "correct" ritual worship honoring the living God of Israel drew directly on the cultic language of Torah – election, sanctification, holiness, offering, and dedication – which Jewish priests performed daily in the blood sacrifices at the Jerusalem temple. In other words, Paul *Judaized* former pagans to fulfill what he saw as the core summation of the Law (see Rom. 13:8–10). Paul's case against circumcision thus belonged to his apocalyptic worldview to be living in the End Times when Gentiles *as Gentiles* enter into Israel's cult to Yahweh.

Though the Galatian believers apparently found Paul more persuasive than his opponents (the letter to the Galatians was preserved, after all), rival missionary preachers of Messiah Jesus once again became a thorn in Paul's side when they happened upon another ritual community in Christ that he was making – the congregation at Corinth. As we shall see, this congregation already had internal problems even before the rival missionaries arrived.

5. PAUL'S QUARRELSOME CONVERTS

Paul faced a number of opponents across his missionary travels, and over issues beyond circumcision. In Greece (the ancient Roman province Achaea), the congregation he founded in the Roman colony of Corinth proved his most problematic. This church had so many problems and conflicts that it nearly collapsed because of its corrosive divisions. The factionalism was, on the one hand, internal within the congregation and, on the other, external from rival Christian missionaries passing through Corinth with powerful speech and teaching. In both instances, Paul's opponents were co-religionists (fellow Jesus followers) and not Jewish synagogue leaders or Roman imperial magistrates, an important point to remember. To deal with these various conflicts, Paul had an extended letter exchange with his congregation over a period of several years (see Appendix 2). The Corinthian correspondence thus has a long and complex history, as the Introduction mentioned.

The narrative that follows reflects one hypothesis that, in my view, provides a suggestive reconstruction of the letters, their events, and their sequence. But, of course, it is only a hypothesis, and competing theories are also plausible. With this caveat, we now turn to a historical reconstruction of Paul's dealings with his most quarrelsome converts.

Paul founded the Corinthian church around 51, shortly after his Macedonian congregations (Philippi and Thessalonica) and a brief stay in Athens (see 1 Thess. 3:1). Learning a few years later about some dispute over moral behavior among the Corinthian believers, Paul commanded them, in a letter, to stop associating with certain people who failed to abide by proper sexual conduct. That letter, apparently Paul's first one to the Corinthians, is lost. It was also unsuccessful with its original audience. Influential believers at Corinth wrote back to Paul, presumably in a lost letter mentioned in 1 Corinthians 7:1, asking for clarification and affirming their own knowledge about sexual conduct. And Paul received additional news about the problems in the Corinthian congregation from Christian travelers passing through his missionary path. Apparently, the initial exchange of letters had only heightened the controversies.

Paul responded with a second letter to Corinth, preserved as our 1 Corinthians, which he sent from Ephesus (an emerging center of his subsequent activity). The letter addressed a host of issues: leadership conflicts; a case of incest; lawsuits among the believers; marriage and gender matters; the questions of eating meat offered in pagan sacrifice, of celebrating the Lord's supper, of displaying charismatic gifts; and debates over the resurrection of the dead; as well as directions on raising the fund for the poor among the Jerusalem believers. Although the various issues may seem disconnected at a first glance, they in fact were instances of a single, overarching conflict over *status*. In the Corinthian congregation, the believers were asserting multiple and competing claims to prestige in relation to their fellows. Coherence emerges when we read closely Paul's description of the Corinthian congregation, which uses terms we would call economic and sociological: "Consider your own call, brothers and sisters: not many of you were wise by human standards, not many were powerful, not many were of noble birth. But God chose what is foolish in the world to shame the wise; God chose what is weak in the world to shame the strong" (1 Cor. 1:26–27). Probably, then, the socioeconomic mix in the congregation included some believers who *were*, indeed, wise (educated), powerful (influential as patrons), and of noble birth (local elite), albeit a minority. The main source of the conflict involved the social betters in the congregation (Paul calls them "the strong") continuing their Greco-Roman norms of hierarchy over their social inferiors (whom Paul terms "the weak"): "the haves" (the affluent) were humiliating "the have-nots" (the poor; the actual terms in 1 Cor. 11:22).

The main goal of this second letter was to urge the Corinthians toward reconciliation: the Strong should give up their status and yield to the Weak, for the sake of edifying the congregation – as a whole "body of Christ." Paul exhorts:

> For just as the body is one and has many members, and all the members of the body, though many, are one body, so it is with Christ. For in the one Spirit we were all baptized into one body – Jews or Greeks, slaves or free – and we were all made to drink of one Spirit.
>
> Indeed, the body does not consist of one member but of many. If the foot would say, "Because I am not a hand, I do not belong to the body," that would not make it any less a part of the body. And if the ear would say, "Because I am not an eye, I do not belong to the body," that would not make it any less a part of the body. If the whole body were an eye, where would the hearing be? If the whole body were hearing, where would the sense of smell be? But as it is, God arranged the members in the body, each one of them, as he chose. If all were a single member, where would be the body be? As it is, there are many members, yet one body. The eye cannot say to the hand, "I have no need of you," nor again the head to the feet, "I have no need of you." On the contrary, the members of the body that seem weaker are indispensable, and those members of the body that we think are less honorable we clothe with greater honor, and our less respectable members are treated with greater respect; whereas our more respectable members do not need this. But God has so arranged the body, giving the greater honor to the inferior member, that there may be no dissension within the body, but the members may have the same care for one another. If one member suffers, all suffer together with it; if one member is honored, all rejoice together with it. (1 Cor. 12:12–26)

Paul's rhetoric of reconciliation conformed to Greco-Roman oratory on the importance of deliberation for the sake of concord (Greek *homonoia*), familiar from ancient political speeches about the town assembly (*ekklēsia*) representing the body politic. As in those speeches, Paul offered up the human body as another recognizable symbol of corporate unity. His use of the symbol in writing to Corinth was particularly apt. The city was known for its famous temple of Asclepius (god of healing), which attracted travelers and displayed numerous body parts on its walls – votive offerings dedicated to the savior god in gratitude for miraculous healing. Yet Paul invoked the symbol of the human body precisely to counter its normally upper-status imagery of hierarchy that placed social betters over social inferiors, to nullify the rhetoric of the Strong in his congregation.

Although Paul made a passing threat to come to the Corinthians like a father to a disobedient child ("with a stick"; 1 Cor. 4:18–21), he nonetheless declared his ultimate confidence in their abilities to achieve their own reconciliation, and so he closed the letter with directions for the collection and a promise of an extended visit in the near future:

> Now concerning the collection for the saints ["holy ones"; Paul's basic term for "believers"]: you should follow the directions I gave to the churches of Galatia. On the first day of every week, each of you is to put aside and save whatever extra you earn, so that the collections need not be taken when I come. And when I arrive, I will send any whom you approve with letters to take your gift to Jerusalem. If it seems advisable that I should go also, they will accompany me. I will visit you after passing through Macedonia – for I intend to pass through Macedonia – and perhaps I will stay with you or even spend the winter, so that you may send me on my way, wherever I go. I do not want to see you just now in passing, for I hope to spend some time with you, if the Lord permits. But I will stay in Ephesus until Pentecost, for a wide door for effective work has been opened to me, and there are many adversaries. (1 Cor. 16:1–9)

Despite Paul's tone of confidence in the closing passages of 1 Corinthians, the letter proved in the end to have failed its purpose, because the congregational factionalism at Corinth only worsened. Paul had misjudged the Corinthians' reaction, and his travel plans changed due to other setbacks. Paul did indeed return to Macedonia but became bogged down in local struggles and ordeals principally in Philippi (mentioned in Phil. 1:29–30).

Unable to visit Corinth as promised, Paul appointed his faithful protégé Titus to carry a new letter, Paul's third to Corinth, on administering the collection for the Jerusalem Christians, a follow-up on his previous directions. Extant only as a fragment (our 2 Cor. 8), this letter recommends Titus as Paul's envoy:

> But thanks be to God who put in the heart of Titus the same eagerness for you that I myself have. For he not only accepted our appeal, but since he is more eager than ever, he is going to you of his own accord. With him we are sending the brother who is famous among all the churches for his proclaiming the good news, and not only that, but he has also been appointed by the churches to travel with us while we are administering this generous undertaking for the glory of the Lord himself and to show our goodwill. We intend that no one should blame us about this generous gift that we are administering, for we intend to do what is right not only in the Lord's sight but also in the sight of others. And with them we are sending our brother whom we have often tested and found eager in many matters, but who is now more eager than ever because of his great confidence in you. As for Titus, he is my partner and co-worker in your service; as for

our brothers, they are envoys (apostles) of the churches, the glory of Christ. Therefore openly before the churches, show them the proof of your love and of our reason for boasting about you. (2 Cor. 8:16–24; see also 12:17–18)

Accompanying Paul's envoy Titus were two other traveling missionaries apparently so famous among the Corinthians that Paul did not need to mention their names. (Attempts in critical commentary to identify these two "brothers" have proven elusive.) Even with these brothers' support, however, Titus's delegation bearing Paul's administrative letter did not receive a positive welcome. Influential Corinthians likely from the Strong became angry about the collection and even more suspicious of Paul as an apostle; after all, Paul's divine claims of apostleship lacked any equivalent letters of recommendation (from, say, the original apostles in Jerusalem). Instead of the collection of money, therefore, Titus brought Paul only the bad news of worsening factionalism and mounting challenges to Paul's apostolic authority.

Paul responded with yet another letter, his fourth to Corinth, in which he defends himself against charges of religious fraud (peddling the gospel for money). This letter survives only as a fragment that is incorporated into the first half of our 2 Corinthians (see Appendix 2). "For we are not peddlers of God's word like so many," Paul swore in this letter, "but in Christ we speak as persons of sincerity, as persons sent from God and standing in his presence. Are we beginning to commend ourselves again? Surely we do not need, as some do, letters of recommendation to you or from you, do we? You yourselves are our letter, written on our hearts, to be known and read by all" (2 Cor. 2:17–3:1). Paul called on the Corinthians to receive him properly when he finally arrives in person. He wrote, "Make room in your hearts for us; we have wronged no one, we have corrupted no one, we have taken advantage of no one" (2 Cor. 7:2).

Humiliation at Corinth and Paul at War

When Paul finally arrived in Corinth to deal with the mistrust and factionalism in person, he walked right into a head-on confrontation with the entire congregation. At the full assembly of all the local house churches, a powerful Corinthian believer condemned Paul with such devastating force as to humiliate him publicly, thereby cutting Paul's visit short (see 2 Cor. 2:5–8). Unfortunately, we do not know the identity of this individual; Paul left him unnamed. Yet the content of his attack is relatively clear from Paul's responses: the man invoked the powerfully appealing "wisdom" of competing Christian missionaries, who had been long frequenting Corinth, as the true standard of apostolic authority against which to condemn Paul's noticeable "weakness" in person (see 2 Cor. 10:10). The historical context of this critique is complex: multiple and competing missionaries moving in and out of Corinth for many years, some of whom cooperated with Paul and others not. Another missionary named Apollos, independent of but sometimes cooperating with Paul, also traveled through and preached in the city, for example (1 Cor. 3:4–6; 16:12). The conflicts, as we saw in the Introduction, were on a different order from those at Galatia; Paul never mentioned circumcision as a point of dispute in any of the Corinthian correspondence. Rather, the Corinthians' conflicts centered on Paul's self-professed weakness in showpiece oratory and wisdom (see 1 Cor. 2:1–5), and also their own factionalism.

Shocked by the public humiliation in the face-to-face confrontation before his own Gentile converts, Paul departed Corinth in shame – and steeled himself for a major fight with them. Rather than risking another failed visit, however, Paul fired off an angry "letter of tears" (his fifth letter to Corinth), for which Titus once again served as the courier (see 2 Cor. 2:3–4; 7:8, 12). Although this letter is only partially preserved (as our 2 Cor. 10–13), the force of its militant tone is nonetheless both full and intact. In this letter of reprimand, Paul was at war and (we might say) went nuclear:

> I myself, Paul, appeal to you by the meekness and gentleness of Christ – I who am humble when face to face with you, but bold toward you when I am away! – I ask that when I am present I need not show boldness by daring to oppose those who think we are acting according to human standards. Indeed, we live as human beings, but we do not wage war according to human standards; for the weapons of our warfare are not merely human, but they have the power to destroy strongholds. We destroy arguments and every proud obstacle raised up against the knowledge of God, and we take every thought captive to obey Christ. We are ready to punish every disobedience when your obedience is complete. (2 Cor. 10:1–6)

The angry rebuke in this passage shows Paul's deep quarrel with his own congregation at Corinth for accepting the preaching of the outside opponents.

But who were these rival apostles? Four points of identification do appear in Paul's Letter of Tears. First, they were showpiece orators, powerfully persuasive enough for Paul to mock as "super apostles" (2 Cor. 11:5–6; 12:11). Second, they proclaimed "another Jesus," "another spirit," and a "different gospel" (2 Cor. 11:4), the content of which likely emphasized Messiah Jesus as a divine sage and the content of God's wisdom

(Greek *sophia*). In contrast, Paul proclaimed a nonsage Jesus whose *weakness* on the cross "made foolish the wisdom of the world" (1 Cor. 1:21). Third, the traveling missionaries were Jewish followers of Jesus, like Paul himself – a similarity that Paul exploited to an advantage in his defense: "Are they Hebrews? So am I. Are they Israelites? So am I. Are they descendants of Abraham? So am I. Are they ministers of Christ? I am talking like a madman – I am a far better one ... " (2 Cor. 11:22–23). And, fourth, they condemned Paul as a religious fraud and worse – Satan's apostle. Paul branded his opponents "false apostles," "deceitful workers," and the actual "ministers of Satan" in disguise (2 Cor. 11:12–13), which fired a series of derogatory epithets back upon the "super apostles" that they had also likely used to condemn Paul. Beyond these four tantalizing references, however, little else about the identity of the rival missionary apostles is known. Whatever the identity of the external opponents, Paul's Letter of Tears proved successful with his target audience – the Corinthians themselves. They eventually welcomed Titus, repented of their hostility, and even rebuked the offending individual who had insulted Paul publicly (2 Cor. 7:5–15).

Yet Paul going nuclear left some radioactive shock effects. The extreme bellicosity of the Letter of Tears hurt the congregation deeply, and residual doubts about Paul as a genuine friend radiated out of the congregation.

Imprisonment "for the Gospel"

By this time, Titus reached Paul with the welcome news from Corinth, which consoled the apostle. But elsewhere, events were not otherwise going well for Paul. In Macedonia, he was still preoccupied with contentious local disputes involving other opponents, perhaps those arriving from Galatia. And, in Ephesus as a direct result of his missionary activities, Paul suffered an imprisonment so perilous that he despaired of his own life (2 Cor. 1:8–9; cf. Phil. 1:21–23).

The Roman law and justice system did not normally use public imprisonment of free persons as a form of punishment. Rather, public "prisons" served as temporary incarceration before a trial and were located in larger households or military barracks. Paul refers specifically to a *praetorium* ("imperial guard"; Phil. 1:13), which outside Rome might have referred to a commander's tent in a military camp, the headquarters of a provincial governor, or a hostel for officials along main roads.

We do not know the charges. Contrasting the truth of his bold speech with "some" who "proclaim Christ from envy and rivalry," Paul wrote that he "had been put here for the defense of the gospel" (Phil. 1:15–16), the terms of which suggest that Paul believed his imprisonment resulted from his conflicts with rival Christian missionaries envious of his gospel's success. Whatever the charges, Paul's jailers allowed him to receive guests and financial assistance and to write at least two letters (ca. 56), which were routine privileges for prisoners of means in the Roman world. Indeed, ancient jailers expected bribes to supplement their income. One letter, to the Philippians, thanked the congregation for the money sent by their envoy Epaphroditus; the other letter, to a fellow believer and householder named Philemon, recommended Philemon's slave Onesimus, whom Paul had baptized in prison and was returning home, for service in Paul's mission. These two letters from prison share common themes of friendship and "partnership" (Greek *koinōnia*), and each anticipates Paul's release. Paul was eventually released from prison, a moment that he described as a life-giving "rescue" analogous to Christ being raised from the dead (2 Cor. 1:9–11).

Once released from prison, Paul wrote a new letter to Corinth (his sixth), which survives only in fragments (see Appendix 2). Defending his sincerity and goodwill despite his changed travel plans, Paul expressed joy over the Corinthian reconciliation with and acceptance of him as their apostle over potential rivals. Having resolved the conflicts with the Corinthians, Paul wrote another administrative letter (his seventh to Corinth) around 56, which restarted his collection effort for the poor among the Jerusalem believers – this letter is our 2 Corinthians 9.

5. THE COLLECTION: PAUL'S CROWNING ACHIEVEMENT OF THE AEGEAN MISSION. WHAT'S NEXT?

When he arrived in Corinth to receive the collection, Paul was in his early to mid-fifties (ca. 57) and according to ancient culture an "old man" (Greek *presbutēs*; see Philem. 9). He enjoyed a restored position of authority and respect. Several high-status Corinthians welcomed him personally. An affluent convert named Gaius hosted Paul in his house, which was apparently large enough to accommodate a meeting of all the congregations together at Corinth (Rom. 16:23). In his greetings, Paul associated Gaius with another convert and prominent figure at Corinth, Erastus the "city treasurer" (Greek *oikonomos*). A first-century inscription of a civic official named Erastus, very likely the same person Paul mentioned, survives today among the ruins of ancient Corinth (see Figure 3).

Figure 3. The Erastus Inscription. ERASTVS·PRO·AEDILITATE·S·P·STRAVIT ("Erastus in return for his aedileship laid [the pavement] at his own expense"). This large, first-century inscription on paving slabs of gray limestone lies uncovered in its original position at the Roman theater in ancient Corinth. It bears the name *Erastus*, the city's aedile. The Latin *aedile* (Greek *oikonomos*) designated the municipal officer in charge of administering the civic treasury and public markets. This Corinthian aedile named Erastus is probably the same person from whom Paul sent greetings in Romans (16:23), and so the Erastus inscription offers the only direct archaeological evidence for any Christian figure whom Paul mentions in his writings. (See Gillman 1992; Kent 1966, 99–100. Friesen 2010 argues against the identification. *Photo: Dietrich-Alex Koch*.)

The welcome from the high-status believers at Corinth (the so-called Strong) must have been especially gratifying for Paul. Gaius was, after all, among the first converts whom Paul had baptized on his initial missionary travels in Corinth more than half a decade before (see 1 Cor. 1:14). Paul enjoyed also the hospitality of another local church leader and patron, Phoebe, and the church in her house at Cenchreae (modern Kechries), the eastern port of Corinth on the Saronic Gulf (Rom. 16:1–2). Then Phoebe, Gaius, and the rest of the Corinthian congregation said farewell to Paul as he boarded a ship with the sealed bags of money, the collection of the Gentiles – the crowning achievement of his Aegean mission. This fund, a gift for the poor in the Jerusalem churches, had played such a major role because Paul intended to honor the deal that he had made more than a decade before with Peter, James, and John – the Pillars of the Jerusalem churches – for his Gentile mission (see Gal. 2:10). Paul sailed for Jerusalem likely from Cenchreae and Phoebe for Rome from Lechaeum, Corinth's northern/western port on the Corinthian Gulf.

Paul appointed his local patron Phoebe as his envoy to head a delegation to the Roman Christians, in preparation for his arrival in the imperial capital when he had finished his task of delivering the collection in Jerusalem. To that end, Phoebe carried Paul's extended letter of self-introduction, our Letter to the Romans. In Romans, Paul introduced his gospel with the clear hope that the exhortations in the letter would garner the support of the Roman Gentile believers for both his Jerusalem collection and a new mission to Spain (Rom. 15:22–33; see Figure 4). In the end, however, the collection effort proved disastrous for Paul and very likely led to his arrest and a violent death.

Paul's Final Days: A Likely Violent Death

For an account of Paul's final days, we might turn from Paul's letters to the Acts of the Apostles (see Chapter 4), which narrates a dramatic tale of Paul's end but without apparent knowledge of the collection. Acts describes Paul being attacked by a mob in Jerusalem, his arrest by Roman troops (for disturbing the peace) and confinement in their barracks, a series of trials before Jewish and Roman authorities (during which Paul makes a legal appeal as a Roman citizen to move the hearing to Rome with the emperor as the final judge), his transport to Rome as a prisoner for trial on capital charges before an unnamed Roman emperor (presumably Nero), and Paul's final days under house arrest in a Roman apartment awaiting the trial (Acts 21–28). The last lines of Acts imply strongly that Paul will be found guilty and executed in the near future (ca. 62).

Because the implication of Paul's martyrdom in Acts so stereotypically parallels Jesus' death as martyrdom in Luke's Gospel (see Chapter 4), the narrative is likely an artificial literary creation. Why did Luke not include an account of Paul's death? Perhaps he did not actually know how Paul died. Indeed, ancient Christians in the second and third centuries wrote multiple and conflicting accounts of Paul's last days. The Pastoral Epistles posit a scenario in which Paul was released from prison and returned to the *eastern* regions of his earlier Aegean mission – coastal Greece (Titus 3:12) and Asia Minor (2 Tim. 4:13), Macedonia and the seaport of Ephesus (1 Tim. 1:3) – a direction the very opposite to that described in his final plans (Rom. 15:19–28). Other second-century accounts, most famously

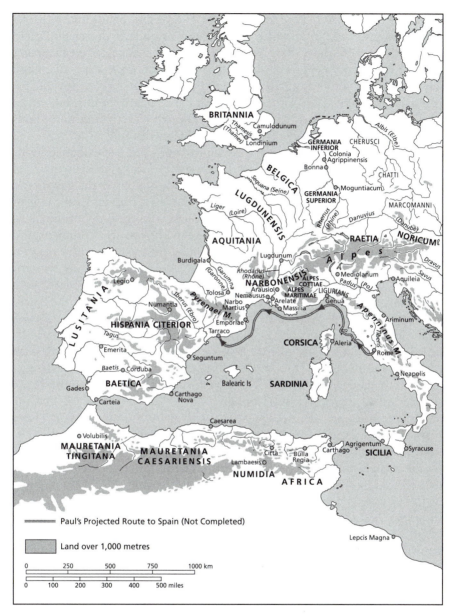

Figure 4 (Map 3). Paul's Unrealized Dream: A Mission to Spain. Given that Paul tended to follow major trade routes and to visit largely Romanized cities, his projected destination probably was the port of Tarraco (modern Tarragona) on the north-east coast of Spain, a Roman colony and provincial capital.

The Martyrdom of St. Paul, describe Paul's trial and beheading in Rome under the emperor Nero, which has become a standard church tradition. Still other legends have Paul realizing his earlier hope to go to Spain. The various accounts of Paul's last days thus changed the story again and again, resulting in contradictory sources of little or no historical value for reconstructing the actual circumstances of Paul's death. In the end, we do not know how or where Paul died, even though church tradition places Paul's death firmly in Rome (see Part II and Conclusion).

The overarching theme of this sketch of Paul's life has emphasized his controversies with his fellow Jesus followers. He was one of many rival missionary teachers, all of whom had competing claims on the gospel and legacy of Messiah Jesus. This fact suggests the instigators of Paul's violent death: his opponents. In this scenario, when Paul returned to Corinth in his mid to late fifties and decided that his Aegean mission was complete, and that his collection was ready for Jerusalem, he planned for a new mission in Spain on the opposite side of his Roman world. But he was worried about what might happen first in Jerusalem. As he wrote, "I appeal to you, brothers and sisters, by our Lord Jesus Christ and by the love of the Spirit, to join me in earnest prayer to God on my behalf, that I may be rescued from the unbelievers in Judea, and that my ministry to Jerusalem may be acceptable to the saints, so that by God's will I may come to you with joy and be refreshed in your company" (Rom. 15:30–32). In this passage, Paul asked the Roman believers to pray for his Jerusalem mission. Those worries were, apparently, well founded.

To continue our scenario, when Paul arrived in Jerusalem, he may have intended to deliver the collection *inside* the Jerusalem temple and *in the same way* that he had delivered his gospel to the Pillars (Peter, James, John) on his earlier, and fateful, visit – namely, with an uncircumcised Gentile by his side. Paul could have intended to pass beyond the temple's Court of the Gentiles (where vendors sold pigeons and exchanged money) into the more exclusive Court of Israel (open only to Jewish men), to make his offering in solidarity with uncircumcised Gentiles as members of "all Israel." Enacting his Gospel for the Foreskin in this provocative move at the temple would have led to a riot, especially from his fellow Jesus followers who demanded circumcision for male Gentile converts. Paul's diction in Romans supports such a reconstruction of his assault and likely murder by the faction of believers in Jerusalem demanding circumcision for a number of reasons. First, Paul writes: "Nevertheless on some points I have written to you rather boldly by way of reminder, because of the grace given me by God to be a minister of Christ Jesus to the Gentiles in the priestly service of the gospel of God, so that the offering of the Gentiles may be acceptable, sanctified by the Holy Spirit" (Rom. 15:15–16). To describe the aims of his collection, Paul chose language specific to the temple and its priesthood.

Second, Paul's plan likely followed the Diaspora synagogue practice of collecting money to send to Jerusalem for the express purpose of offering sacrifices inside the Jerusalem temple. It was the common practice of a local Jewish community in the Diaspora to collect and send money to Jerusalem in contribution of the priestly sacrifices at the temple. According to Philo of Alexandria, Gentiles (even the Roman emperor) knew of such collections.

> (The emperor Caligula) knew therefore that they (the Jews in Rome) have houses of prayer (synagogues) and met together in them, particularly on the sacred Sabbath days when they receive instruction in their ancestral philosophy. He knew also that they collected money for sacred purposes from their first-fruits and send them to Jerusalem by persons who would offer the sacrifices (at the temple). (Philo, *On the Embassy to Gaius* 156–157; trans. Colson 1962, 79–81, altered)

This Diaspora synagogue practice was the likely model for Paul's collection. The priestly diction of his language and the worry in his tone suggest that Paul intended to offer *provocative* sacrifices at the Jerusalem temple, the "first fruits" of *uncircumcised* Gentiles given in solidarity with all Israel, which he feared both the believers and the unbelievers in Judea might find totally unacceptable (Rom. 15:25–33).

Third, even the Acts of the Apostles hints at this hypothesis: Acts describes Paul's arrest at the Temple accompanying a serious charge: "he has actually brought Greeks into the temple and has defiled this holy place" (Acts 21:28). Yet the author of Acts presents this charge as *false*. The charge thus runs counter to the narrative agenda of the text, and its very oddness suggests it to be historical. Because this allegation against Paul contradicts the theological agenda of the author of Acts, it seems likely that it has some basis in historical fact. The author knew that Paul had been accused of bringing a Gentile into the area of the Temple restricted to Jews (the Court of Israel) and felt obliged to refute the charge.

In the end, Paul's delivery of the collection in Jerusalem proved disastrous. His own provocative act to promote his Gentile mission at the temple likely caused a local riot from both nonbelieving Jews and from believers in Jerusalem who had long been hostile to Paul and who advocated that Gentile members of the faith be circumcised and fully converted to Judaism. Paul probably thus suffered a violent death in the early 60s, turned over to authorities by his own fellow believers, as a direct result of his controversial mission activities.

6. Wrapping Up the Historical Paul

Chapters 1 and 2 have sketched Paul's life (and death in part) to show the problems of and gaps in what we can claim to know. We are especially ignorant of Paul's early life and his death. My timeline of events is, of course, hypothetical. Yet I hope that the reader has seen the historical evidence in Paul's own letters that clearly show how an uncritical reliance of the book of Acts is the wrong way to conceive of his biography.

Paul had a Greco-Roman education in classical rhetoric and allegory. He also had Jewish training as a Pharisee who favored flexible, revisionist readings of Scripture. He remained proud of his Jewishness and considered himself not to have "converted" to a different religion, but to have had a "calling" in the same sense that Hebrew prophets received "callings" as messengers of the Lord. Paul's Gospel for the Foreskin participated in a specific apocalyptic hope of his day, debated within ancient Judaism – the eschatological pilgrimage of uncircumcised Gentiles who turn from idols to worship the God of Israel, a portent of the Final Judgment. This sustained apocalyptic hope led to direct confrontations with Jesus' original apostles and other Jerusalem church leaders, who had revised their gospels to include proper observance of the Jewish Law in light of the disappointment of Christ's return being an unfulfilled promise. Church conflicts at Jerusalem and Antioch divided believers and forced Paul to embark on a new plan – his own mission to the Gentiles, free from the authority of the Jerusalem church leaders.

The period of Paul's Aegean mission, little more than a decade, generated the greatest productivity of Paul's life. All his letters come from this relatively compressed period of his career, when he founded his own international network of tiny apocalyptic cells of Gentile believers in Galatia, Thessalonica, Philippi, and Corinth. Romans, his last known letter, records Paul's confidence at the crossroads of his career – and his unrealized dream for a mission to Spain at the other end of his Roman world. That period also saw Paul's greatest opposition emerging in the form of various other traveling missionaries bearing gospel messages sharply different from his. Those rival apostles or their partisans likely had a strong hand in Paul's untimely and violent death, which probably involved a disturbance in Jerusalem related to Paul's attempt to deliver his collection of money – the fruit of his decade-long labor – as an "offering of the Gentiles" (Rom. 15:16) at the Temple Mount.

A major theme emerging from this life sketch is that Paul had both Jewish and Greco-Roman identities. How do we bend our minds around a plural identity? The issue for the next chapter will be to ask this question in light of the evidence in Paul's letters that reproduce a Roman discourse of authority. In the process, we shall also assess Paul's impact on his contemporaries in greater detail.

3

PAUL'S LIFE IN ITS ROMAN CONTEXT

My aim in this chapter is to delineate the strategies by which Paul's language both participated in Roman culture and created distinct claims to authenticity in response to conflicts and reprisals. This approach shifts the scholarly paradigm from Paul *against* Roman culture, or Paul *and* Roman culture, to Paul *within* Roman culture. Paul's letters show that he was a full participant in his cultural home of the Roman world. This point reflects back on and adds to my opening list of paradoxes in Chapter 1: modern people may imagine that Paul subverted the imperialism of the ancient Romans, but in fact he relied on their rhetoric and ideologies. The so-called paradoxes are creations of modern readings that this book challenges. I do not see contradictions in Paul, but consistencies. The consistencies extend even between Paul and Roman culture.

Chapter 2 focused on Paul's founding and nurturing of Christian communities, and on the various internal and external conflicts to which his letters responded. We saw that Paul's greatest adversaries arose from within the Jesus movement – rival apostles proclaiming to Gentiles a different gospel about the Messiah Jesus. This finding raises a central question for this chapter: How can we understand Paul as a "key figure" not just in early Christianity but also in classical antiquity?

For a number of modern interpreters, the answer is both straightforward and obvious: Paul was famous in his own lifetime, and he worked to subvert the dominant culture of Roman imperialism. On this view, his essential identity was revolutionarily anti-Roman. This hypothesis sets Paul over against the "pagan" imperial background of the first century, effectively placing the apostle outside the culture of the Roman Empire (presented as a single, homogenous entity), in order to emphasize the distinctiveness and importance of Paul's thought. Such an opposition between Paul and Rome supposedly offers a biblical resource for Christians challenging the political hegemonies of today.

Despite my wishes to accept its liberal theological appeal, I argue that this "anti-Roman" hypothesis about Paul does not hold. Matters are much more complicated than simply asking an either/or question – whether Paul was for or against the Roman Empire – because he likely was both. In any case, a more important agenda occupied his preaching: God's final judgment and the imminent end of the world. To be sure, Paul was controversial in his preaching. But this controversy came largely from his language, which advanced a particularly Roman discourse of authority that provoked the conflict of rivals.

1. Roman Culture and Imperialism

Understanding Paul's life in its Roman context begins on the basic level of studying culture. What is "culture"? Older definitions focused on the nobility in a particular society and its allegedly stable and harmonious set of aristocratic values. More recent research in cultural anthropology has recognized that all people, not just the aristocratic elite, have a culture, and so a better meaning for the term has emerged. Avoiding the aristocratic sense of "high culture," a new generation of scholars today extends the application of the concept to non-elites, popular culture, and subcultures. Understanding culture as unstable and contested, rather than stable and harmonious, we can investigate a culture ethnographically and seek to capture the whole complex of behavioral values and characteristics that identify a group of any sort. For biblical studies, this approach (known throughout the humanities as the Cultural Turn) challenges all of us to keep in mind the literary and rhetorical nature of Paul's letters before reading them as straightforward fact and social description. A cultural study of Paul thus moves beyond analyzing the writings of the New Testament evidence as objective (unmediated) sources of early Christian life to examining them as rhetorical strategies of ancient discourse.

I discuss this cultural studies approach in some detail as a response to the biblical scholarship on Paul and empire, which perpetuates outdated clichés born of the previous "elite meaning" of the term *culture*. Rather than asking how Paul reacted to the background of elite Roman culture – a question both leading and narrow – we should make a broader inquiry. Culture is a diverse set of values and practices, which non-elites also possess. In this regard, my thesis about Paul's rhetoric and theology reflecting the influence of Roman culture does not depend on Paul's supposed Roman citizenship (attested only in the Acts of the Apostles; see Chapter 4). Paul's language could have been Roman even if he himself was not an actual citizen.

I need also to address the modern terms tossed around in the current debate, which function more to label rather than to explain the ancient evidence. For example, *imperialism*. The term does not have self-explanatory meaning, nor is it a single, uniform phenomenon across world history, literature, or geography.

The modern notion of imperialism comes from the European nation-state building in the nineteenth and early twentieth centuries, which creates the polarizing categories of "colonizers" and "colonized." I do not find this modern meaning directly applicable to classical antiquity. In fact, Rome used the term *colonies* for communities of its own citizens abroad, as opposed to subjugated local populations. While some post-colonialist studies may be suggestive when they are carefully nuanced for the dramatically different context of the ancient world, it is not clear that Rome's rule of local populations can be readily labeled "colonial," according to modern definitions. Unlike modern empires (eighteenth-century imperial Russia may be a possible exception), ancient Rome ruled local populations with much less imposition of its central institutions abroad, leaving cities and entire nations largely autonomous as long as they supplied Rome with taxes and military support. Governors and military commanders did not systematically replace native cults with Roman religion, for example. The Romans in the first century had no professional bureaucracy to match the scale of their empire. Government was limited and provincial magistrates were few, being aristocrats without formal training in civil service – in other words, amateurs – who directed the slaves and freedmen of the emperor's household to handle the daily affairs of overseas administration. As well, the Roman government cooperated with the leaders of local populations through a traditional patronage-and-client system, which offered certain political exchanges and favors from the Roman governor as a benefactor to the local aristocratic elite and its self-governing rule. After all, the original meaning of the Latin word *provincia* was not a bounded geography under uniform administration but a sphere of military duties (called *imperium)* granted to a Roman magistrate overseas – collecting taxes and maintaining order. In this way, modern maps of the Roman Empire can mislead. (We shall return to the question of Roman maps in a moment.)

Likewise problematic when applied to the Roman Empire is the modern notion of propaganda. A representative definition of the modern term holds that *propaganda* is the practice and art of inducing people to behave in a way differently than they would in its absence. More recent studies find that the real power of propaganda lies in its capacity to conceal itself. This modern use of propaganda first occurred as a critical term of analysis for Roman historians in the 1920 and 1930s, when they began to see in the

Augustan age a mirror for the dramatic political changes of Europe: the rise of the military dictatorships of Benito Mussolini, Francisco Franco, Adolf Hitler, and Joseph Stalin. In this analysis, Augustus Caesar thus emerges as the prototypical *Führer* and *il Duce*, who rules by propaganda (organizing public opinion) through his operatives (poets such as Virgil). This modern propaganda thesis encourages simplistic dichotomies like "pro-" and "anti-Augustan" to describe the literature of the era. The problem with this thesis is that Rome had no central office in its imperial government to coordinate a single propagandistic message, nor the technology of mass media. Without careful definition, the term labels the ancient evidence with misleading connotations. Using propaganda to describe Roman imperialism often constructs an interpretation consistent with today's negative assumptions about modern totalitarian regimes. It thus drives a reading of the ancient evidence to confirm a predetermined modern narrative about the past.

All this leads us to reexamine what Romanness meant in Paul's ancient context. Since the nineteenth century, the legal definition of citizenship has largely shaped the term's meaning in classical scholarship. The origins of this legalistic approach began in the nineteenth-century use of inscriptions in Roman history, to argue for the spread of certain Roman institutions (colonies, citizenship, language, law, and coinage) as the features common to all the provinces. Those similarities then provided what appeared as objective, straightforward criteria for measuring the level of acculturation in a particular region. On that view, *Roman* is a clearly bounded identity in cultural opposition to "native" and *Romanization* an active (top-down) force to which natives "reacted." In that analysis, the meaning of Roman is obvious; the task of scholarship is simply to measure the level of acculturation in a particular individual or group among local populations. Much Pauline scholarship that attempts to measure the level of Roman acculturation (or lack thereof) in the apostle unfortunately follows an essentialism that mistakenly regards Roman identity to have an innate existence as a stable set of characteristics rather than a social and cultural construct composed of various and competing forms.

We need to move beyond thinking about Romanness as a bounded entity against which the "opposing" cultural identity of Paul can then be contrasted or otherwise measured. Paul's experience of Roman culture, his way of "being Roman," involved various subcultures, including Jewish ones. As previous chapters have explained, being Jewish and being Roman were not mutually exclusive. There was no single (homogenous) Roman identity, but rather multiple identities, experiences, and possibilities of being Roman. Indeed, by the late Republic and early Empire, "Roman" had expanded beyond its ethnic sense of Latin-speaking natives of the Italian mainland. Being Roman had become a way of organizing knowledge rooted in particular discourses. Such discourses are what I mean by "ideologies" in that they collude with, support, and make sense of the existing structures of authority and domination, whether or not the collusion is altogether conscious. From this perspective, we see that even ancient people legally denied access to Roman citizenship, those provincials "from below," participated in various discourses of being Roman by actively reproducing such styles of communicating ideas in their mundane lives. To repeat my point (above), Paul still shared cultural identities of Romanness even if he was not a Roman citizen.

Rather than focusing on the limited definition of a legal rank (such as citizenship), a cultural studies approach identifies and analyzes the range of Roman ways of thinking that Paul's writings expressed. This approach is better because it allows for different experiences of being Roman through various subcultures, including Jewish ones. Matters are much more complicated, therefore, than simply asking whether Paul was for or against Roman imperialism. On the one hand, no individual in a society can escape or carve out a space apart from the dominant culture. On the other hand, no ideology is completely successful in dominating everything: control always fails somewhere, and thus people can deviate inside the dominant structures without noticeable radicalism.

Paul's mission to the Gentiles operated without noticeable radicalism *within* the wider Roman culture in part because the Pauline movement was very small, and in part because Paul used specific language that colluded with a particularly Roman discourse of authority. This insight explains why Paul's main adversaries were fellow Jesus followers and apostles – those associated with Paul's tiny subculture closely enough to care about or even to notice it – rather than Roman imperial magistrates.

2. PAUL'S LANGUAGE OF AUTHORITY: A ROMAN DISCOURSE

In its day, the Pauline mission was virtually unnoticed by imperial magistrates and other members of Rome's aristocratic elite. Paul and his circle of associates did, however, make a great impact on some small groups of contemporaries – his Gentile converts. Why did Paul's message appeal to them? One reason is that, in part, it played upon politically and culturally charged themes generally familiar in Roman discourse. Paul's language of authority promoted a discourse of mastery widely diffuse in the ancient

Mediterranean world, which the Romans called "clout" or "influence" (Latin *auctoritas*).

The term *auctoritas* denoted the personal attributes of initiative and superiority in an individual (the *auctor*) that subordinates and colleagues had willingly granted. It directed actual power along dynamic patterns of personalized influence rather than through static, abstract institutions (titles, ranks, offices). The meaning recalled the clout of a Roman mother (Latin *materfamilias*) in her family, a traditional attribute of women who lacked official rank in ancient society. The idea created a crucial distinction between one's influence (*auctoritas*) achieved by personal leadership qualities and one's official authority (*potestas*) transacted as a result of office or rank. The ancient value of *auctoritas* was deeply moral, belonging to Rome's "conflict culture" that required a person's merit to be constantly earned, validated, and regained. Ancient writers remarked that the Latin term *auctoritas* was quintessentially Roman and untranslatable into a single Greek term. Greek writers typically had to use multiple terms to describe it, which means that native Greek speakers like Paul could have known and used the cultural idea even if they did not speak Latin. The traditional attribute of a *materfamilias'* real power in the family was widespread in the ancient Mediterranean world. Indeed, Paul evoked it a number of times, to honor a mother who personally influenced him (Rom. 16:13) and to remind his congregations of the influence that his maternal birthing of them exercised (Gal. 4:19).

The idea of *auctoritas* belongs to the Roman discourse of both identities and politics. The emperor Augustus declared that his authority to rule came not from holding any particular office but, quite naturally, from the influence of his deeds. Augustus used *auctoritas* as the central concept to express his *imperium* (power) because the term had wide currency as *the* moral value of leadership in the earlier Republic. By deliberately emphasizing *auctoritas* as the principle of his rule, Augustus positioned himself as the best yet in a long-standing Roman tradition. Augustus thus made clear his intention to lead the Roman state, after the destruction of the decades-long civil wars, on a moral authority higher than that of merely a titleholder, government functionary, or magistrate.

In a public writing celebrating his deeds, called the *Res Gestae Divi Augusti* ("The Achievements of the Divine Augustus") and published in monumental inscriptions throughout the whole Roman world after his death (14 C.E.), Augustus wrote, "I excelled everyone in influence [*auctoritas*], but I had no more power [*potestas*] than the others who were my colleagues in each magistracy" (*Res Gestae* 34.3). (The Greek version rendered *potestas* as *exousia* and *auctoritas* as *axiōma*, the latter

Greek word being a common translation for the Latin *dignitas*.) Importantly for our study of Paul, the emperor Augustus repeatedly emphasized his refusal of official "rights":

> I *did not accept* absolute power that was offered to me when I was both absent and present by both the people and the senate . . . I *did not accept* the annual and lifetime consulship being offered to me at that time . . . [W]hen both the senate and the people of Rome were in agreement that I alone should be appointed supervisor of both laws and customs possessing the greatest authority, I *adopted no power* that was being offered contrary to ancestral customs. (*Res Gestae* 5.1–6.1; trans. in Brunt and Moore 1967, 36–37, emphasis added; see also Cooley 2009, 127–31)

The language of repeated refusal routed real authority through one's personal deeds rather than through the formal "powers" of office that lesser leaders would have accepted. According to the Roman ideology, a true leader gained clout (*auctoritas*) by giving up official "power" (*potestas*).

Paul's language of apostolic authority advanced a similar discourse of "clout" and thereby participated in Roman cultural identities. As did Augustus, Paul claimed that one of the significant roots of his authority was the influence of his deeds. Paul connected his legitimacy as an apostle to his personal apostolic activity – converting Gentiles and establishing congregations – and not to official power or "rights" granted by the title or office of "apostle":

> Am I not free? Am I not an apostle? Have I not seen Jesus our Lord? Are you not my work in the Lord? If I am not an apostle to others, at least I am to you; for you are the seal of my apostleship.
>
> This is my defense to those who would examine me. Do we not have the right to our food and drink? Do we not have the right to be accompanied by a believing wife, as do the other apostles and the brothers of the Lord and Cephas? Or is it only Barnabas and I who have no right to refrain from working for a living? . . . If others share this rightful claim on you, do not we still more?
>
> Nevertheless, we have not made use of this right, but we endure anything rather than put an obstacle in the way of the gospel of Christ. Do you not know that those who are employed in the temple service get their food from the temple, and those who serve at the altar share in what is sacrificed on the altar? In the same way the Lord commands that those who proclaim the gospel should get their living from the gospel.
>
> But I have made no use of any of these rights, nor am I writing this so that they may be applied in my case. Indeed, I would rather die than that – no one will deprive me of my ground for boasting! If I proclaim the gospel, this gives me no ground for boasting, for an obligation is laid on me, and

woe to me if I do not proclaim the gospel! For if I do this of my own free will, I have a reward; but if not of my own free will, I am entrusted with a commission. What then is my reward? Just this: that in my proclamation I may make the gospel free of charge, so as not to make full use of my rights in the gospel. (1 Cor. 9:1–6, 12–18)

Paul's rejection of "official" apostolic rights resembles Augustus's refusal of honors in the *Res Gestae*. Paul tried to persuade the Corinthian congregation that his authority to be *their* apostle was both real and legitimate. He hammered on the term *rights* in one rhetorical question after another, taking special pride in his refusal to accept the rights that other (rival) apostles of the Lord have accepted. Others such as Peter demanded pay ("food and drink") and the right to have an accompanying wife. But Paul "would rather die" than use these "official" rights. Instead of apostolic rights, Paul placed his real authority in the actual work of his gospel that his divine commission obligated him to perform; in other words, his personal deeds. "If I am not an apostle to others," Paul wrote to the Corinthians, "at least I am to you; for you are the seal of my apostleship." Paul thus used the Roman discourse of clout throughout his letters to respond to challenges of his apostolic authority.

We now return to the question of Roman maps. In his *Res Gestae* (26.1), Augustus gives a mental map of his expansion of Rome's empire and influence throughout the world: "I enlarged the territory of all the provinces of the Roman people, which had neighboring peoples (outsiders) that were not subject to our rule." In the Greek version, the term for outsider peoples is *ethnē* – the same word we find in Paul's letters that appears in modern translation as "Gentiles" (a religious term). A comparison with the *Res Gestae* suggests *ethnē* to be a *geographic* term in the Roman language of mapping: *ethnē* defines a unity of different peoples under a single *imperium*. We see this geographic meaning in Paul's description of his own accomplishments among the *ethnē*:

In Christ Jesus, then, I have reason to boast of my work for God. For I will not venture to speak of anything except what Christ has accomplished through me to win obedience from the Gentiles (*ethnē*), by word and deed, by the power of signs and wonders, by the power of the Spirit of God, so that from Jerusalem and as far around as Illyricum I have fully proclaimed the gospel of Christ. Thus I make it my ambition to proclaim the gospel, not where Christ has already been named, so that I do not build on someone else's foundation. . . . This is the reason that I have so often been hindered from coming to you [in Rome]. But now, with no further place for me in these regions, I desire, as I have for many years, to come to you when I go to Spain. For I do hope to see you on my journey and to be sent on by you, once I have enjoyed your company for a little while. At present, however, I am going to Jerusalem in a ministry to the saints; for Macedonia and Achaia have been pleased to share their resources with the poor among the saints at Jerusalem. (Rom. 15:17–20, 22–27)

The mental map of Paul's itinerary was a distinctly Roman world. It was a unified partnership (Greek *koinōnia*) of manifold provincials (*ethnē*) under a single *imperium*. Like the imperial map of the *Res Gestae*, Paul's itinerary had the language of reaching limits, and it deployed the particularly Roman meaning of *imperium* as a sphere of duties granted to an overseas envoy (Greek *apostolos*). In this Roman sense, the world of Paul's missionary imagination would have sounded imperialistic to his contemporaries.

When Paul's congregations questioned why he acted as an overseas envoy (apostle) without official credentials to present, Paul reminded them that he needed nothing of the sort, especially letters of recommendation. His work as their founder provided sufficient proof of his apostleship. Using startling imagery of the human body, Paul called the Corinthian congregation *his* letter, written on *his* heart, for Christ writes on tablets of *human hearts*:

Are we beginning to commend ourselves? Surely we do not need, as some do, letters of recommendation to you or from you, do we? You yourselves are our letter, written on our hearts, to be known and read by all; and you show that you are a letter of Christ, prepared by us, written not with ink but with the Spirit of the living God, not on tablets of stone but on tablets of human hearts. (2 Cor. 3:1–3)

The reference to tablets of stone may have alluded to the Mosaic Torah, but it also may have mocked the Greco-Roman epigraphic habit of erecting monumental inscriptions attesting to a patron's generous benefaction. Whatever the case may be, the body metaphor pertains to authority in imagining a personal participation in the divine. Indeed, Paul claimed a godlike authority of sorts by virtue of his commission as an apostle (envoy) of his divine lord.

Although Paul asserted the divinity of his calling and his witness of the risen Lord as the bases of his authority in other places (Gal. 3:1, "Paul an apostle – sent neither by human commission nor from human authorities, but through Jesus Christ and God the Father"; Rom. 1:1, "Paul, a slave of Jesus Christ, called to be an apostle, set apart for the Gospel of God"; 1 Cor. 9:1, "Have I not seen Jesus our Lord?"), he did not rest his apostolic authority solely on such claims, for that would not have distinguished him from other apostles of Messiah Jesus, such as Peter and James. Rather, Paul asserted that his authority over his congregation was a higher and more moral one than that which other church leaders and apostles have: the personal influence of his deeds, which created the congregation in the first place. Paul thus routed his leadership claims very specifically through his clout, which he attributed to God working through him (1 Cor. 15:10, "But by the grace of God I am what I am, and his grace toward me has not been in vain. On the contrary, I have worked harder than any of them [the other witnesses of the risen Lord] – though it was not I, but the grace of God that is with me."). This evidence suggests that the Roman discourse of *auctoritas* formed the language of Paul's apostolic authority – and even shaped his thinking about God's authority.

The Roman *auctoritas* appears not only in expressions of Paul's apostolic authority but also in his description of God's ultimate authority:

> But who indeed are you, a human being, to argue with God? Will what is molded say to the one who molds it, "Why have you made me like this?" Has the potter no right over the clay, to make out of the same lump one object for special use and another for ordinary use? What if God, desiring to show his wrath and to make known his power, has endured with much patience the objects of wrath that are made for destruction; and what if he has done so in order to make known the riches of his glory for the objects of mercy, which he has prepared beforehand for glory – including us whom he has called, not from the Jews only but also from the Gentiles? (Rom. 9:20–24)

In this passage, Paul recasts the Old Testament theme of God as a potter (Jer. 18:1–11) into contemporary Roman terms. God has certain rights as the divine Creator to destroy his creation at will, just as a potter can reshape and destroy his pottery, but God refuses to exercise those official (creator) rights in favor of making known the influence of his mercy – a higher and more moral form of authority. By routing real power through personal influence rather than through bureaucratic office (even that of Creator), Paul reads Jewish Scripture through Roman ways of thinking about the highest authority.

Paul's language both participated in Roman culture and created distinctive claims to authenticity. Unlike Augustus and other aristocratic Romans, for example, Paul used a metaphor of slavery to describe his authority and that of Messiah Jesus. Paul called himself a slave of Christ and the "slave of all." This self-description is Protean, like the Homeric shape-shifter who adopted several identities. And, paradoxically, Paul claimed that his slavery signaled his freedom as an apostle:

> For though I am free with respect to all, I have made myself a slave to all, so that I might win more of them. To the Jews I became as a Jew, in order

to win Jews. To those under the law [Torah] I became as one under the law (though I myself am not under the law) so that I might win those under the law. To those outside the law I became as one outside the law (though I am not free from God's law but am under Christ's law) so that I might win those outside the law. To the weak I became weak so that I might win the weak. I have become all things to all people, that I might by all means save some. I do it for the sake of the gospel, so that I might share in its blessings. (1 Cor. 9:19–23)

Paul repeated this oddly honorific metaphor of slavery multiple times for himself, his followers (see Rom. 6:16–22), and Messiah Jesus:

Let each of you look not to your own interests, but to the interests of others. Let the same mind be in you that was in Christ Jesus, who, though he was in the form of God, did not regard equality with God as something to be exploited, but emptied himself, taking the form of a slave, being born in human likeness. And being found in human form, he humbled himself and became obedient to the point of death – even death on a cross. Therefore God also highly exalted him and gave him the name that is above every name, so that at the name of Jesus every knee should bend, in heaven and on earth and under the earth, and every tongue should confess that Jesus Christ is Lord, to the glory of God the Father. (Phil. 2:4–11)

Paul's ritual song to Messiah Jesus thus sang the story of the cross in the tones of slavery: Jesus "emptied himself, taking the form of a slave," and so "humbled himself," and "became obedient to the point of death."

Was all this language countercultural? Did it overturn *slavery*, one of the basic hierarchies by which the Romans structured their world? Modern scholars disagree on this point, as well as on the very meaning of the metaphor in ancient Roman discourse (see Harrill 2003, 596–98; Martin 1990). To be sure, the apostle's metaphor of slavery has seemed to many modern readers to go against ancient culture, which fundamentally dishonored slaves. Famously, nineteenth-century British and American abolitionists ransacked Scripture to support their Christian antislavery theology and so "found" in Paul's metaphor an egalitarianism of "mutual servanthood" that they read as condemning slavery (see Harrill 2006, 165–92). But, from a historical perspective, Paul did not actually escape or carve out a space apart from his dominant culture, because (as we shall see) the metaphor, too, participated in the Roman hierarchical language of *auctoritas*, even if not all elite writers used it that way.

A case in point is the Roman use of slaves as stock figures to teach ethics. Roman moral instruction deployed storytelling in handy collections of illustrative tales (Latin *exempla*). Such morality tales exhibited a fascination with inversion, which engaged the traumatic upheavals of the Roman civil wars through which Julius Caesar and Augustus, in turn, came to power. In the tales, social inferiors like slaves gave up personal gain and even their lives for the greater good of the community. Completely detached from self-interest, the good slave (Latin *servus frugi*) saved the master's household by enduring torture to the point of death.

A collection of such tales appears in the ancient Roman moral handbook *Nine Books of Memorable Deeds and Sayings*, which Valerius Maximus compiled for the emperor Tiberius (ca. 14–37 C.E.). These stories praised the fidelity of slaves toward their masters all the more, because it was not expected. For example, a famous orator was once accused of incest, and the prosecutors demanded one of his household slaves for interrogation by torture (as Roman law required). The slave chosen was a youth, who assured his master that he would not betray him. "And he kept his word with marvelous endurance," despite the brutality of the interrogation. Valerius ends the tale by praising the goddess Fate (Latin *Fortuna*) for placing such a "loyal and brave" spirit in the body of a slave. Through specific and concrete acts, the "faithful slave" expressed acceptance of the master's point of view so fully as to have become an extension of the master's self. The admirable fidelity of slaves appeared in further tales of domestics enduring horrendous torture bravely and obediently to the point of death. The plot of the stories depended on *inversion*, the slave's morality proving greater than that of the master. Such unlikely heroes urged aristocratic Romans toward the faithful valor in the face of death that even a lowly slave could attain (Latin *fidelitas*, comparable to what Paul meant by "faith"). Valerius used the figure of "the slave" to think about and promote greater *auctoritas* in masters, a rhetorical strategy in the overall project of his moral handbook.

Paul's metaphor of slavery participated in a similar moral project through his use of the slave persona for himself (1 Cor. 9:19–23) and for Christ (Phil. 2:6–8), which taught that true authority lies along analogous patterns of inversion, personal clout, and ironic heroism. The heroic language of inversion advanced a known rhetorical trope about the slave within ancient discourse and supported Roman thinking about power and authority – a true leader gives up rights to gain real status and shows fidelity to a higher authority even to death. I want to be clear that my parallel to Roman slave *exempla* does not suggest that Paul necessarily read the writings of Valerius Maximus (which I doubt). Rather, I claim that Paul's writing illustrates the same cultural reasoning that we find in Roman moral discourses of leadership and power. I thus ask how audiences in the Roman world would have likely heard and made sense of Paul's slave metaphor. This methodology is concerned less about Paul's authorial intention and more with the content of the logic in Paul's discourse. Placing Paul's language in its Roman context therefore provides a new insight into the old chestnut of why Paul's preaching appealed to urban, and Romanized, Gentiles.

But one might object that Paul "subverts" Roman imperialism by his use of the epithet "Lord" (Greek *kurios*) for his Messiah Jesus. Doesn't Paul calling Jesus Lord challenge and ultimately overturn the supreme lordship of the Roman emperor? My reply points to the ancient context of the term. "Lord" was an epithet common of all deities in the ancient Mediterranean world, not unique to Roman emperor worship. It characterized, for example, the god of healing ("Lord and Savior Asclepius"), the Egyptian goddess Isis ("Lord and Queen Isis"), the supreme father Zeus, and even the youthful Apollo. Moreover, in Rome's fundamentally hierarchical society, *kurios* had regular use in the daily speech of slaves to masters, commoners to aristocrats, soldiers to commanders – as illustrated even in the New Testament (Luke 7:6–8); virtually all ancient people spoke this way to their social betters. Analogous are the traditional British address of a nobleman as *lord* and the aristocratic connotations of *Señor* in formal Spanish. Paul calling his Messiah Jesus "Lord" does not prove anything about an anti-imperial stance to Rome, because the term specified not the emperor alone but was a commonplace epithet of respect for both noble society and deities. If anything, Paul exploited the linguistic flexibility of the term when he affirmed the existence of "many gods and many lords" (1 Cor. 8:5), albeit to refuse worship of them. In ancient Mediterranean religions, worshippers routinely called themselves "slaves" of their divine "lord" (master), a pledge of special devotion to a patron deity.

In short, Paul's use of the slave persona belongs to the same discourse of apostolic authority found in his repeated refusal of certain "rights" (1 Cor. 9:1–18) and his denial of needing human credentials such as recommendation letters (2 Cor. 3:13). All these passages route real apostolic power through Paul's accomplishments and personal influence. Whether consciously or not, Paul's language thus advances, participates in, and colludes with particularly Roman ways of exercising power. Rather than subverting the logic of Roman imperialistic thinking, Paul's letters provide instances of it.

3. Paul's Jewish Apocalypticism in Its Roman Context

Modern scholars who claim that Paul subverted Roman imperialism for his contemporaries typically point out his particularly Jewish apocalypticism. The allegedly best explicit evidence is said to be in 1 Thessalonians. When Paul reminded his congregation that the time of the Final Judgment was unpredictable – "For you yourselves know very well that the day of the Lord will come like a thief in the night. When they say, 'There is peace and security,' then sudden destruction will come upon them, as labor pains come upon a pregnant woman, and there will be no escape!" (1 Thess. 5:2–3) – the key phrase, "peace and security," seems to parody a Roman imperial slogan. Indeed, the same phrase appears in the legends "Augustan Peace" (Latin *paci Augusti*) and "Augustan Security" (*securitas Augusti*) on Roman coins. Wasn't Paul evoking and thus subverting the Roman peace (*pax Romana*) seemingly made sure by the emperor Augustus? Such a question leads this Paul and Empire scholarship to the conclusion that Paul wrote hidden transcripts into his letters.

A "hidden transcript" refers to language that subordinated people speak in private beyond the ears of their social betters, in contrast with the "public transcript" that subordinated people and their social betters speak together when interacting with each other. The term is useful when studying total institutions (slavery, serfdom, caste subordination, and living conditions under military dictatorships or in jails and prisoner of war camps) because those particular forms of domination bear a family resemblance to each other – institutional extraction of labor enforced by an authoritarian terror in the form of arbitrary beatings, sexual violations, and powerful surveillance of the weak. We identify certain speech and actions to be subversively "coded" against the dominant ideology best when we have direct testimonies of subordinated people that tell us this information. The totalizing institutional framework of the term, however, imposes a serious methodological constraint on scholars who wish to find hidden transcripts in ancient literature like the New Testament writings. Rome was not a "total institution" of oppression. We lack testimonies from early Christians explaining what their coded discourse might have been when spoken in the presence of outside authorities.

Let me be clear. I do not dispute the evidence of peace and security as a slogan on Roman coins. Rather, I challenge the claim that Paul quoted this slogan as a hidden transcript of resistance against Roman imperialism. How can modern scholars know that this phrase articulates a hidden transcript? After all, the phrase is not very hidden in the text! To be sure, the slogan "peace and security" would have likely evoked the pax Romana, but not as a hidden message of resistance. Paul's apocalyptic language advanced a Roman discourse of peace as a *pax* (Latin for "pact, settlement") that came only after conquest and war. The language simultaneously engaged Roman cultural themes as it asserted apocalyptic distinctiveness. This process is not one of cultural "negotiation" either, because that model suggests that Romanness and Jewishness had completely separate existences like two different entities, which could then be said to "interact" with each other. A better approach understands the multiple identities and possibilities of being Roman.

Paul's preaching of Jewish apocalypticism both subverted and supported Roman authority. It expressed Paul's plural identities within his Roman culture. As Chapter 2 has shown, Paul in 1 Thessalonians urged his congregation to see their local "afflictions" (Greek *thlipsis*) as a necessary part of God's apocalyptic war. The language constructed a dichotomy of forces – "light" and "dark" – in a conflict of cosmic dimensions, which defined the proper identity and role of Paul's Gentile congregations over against outsiders. Paul wrote that God's Final Judgment would bring "wrath" and "sudden destruction" upon outsiders, from which "there will be no escape" (1 Thess. 5:3–10). Those references emphasized the psychological terror of witnessing catastrophe – global slaughter by God's weapons of mass destruction. Paul called on his followers to steel themselves for God's onslaught against the divine powers and rulers of this world, with an assured military victory: the entire community will receive salvation, even members who have died before the decisive battle. "For the Lord himself," Paul exhorted, "with a cry of command, with the archangel's call and with the sound of God's trumpet, will descend from heaven, and the dead will rise first. Then we who are alive, who are left, will be caught up in the clouds together with them to meet the Lord in the air; and so we will be with the Lord forever" (1 Thess. 4:16–18). According to Paul, the Day of the Lord will bring a peace established by the bloody wrath of the Final Judgment. Paul thus spoke of "peace" in the military sense of conquest by a "kingdom." Paul's apocalyptic imagery of peace was culturally Roman in its valorization of war. It celebrated a lasting peace that came only through violent mastery of the world: the triumphant coming of the Lord will be *like* the dominion of Rome. Paul's language thus advanced an imperialist ideology that was very Roman in its model of peace.

4. Paul Living within Roman Authority

Now we are ready for an analysis of the only Pauline passage that gives explicit attention to imperial authorities, Romans 13:1–7. There, Paul spoke directly about Christian behavior toward the governing authorities of the Roman Empire. Much modern biblical interpretation has found the passage somewhat of an embarrassment, because it has historically been cited to support royal absolutism (the divine right of kings) and modern totalitarian regimes (see Box 16).

Box 16 Paul on Roman Imperial Authorities

Let every person be subject to all governing authorities; for there is no authority except from God, and those authorities that exist have been instituted by God. Therefore whoever resists authority resists what God has appointed, and those who resist will incur judgment. For rulers are not a terror to good conduct, but to bad. Do you wish to have no fear of authority? Then do what is good, and you will receive its approval; for it is God's servant for your good. But if you do what is wrong, you should be afraid, for the authority does not bear the sword in vain! It is the servant of God to execute wrath on the wrongdoer. Therefore one must be subject, not only because of wrath but also because of conscience. For the same reason you also pay taxes, for the authorities are God's ministers, busy with everything. Pay to all what is due them – taxes to whom taxes are due, revenue to whom revenue is due, respect to whom respect is due, honor to whom honor is due. Owe no one anything, except to love one another; for the one who loves another has fulfilled the law. The commandments, "You shall not commit adultery; You shall not murder; You shall not steal; You shall not covet"; and any other commandment, are summed up in this word, "Love your neighbor as yourself" [see Lev. 19:18]. Love does no wrong to a neighbor; therefore, love is the fulfilling of the law. Besides this, you know what time it is, how it is now the moment for you to wake from sleep. For salvation is nearer to us now than when we became believers; the night is far gone, the day is near. Let us lay aside the works of darkness and put on the armor of light; let us live honorably as in the day, not in reveling and drunkenness, not in debauchery and licentiousness, not in quarreling and jealousy. (Rom. 13:1–14)

Some biblical commentary has attempted to neutralize the text or make anti-imperialist sense of it through a modern liberationist ethics on government. Various interpreters have tried, among other things, to identify the passage as either a later scribal addition (interpolation) or, if genuine, a very particular piece of advice about paying taxes in the specific local and historical context of a tax protest in the city of Rome under the Emperor Nero. While most scholars have rejected the recourse to textual interpolation, many find the hypothetical reconstruction of taxation unrest in Rome to be a plausible if admittedly a speculative context in which to understand the passage's meaning.

Yet, in recent years, scholarly discussion has moved from finding a social context to unveiling the point of the passage, said to lie *behind* the straightforward meaning of the text. One form of this hypothesis proposes that Paul used *counterfeit* praise for Roman imperialism in order to say the very opposite of what he actually meant. To confirm this ironic view of the passage, such commentators cite other texts in Paul's letters that condemned the "rulers of this age" as "doomed to perish" in the apocalyptic wrath to come at the Final Judgment (1 Cor. 2:6–8). On this interpretation, Paul covertly subverted the very Roman authorities that the surface meaning appears to have commended. But such *presentism* (interpreting the past exclusively through the present) understands Paul's writings through a modern liberationist theology. It is highly problematic for doing history, being little more than wish fulfillment. More *historical* commentary takes seriously that fact that Paul was self-consciously writing to Rome. It is no surprise to find Paul sounding quite different in 1 Corinthians about the "principalities and powers" and gleefully predicting their imminent ruin. Besides, in Paul's apocalyptic worldview, the phrase "rulers of this age" points also to evil angels. The "rulers," after all, control the entire "age," a sphere of influence much broader than the Roman Empire, and are coupled with "angels" in a list of celestial "powers" (Rom. 8:38), a suprahuman identity. Paul likely took the evil principalities and powers to be both the demonic powers and their puppets on earth, which include Roman and all other human rulers – and even Paul's opponents within the Jesus movement.

Paul's belief in the divine appointment of human rulers and his simultaneous belief in God's overthrow of those same rulers should not be surprising to readers familiar with the Old Testament and ancient Judaism. The tension was present in Jewish apocalypticism generally. After all, a core belief of Jewish apocalyptic eschatology held that God was in charge of all events and that nothing happened apart from his divine will. A good example is the political oracle about the rise and fall of world kingdoms in the apocalyptic book of Daniel, which affirmed both that God gave each king the authority to rule (Dan. 2:37–45) and that God will ultimately destroy all earthly rulers and establish his own kingdom (Dan. 7). Paul's support of human governing authorities (in Rom. 13) and his apocalyptic condemnation of human governing authorities in other passages (Rom. 8:38–39; 1 Cor. 15:24) were not culturally contradictory, but go hand in hand.

Yet another form of the anti-imperialist argument proposes reading what the text of Romans 13 insinuates. According to this hypothesis, Paul's apparent advice about Christian loyalty to Roman imperialism uses the coded and ambiguous language "of the oppressed" in order to avoid detection from Rome's authorities, who presumably might have read it. The argument tries to neutralize Paul's seeming acceptance of Roman authority by applying, once again, the modern political theory of hidden transcripts. But, as we saw concerning 1 Thessalonians 5, the hypothesis about a hidden transcript poses serious difficulties without insider testimony of how such discursive strategies were articulated. We thus face the same insurmountable problem as before: If Paul wrote coded and ambiguous speech in order to avoid detection, how can modern readers detect his "real" message in Romans 13? After all, it's supposedly *hidden*!

A better approach offers a more contextual analysis of the passage as part of the discourse of its contemporaneous culture, which leads to a closer reading of the text. More clearly than any other passage, Romans 13 supports the thesis that Roman ideologies of authority shaped Paul's language of mission. The language went beyond urging the mere payment of taxes and belonged to the moral exhortation within Roman culture that Jewish communities had already formulated and preached in Diaspora synagogues. Opening Paul's moral exhortation is the term *(governing) authority* (Rom. 13:1, Greek *exousia*; equivalent to Latin *potestas*, against which *auctoritas* was contrasted in Roman culture). Unfortunately, modern translations mask the specific civic duties that Paul's ancient Greek words described. *Exousia* designated the multiple forms of leadership needed to run an ancient Roman city: holding elected office (Rom. 13:3, Greek *archontes*), administrating bureaucratic functions (Rom. 13:4, *diakonos*), and performing liturgical duties (Rom. 13:6, *leitourgoi*). Paul's use of *exousia* thus referred to the specific rights granted to municipal magistrates in a *fixed term of office*. The end of those "official" civic rights will come, Paul believed, at the Final Judgment.

Official rights of governing rulers expressed only one kind of authority in Roman cultural understanding. The other kind was the ability to have "clout" (*auctoritas*), as explained previously. Paul in Romans 13 mentions the former as subordinate to the latter: *bureaucratic office* granted formal rights such as taxation, which deserved respect (v. 7, "honor"), but personal *clout* expressed a higher and more moral authority. The exhortation thus urged the whole Christian congregation at Rome to fulfill civic duties, such as paying taxes and giving respect to the official rights of government authorities, and then to forget about them because such duties to outsiders are not what mattered; the ultimate obligation is mutual love that builds up the Christian congregation. Paul wrote a summary of all the Torah commandments as follows: "owe no one anything, except to love one another" (Rom. 13:8). He thus urged the congregation to influence each other through love of neighbor (fellow believers). The language sets up a hierarchy of clout, mutually exercised, over official rights, which would have been familiar to an ancient Roman audience.

This chapter has tried to provide a response to the growing anti-imperialist literature on Paul. The apostle influenced his contemporaries by reproducing a Roman discourse of authority in the language of his mission. Paul, therefore, was not a revolutionary, proliberation activist in the modern sense; he was not making a theological case against "imperialism." Yet he also was not a pacifist in the modern sense, either. Indeed, Paul expected the imminent coming of a *divine* empire ruled by Christ and God. He thus was not completely comfortable with Roman imperial rule or ideology. In place of a totalizing "either/or" (Paul *either* for *or* against Rome), a more useful approach situates Paul *within* Roman culture. My analysis has deployed a broader idea of culture that rejects the facile use of "imperialism" and "propaganda" to label rather than to explain the evidence. Being Roman was a discourse that routed authority less through the official power of rank than through the informal patterns of personal clout – one's *auctoritas*. Paul's letters illustrate his full implication in this Roman discourse even if he preached a distinctly apocalyptic message. We must not separate Jewishness and Romanness into separate containers as if they were different and bounded cultural identities.

This Roman context will be crucial also in Part II, in which we explore the many different "Pauls" that appeared in writings of his interpreters.

PART
II

THE LEGEND

4

COMPETING STORIES ABOUT
PAUL IN LATE ANTIQUITY

If Paul was controversial in life, he was even more so after his death (ca. 62). We saw in the first part of this book, on the life of Paul, that his mission to Gentiles provoked conflicts with other Christians. As he defended himself, Paul advanced a particularly Roman discourse of "clout" (*auctoritas*) that asserted his personal authority over potential rivals. In this cultural sense, I argued, we may call Paul *Roman*. We now turn to the legendary Paul. Over time, the figure of Paul became Roman in a different way – in legal and political senses that imperial officials and other members of the aristocratic elite would have more likely acknowledged as one of their own. To support my thesis in this chapter and the next, I shall discuss quite different texts, from works attributed to Paul to arguments against his teaching, to uses of his writings in discourses and doctrines advanced by powerful ancient church figures (a full list appears in Appendixes 1 and 3). Despite their diversity, the texts represent Paul's growing influence on and significance in vastly different kinds of early Christianity.

We meet, first, Paul the Roman hero and model imperial citizen; in death, the apostle became a martyr venerated as the new Romulus and "second" founder of Rome. Next comes Paul the sexual role model, with whom early Christians debated the value of family, asceticism, and patriarchy. The third Paul in our survey is the Deceiver – Satan's apostle and the mad magician – whose details reflect late ancient anxieties about the figure's emergent fame.

1. Paul the Roman Hero: Christians as Model Imperial Citizens

The Acts of the Apostles (ca. 95–115)

My antibiography of Paul uses the canonical Acts of the Apostles merely as one of the first interpretations of Paul, rather than as a primary source providing independent information about his life. Importantly, the book of Acts neither mentions a collection of Paul's letters nor presents Paul as a letter writer. Removing all letters from Paul's story may have been a strategy on the part of the author of Acts to resolve the obvious tensions that Paul's letter corpus had caused for ancient Christians. Instead, what Acts emphasizes about Paul is a detail never mentioned in his letters – his alleged Roman citizenship. Of all the Christian apostles, only Paul is said to have been a Roman citizen. This detail from Acts has great thematic importance because Roman citizens in the time of Paul were less than one percent of the total Mediterranean population and enjoyed special privileges in law and society. Such high rank confirmed for later Christian interpreters that Paul must have had a social prominence in the Roman world that matched his high theological standing in the church.

The book of Acts narrates a highly theological history of the first three decades of the early church, from its inauguration in Jerusalem after Jesus' death to its arrival in the imperial capital of Rome with the apostle Paul. The narrative contains scenes that present the church as unthreatening to and at home in the Roman Empire. Key episodes show Paul to be innocent of any crime, especially that of political sedition. The juridical processes heighten Paul's status not only as a hero but also as a Roman, often with a touch of narrative irony. In Acts, Paul is more authentically Roman than even some of the Roman magistrates and army officers he encounters on his travels.

The author of Acts develops this theme in Paul's first encounter with imperial authority (Acts 13:4–12). In the scene, Paul appears before a Roman governor (proconsul) named Sergius Paulus, who just so happens to share Paul's surname (no historical evidence of a historical Sergius Paulus survives; the figure is perhaps a Lukan fiction). Described in the text as a "discerning" man, Sergius summoned Paul to his court to hear "the word of God" (Acts 13:7). A contest of religious power ensues before the governor's eyes: a local Jewish magician named Bar-Jesus (alias Elymas) – whom the text identifies explicitly as a "false" prophet – attempts to turn the proconsul away from the new faith by a display of magical power. But when Paul and Elymas face each other, it is no contest. Paul looks intensely at Elymas and utters a curse that at once reduces the court magician into a blind, pathetic figure who must grope for help even to walk. The contest thus establishes the superiority of Christianity over inferior magic, which evokes a stock Roman opposition between *religio* (the legitimate, public worship of loyal subjects) and *superstitio* (the foreign, private practices of dangerous outsiders). This inaugural episode of Paul's encounter with Roman authority sets in motion not only Paul's missionary journeys (as Christianity's greatest hero) but also a major thematic pattern: Rome ruling wisely and benevolently over the world. Imperial officials repeatedly side with Paul over locals (Jews and Greeks), a narrative trope that depicts Rome as Paul's best friend and patron.

Paul's Roman citizenship in Acts functions as a literary device to heighten dramatic suspense and to move the main character, Paul, to his ultimate destination of the imperial capital. In Acts, Paul declares his Roman citizenship in two episodes (Acts 16:37–38; 22:25–29), setting up the climax of Paul's celebrated appeal to Caesar (25:11–12; 26:32), which in turn leads him (and thus the church) to Rome. In each episode, the news of Paul's Roman citizenship comes as somewhat of a surprise, out of the blue and at the last minute.

The episode of the Philippian slave girl (Acts 16:16–40) appears in an appropriate setting for the book's overarching theme – the text identifies the city explicitly as a "Roman colony" (Acts 16:12). Paul exorcises a slave girl who "had a spirit of divination and brought her owners a great deal of money by fortune-telling" (Acts 16:16). The loss of the spirit renders the slave no longer a soothsayer, and her owners without their former source of income. "But when her owners saw that their hope of making money was gone, they seized Paul and Silas and dragged them into the marketplace before the authorities" (Acts 16:19). In the judicial hearing that ensues, the browbeating owners lie: "These men are disturbing our city; they are Jews and are advocating customs that are not lawful for us as Romans to adopt or observe" (Acts 16:20). For their part, the city's Roman magistrates respond to the charges and a growing angry mob by ordering Paul and Silas to be publicly beaten and thrown into prison overnight, which was a routine sentence for breaking the peace under Roman rule. But, after a miraculous prison break, Paul converts his jailer and protests his mistreatment.

This scene of last-minute rescue has Paul lecturing Roman officials about the legal protections of Roman citizenship from such arbitrary beatings and imprisonments (Acts 16:37). The magistrates thus release Paul and Silas after only one night in prison and apologize for the city's mistreatment of them as Roman citizens (Acts 16:39), which furthers Luke's theological theme that the church's mission does not violate Roman authority in the world. Curiously, Paul could have mentioned his citizenship before his beating and jailing, but the author employs a dramatic device of delay in order to heighten suspense. Hearing the sudden news – and believing Paul at his word without any verification of the claim – the Roman magistrates quickly remedy the injustice caused by Paul's mistaken identity. They come in person to apologize and grant Paul's demand for an official escort out of town in a formal procession. The episode thus presents Paul as the real Roman hero. The Romans once again protect the mission of Citizen Paul over local, and illegitimate, opposition – Luke's theological theme.

This thematic pattern repeats itself in subsequent episodes. For example, in Paul's fateful visit to Jerusalem, locals ambush Paul while he worships at the Jerusalem temple (Acts 21:27–31). A Roman tribune (legionary senior officer) orders his troops to intervene, reestablishing law and order. The Roman soldiers rescue Paul from a lynching only to take him prisoner in the mistaken belief that they have in hand a wanted outlaw known as "the Egyptian." Again, Paul declares his Roman citizenship at the last minute, right before he is about to be beaten. The tribune (with the impressively Roman name of Claudius Lysias) confesses that "It cost me a large sum of money to get my citizenship," to which Paul replies, "But I was born a citizen" (Acts 22:28). The dramatic trope of irony from Paul's previous trial at Philippi recurs: *Which character is the true Roman?* Claudius admits to buying his citizenship later in life, so Paul holds the greater claim to be Roman than even a senior legionary commander does. Paul's Romanness in law being thus established, the commander Claudius sends our hero off to the Roman capital of Judea, the coastal city of Caesarea, with an official letter of introduction as a Roman citizen (Acts 23:27) and a full military guard out of Jerusalem, to the Roman governor for a proper court hearing. The escort scene parallels the one previously, in Philippi. In Acts, Roman authorities lead Paul on his way – literally – which is further evidence of Luke's theology driving his "history."

After a series of delays, Paul finally has his trial before the Roman governor of Judea, Porcius Festus, a figure said to be "rather well informed" about Christianity (Acts 24:22). This episode contains Paul's famous appeal to Caesar, a dramatic climax in Acts.

> Paul said, "I am appealing to the emperor's tribunal; this is where I should be tried. I have done no wrong to the Jews, as you very well know. Now if I am in the wrong and have committed something for which I deserve to die, I am not trying to escape death; but if there is nothing to their charges against me, no one can turn me over to them. I appeal to the emperor." (Acts 25:10–11)

The powerful oration persuades the governor, who then dispatches the prisoner to Rome. The Jewish king of Galilee, Herod Agrippa, visiting Caesarea, also hears Paul's case and concurs with Festus's judgment. Agrippa even says to Festus that they could have each released Paul "if he had not appealed to the emperor" (Acts 26:32). These dramatic speeches of Paul function apologetically, to defend Christianity's innocence before both

Jewish and Roman law (and their representative authorities). The apologetics of Luke-Acts had multiple purposes but most likely aimed to reassure insiders in Luke's community about Christianity's legitimacy in the Roman Empire.

In sum, the author of Acts emphasized Paul as Roman in the same legal and political sense that imperial magistrates would have been recognized as deserving their honor and patronage. The narrative of Paul's appeal to Caesar repeated the same trope found in previous scenes, which functioned to defend the legitimacy of Christianity in the Roman Empire and advanced Luke's theological theme of church leaders as model imperial citizens. The value of the story is thus more literary than historical – a fiction to defend the legitimacy of the early church, here embodied in Paul.

"The Martyrdom of Paul" (ca. 190)

If the book of Acts strongly hints that Paul will die as a martyr in Rome (see later discussion), neither Acts nor any other book of the New Testament narrates his actual death, which left later Christian imagination to invent such stories. The earliest account, also the one most influential on church tradition, is *The Martyrdom of Paul* (ca. 190; see Appendix 3) included within the apocryphal *Acts of Paul*. Advancing a tradition that Paul died as a martyr in the city of Rome, the work made up episodes for Paul's final days in order to fill in this significant gap in the apostle's biography. The work enjoyed great popularity in late antiquity and the Middle Ages, influencing Christian art. Rome's great fire under Nero (64 C.E.), a later artistic theme, does not appear in this particular story, however. Apparently, even at the end of the second century, early Christian imagination had not yet connected the epic horror of that Roman catastrophe to the legend of Paul's martyrdom.

The drama of the *Martyrdom* follows the same narrative pattern that we found in the canonical book of Acts: Paul proves through a series of travails to be more noble and Roman than the imperial leaders he encounters. The theme begins with Paul renting a barn outside Rome as space for his expanding Roman mission. The fame of Paul's preaching in this barn attracts a throng of Roman visitors wishing to hear the apostle preach. The newly converted faithful include a great many household slaves of the emperor; it is they who will bring Paul and Nero together. The emperor's cupbearer Patroclus sits on a high window in the barn in order to listen to Paul, over the crowd, but he unfortunately falls to his death (cf. Acts 20:9–12 for a parallel scene). Upon hearing the news of his favorite's death, Nero laments greatly. But Paul raises Patroclus from the dead – a show of the apostle's power over Satan – and the slave returns to Nero and reports his eager enlistment as a soldier in the new faith and its coming Kingdom. News of an advancing "kingdom" and its soldiers frightens Nero into arresting all Christians in the city for summary execution, without trial – in violation of Roman law, the text emphasizes.

The roundup of Christians brings Paul in chains before Nero, whose interrogation apparently confirms the emperor's suspicions about the apostle's recruitment of Romans in a new army to destroy Rome and its empire. When the enraged Nero has Paul beheaded, a punishment reserved for Roman citizens, milk rather than blood gushes out of the apostle's neck. Later in the day and now raised from the dead, Paul arrives in the imperial court with his head reattached to continue his previous rebuke of Nero. The postmortem Paul reproaches the emperor for executing prisoners without any trials – a crime not only against divine law but also against Roman law. An admonished Nero obeys Paul's command to free the remaining prisoners, including high-ranking guards and slaves of the imperial household. The narrative ends with the released Roman soldiers and slaves pledging their allegiance to Paul, who baptizes them and glorifies God. *The Martyrdom of Paul* thus characterizes Citizen Paul as more Roman than Nero, and better suited to rule the world – the dramatic theme from the canonical Acts of the Apostles.

"The Correspondence of Paul and Seneca"
(Fourth Century)

This same theological theme recurs in *The Correspondence of Paul and Seneca*, a fourth-century Latin forgery (see Appendix 3). The apocryphal work contains fourteen epistles allegedly written and exchanged between Paul and his famous pagan contemporary, the Roman philosopher Seneca. Seneca was the tutor and political advisor to the emperor Nero, which made him a perfect figure for ancient Christians to appropriate as Paul's "friend." The work thus connects Seneca and Paul through their purported mutual ties as noble Roman citizens. The author of the pseudonymous correspondence reimagines Seneca as admiring Paul's letters as a font of moral philosophy greater than his own epistles. Calling Paul "my dearly beloved" and "the peak and crest of all the most lofty mountains," Seneca rejoices in his good fortune to have come across Paul letters, for after reading them he tells Paul, "I am so close to you that I may be considered your second self . . . especially since you know that you are a Roman citizen" (*Letter 12, from Seneca*). The correspondence depicts Seneca himself reading Paul's letters to Nero aloud, an awe-inspiring experience that moves the emperor to accept Paul's moral admonition. The pseudonymous Seneca decries the injustice of Nero's blaming the Roman citizen Paul and his fellow innocent Christians for the great fire in Rome, which evoked a legend (current in the fourth century) about the location and circumstances of Paul's eventual martyrdom.

The New Star: Paul's Martyr Cult at Rome (Fourth Century)

The locations, objects, and stories of Paul's martyrdom in Rome are ancient but doubtful. The stuff of urban myths, the legends grew from the accounts in the canonical book of Acts and the apocryphal *Martyrdom of Paul*, both secondary sources. Paul's farewell address to the Ephesian elders, the only speech to a Christian audience in the book of Acts (20:17–35), indicates that the apostle will suffer, like Jesus, rejection and a martyr's death. For example, the Lukan Paul declares his willingness to die and announces that "none of you, among whom I have gone about proclaiming the kingdom, will ever see my face again" (Acts 20:25), and that God obtained the church with "the blood" of Jesus' death. A consensus of modern biblical scholars holds that the speech is a literary creation by Luke, who aimed in multiple places of his two-volume work to parallel the character of Paul (in Acts) and the character of Jesus (in the Gospel of Luke). Another fictional account, in *The Martyrdom of Paul*, completed Luke's funerary expectations for Paul by specifying Rome as the location of the apostle's death, which in late antiquity led to the invention of a tomb and holy relics. In the fourth century, a Roman cult of Paul had developed, imperially sponsored, which focused its veneration of the apostle on two roads leading out from the city's walls, the Ostian Way (Via Ostiensis) and the Appian Way (Via Appia). Roadside shrines rebuilt as church basilicas, these imperial monuments of a new civic hero reshaped Roman identity and public memory. In a revised sense of their history, fourth-century Romans displaced Romulus and Remus, Aeneas, and the Gemini (Greek Dioscuri, the twin "sons of Zeus" known as Castor and Pollux) by venerating Paul, along with his "twin" saint (Peter), as *the* earthly founders and heavenly guardians of the Eternal City.

The invention of this wholly Roman Paul came from the religious change that Constantine the Great (ca. 272–337) had begun during his reign over a newly reunited Roman Empire. His imperial patronage of Christianity brought the faith from a persecuted minority to near preeminence in Roman religious and political life. Constantine's many building projects attempted to discover an eternal Christian identity in Rome's past by memorializing in public architecture the places of Paul. The imperial church basilica on the Ostian Way marked out the sacred space of Paul's (alleged) tomb and, because it lay outside the city's walls, restructured Rome's sacred landscape to celebrate beliefs in the everlasting unity between the apostle and the imperial order.

Civic rituals took on revised meanings as well. For example, each February 15, Rome's annual state festival, the lewd Lupercalia, honored the suckling of Romulus and Remus by a she-wolf. Skimpily clad teams of youths ("little wolves," Latin *luperci*) would run amuck around the seven hills of the city, lashing anyone in their path, especially pregnant girls. By the late fifth century, this celebration included large numbers of Christians who associated the annual circuit run around the city's walls with the cult of Paul as the founder figure Romulus. Almost two hundred years after Constantine had legalized Christianity, the vast popularity and debauchery of the Lupercalia ultimately led Rome's bishop (Pope) Gelasius around 495 to ban Christians from participating in the old pagan ritual. This effectively ended public worship of Rome's very origins, which the fertility festival had performed annually.

Outside the city's walls at Paul's cult site on the Ostian Way, the earlier Roman bishop Damasus (ca. 366–384) inaugurated a more grandiose basilica worthy of the pilgrimage destination that the sacred space had become. Pilgrims traveled from all over the Mediterranean world to see, touch, and receive miraculous healings (and souvenirs) from what they were told were the mortal relics of Paul's body – bones, ashes, a bloodstained shroud, and some chains. The shrine's decorative iconography recalled Roman military laurels and athletic trophies. Paul's relics received official veneration by Rome's whole population annually, in a state feast day of the imperial Roman calendar (July 29). The cult followed a cultural habit, going back to traditional Roman religion, of a family gathering for a commemorative meal (Latin *refrigerium*) at its gravesite to feed the "grateful dead" of the household ancestors and so to cultivate their divine protection for another year. (Indeed, the marble sarcophagus allegedly containing Paul's body, which I discuss in the Conclusion and which dates to the reign of the emperor Theodosius I [347–385], has small openings in the top for feeding tubes.) The city's population and pilgrims thus venerated Paul as their collective ancestor and divine protector, Rome's father and true estate owner (Latin *paterfamilias*).

Such new religious modes of Roman self-understanding found expression in another practice of Paul's martyr cult, its mythmaking stories.

Prudentius (late fourth century), the greatest of the ancient Christian Latin poets, echoed Virgil to recast Paul as Rome's legendary hero and founder figure in a lyrical representation that relied as heavily on remembering as forgetting. Prudentius's classicism conceptually rearranged Roman memory. He exploited, for example, the mythic significance of the Tiber River, which flowed through the city, for Roman civic identity: on its banks the discouraged wanderer Aeneas had slept and into its waters the twins Romulus and Remus had been thrown. The Pauline tomb on the Ostian Way, near the banks of the Tiber, facilitated the Christian poet's link of Paul and "Father Tiber," personified in Roman myth and cult as a river-god ready to assist Rome's founders and heroes. For Prudentius, the Tiber had once again witnessed the apparent deaths of Rome's founding figures – Paul and Peter. Closely associated in martyr cult, Paul and Peter displaced Rome's former tutelary deities and twin astral guardians, Castor and Pollux (a pair of apotheosized heroes from the East, often depicted as disembodied stars hovering above the city). Paul together with Peter thus received the astral immortality evocative of the apotheosis reserved for Romulus, the Gemini, and deified emperors. Roman myth and cult now acclaimed the apostolic twins as the city's new stars.

Christians excavated their Roman identity and memory in martyr relics and ruins also at the city's other Pauline cult site, the catacombs on the Appian Way. The emperor Constantine had built a basilica there too, and afterward the bishop Damasus dedicated a Latin poem on a marble plaque at the cult area, which essentially naturalized Paul as Rome's premier citizen ("one of us," the bishop inscribed). The memorialization transformed the catacombs into what we might call a national cemetery for the heroic dead and made Paul's body Roman property. The Latin poem recalled the specific language of Rome's traditional war ritual, known as evocation, which great Roman generals had used in the past to entice (Latin *evocatio*) a foreign deity to leave its native land with formal promises of a new home and state-sponsored cult at Rome. *Evocatio* participated in a wider cultural habit of Romans using *foreignness* to define their own religious traditions. In the fourth century b.c.e., for example, a Roman general enticed the goddess Juno to depart her patronage of an enemy city (Veii) for a better temple and better worship in Rome. In the religious logic of *evocatio*, the immigrant Saint Paul had left the East and was now Roman.

The Roman ownership of Paul's body was set down in a later legend, an etiology explaining why Paul has *two* martyr cult sites. According to the sixth-century legend, Christians from the eastern part of the Roman Empire once tried secretly to steal back for their home region the bodies of Paul and Peter, only to be stopped in their tracks along the Appian Way by God in a violent earthquake, as a posse of alarmed Romans rushed out of the city to catch up with the thieves. Recovering the stolen bodies, the posse placed the bodies of their city's martyrs in the nearby catacombs for temporary safekeeping, and later translated them into their permanent cult locations on the Ostian Way (Paul) and in the Vatican (Peter).

The legendary etiology did not end competition over rival Pauline holy places, however. The Roman estate Aquae Salvias, later a monastery, housed a memorial for Paul's fallen head, with a legend that its three springs marked the three spots on the ground where the head had bounced upon its decapitation by a Roman soldier at Paul's martyrdom. Apparently, Paul's head became a relic of choice in late antiquity; throughout several centuries, Rome had two separate basilicas with altars for Paul's holy cranium.

For our purposes, the significance of Paul's martyr cult lies in its proliferation at Rome. The legends of the cult reshaped Roman identity and public memory. Paul displaced the old pagan founders to reign as the Eternal City's new monumental hero and divine patron, who was believed to be present simultaneously in the grave(s) and in the heavens.

2. Paul the Sexual Role Model: Ascetic or Family Man?

Many Christian writings depict Paul and his circle of associates as model local citizens and the best family supporters. Yet the historical Paul was not a family man, nor did he teach that believers should marry and have children as the best practices for total devotion to God. Not a romantic fellow, Paul believed in sexual renunciation over marriage as the Christian ideal. Though he urged all believers to strive for strict sexual renunciation as the best virtue, he did not make asceticism a blanket rule for the Christian life. He described celibacy as a divine "gift" (Greek *charisma*) that God did not bestow on all. Paul diagnosed some people to have a bodily incapacity for self-control, always falling short of the ascetic ideal. He taught that such "weak" believers, without the gift of celibacy, could still be full members of the church as long as they continued to strive toward God with their best moral behavior. This teaching appears in 1 Corinthians, a letter that Paul wrote in part to oppose the strict ascetic teachings among the believers at Corinth (see Box 17).

Paul conceded a place in the church for the married by qualifying the strong ascetic position at Corinth (quoted in 1 Cor. 7:1, "It is well for a man not to touch a woman"). Paul argued that a family man or woman

---

Box 17 Paul on Marriage and Celibacy

I wish that all were as I myself am. But each has a particular gift from God, one having one kind and another a different kind.

To the unmarried and the widows I say that it is well for them to remain unmarried as I am. But if they are not practicing self-control, they should marry. For it is better to marry than to be aflame with passion. . . .

I want you to be free from anxieties. The unmarried man is anxious about the affairs of the Lord, how to please the Lord; but the married man is anxious about the affairs of the world, how to please his wife, and his interests are divided. And the unmarried woman and the virgin are anxious about the affairs of the Lord, so that they may be holy in body and spirit; but the married woman is anxious about the affairs of the world, how to please her husband. I say this for your own benefit, not to put any restraint upon you, but to promote good order and unhindered devotion to the Lord. (1 Cor. 7:7–9, 32–35)

---

could still be a Christian, but not the best Christian. He did not lay down a firm rule about marriage, which he viewed primarily as a means of satisfying (extinguishing) the sexual urge and thus as protection against possible immorality (1 Cor. 7:9). Because of this tendency to side with everyone, Paul posed difficulties for later Christians wanting to read his epistles for clear ethical guidelines on family values.

"The Acts of Paul and Thecla" (Second Century)

In antiquity, too, the question of family values was contested. It is not surprising, then, that we find two contradictory views of Paul as a sexual role model. One view, which *The Acts of Paul and Thecla* represents, promoted a strict asceticism as the best measure of citizenship and family life in the Roman Empire. A second view, flourishing in the same period of the early second century, appeared in rival works also falsely bearing Paul's name (Colossians, Ephesians, the Pastoral Epistles), which promoted marriage under a traditional male patriarchy as the only way to support a society. Christians in late antiquity, therefore, reinvented Paul in multiple and conflicting ways in order to promote their cultural acceptance within the Roman Empire. On family values, Paul's legacy divided his interpreters.

The apocryphal *Acts of Paul and Thecla* narrates the adventures of its namesake female convert, who at the narrative's end gets a call from Paul to be an apostle in her own right. Highly popular in late antiquity, the work generated the widespread cult of Saint Thecla in its multiple venerations and traditions throughout the Mediterranean world (see Davis 2001); her feast day still receives celebration in September, in the Roman Catholic and Eastern Orthodox liturgical calendars respectively.

For Christian art, the work offers the only surviving description of what ancient Christians imagined Paul looked like: short, bald, bowlegged, having knit eyebrows and a crooked nose (*Acts of Paul and Thecla* 3). Though preserving no accurate historical memory of Paul's actual physical appearance, the description is nonetheless important for reconstructing how ancient Christians viewed Paul. In the modern era, the inaccurate assumption grew that this portrait was negative and typical of "the ugly Jew," but in recent years, a consensus of scholars now agrees that the portrait advances a stock piece of Greco-Roman rhetorical praise of what the ancient Romans called *dignitas*, the positive physiognomy of a statesman and general – the ultimate good citizen. The physical description serves also the narrative function of enabling the Christian host in the story to identify Paul on the street.

In the narrative, Paul settles into a host's apartment in the Asia Minor city of Iconium to preach daily on the holy asceticism of strict sexual renunciation. Within earshot, the heroine Thecla sits in a window of the neighboring apartment on the eve of her wedding. She is betrothed to a certain Thamyris, a fellow Iconian citizen. Thecla overhears Paul's preaching on virginity and becomes so enthralled that she refuses to eat or move from the window for days on end. In hysterics over Thecla's newly ascetic behavior, her desperate mother Theoclia sends for the betrothed Thamyris and warns him that Paul "will overturn the city of the Iconians" with such preaching on virginity (*Acts of Paul and Thecla* 9; trans. in Meeks and Fitzgerald 2007, 297). Thamyris, for his part, goes to the local Roman governor to accuse the "sorcerer" Paul of being a foreign villain whose preaching urges young women to violate their civic marriage duties. Indeed at the hearing, the Roman proconsul questions Thecla explicitly about the specific accusation of bad citizenship: "Why do you not marry Thamyris, according to the law of the Iconians?" All the talk of civic patriotism leads Theoclia to renounce her daughter, shouting, "Burn the wicked one; burn her who will not marry in the midst of the theater, that all the women who have been taught by this man may be afraid" (*Acts of Paul and Thecla* 20; trans. in Meeks and Fitzgerald 2007, 299). The governor condemns Thecla to death by a public burning in the city's theater, and Paul to be flogged and banished from the city.

The domestic dispute of Thecla's family becomes a public spectacle about proper citizenship in a city. But who is the real "citizen" in the story? The spectacle in the city's theater provides a lesson in divine justice for the onlookers. God sends a miraculous rainstorm that saves Thecla from the fire, and the almost martyred Thecla leaves town to travel with Paul along his missionary journey. The miracle exposes the evil Thamyris as the real "bad citizen" who abuses his civic privileges and the legal system to avenge an unrequited love.

The scene in Antioch, the next city on this apocryphal Paul's itinerary, repeats the plot's dramatic cycle of unrequited love. A private crush once again becomes a public spectacle on proper citizenship before the theater audience of an entire city. The obstructing character in this episode is explicitly identified as "a leading citizen of Antioch," a certain Alexander, who pursues the beautiful Thecla as the next suitor for her hand in marriage. Yet, always the model ascetic, Thecla refuses Alexander's amatory embraces with an extraordinary display of female honor over male shame: she tears his aristocratic cloak and knocks off his civic crown, rendering him a public laughingstock. To avenge his humiliation, Citizen Alexander hauls Thecla before his local Roman governor who, in turn, condemns the young virgin to death by wild beasts in the city's amphitheater and to bear the placard "sacrilegious [one]." Once again, Thecla suffers from local male injustice. But, while imprisoned, she enjoys the female patronage of a royal citizen ranking higher than Alexander – Queen Tryphaena, who belongs to the Roman imperial family. Protecting the imprisoned Thecla from further sexual assaults, Queen Tryphaena adores Thecla as a surrogate for her dead daughter Falconilla, whose postmortem self has asked her mother in a dream to "receive this stranger, the forsaken Thecla, in my place" (*Acts of Paul and Thecla* 28; trans. in Meeks and Fitzgerald 2007, 300). Thecla's asceticism thus restores lost family ties in a piety and love higher than Alexander's lustful desire for a quick marriage simply for sex.

But Thecla must still face death. During her attempted execution in the civic amphitheater, the roars from the crowd divide along gender lines. The city's men shout "Away with the sacrilegious person," but the city's women lament the injustice of the whole evil spectacle. The female solidarity extends even into the animal kingdom, when a brave lioness sacrifices herself to protect Thecla from an attacking lion – the first animal Christian martyr on record. Then, in another stunning spectacle of God's salvation, Thecla baptizes *herself* on the arena's field by jumping into its water reservoir of death, full of what are identified as carnivorous seals. A divine lightening bolt electrocutes the marine predators but leaves

Thecla unscathed and newly baptized. When even more wild beasts are sent into the arena to eat her, the women in the audience join God in saving Thecla by throwing their flower petals, fragrant ointments, herbs, and other aromatic plants onto the field so that the abundance of perfumes would sedate the beasts into hypnotic stupors (see Box 18).

Box 18 The Female Apostle Thecla: Celibate and (Would-be) Martyr

And there arose a tumult: the wild beasts roared, the people and the women sitting together were crying, some saying, "Away with the sacrilegious person!", others saying, "O that the city would be destroyed on account of this iniquity! Kill us all, proconsul; miserable spectacle, evil judgment!"

And Thecla, having been taken from the hands of Tryphaena, was stripped and received a girdle and was thrown into the arena. And lions and bears were let loose upon her. And a fierce lioness ran up and lay down at her feet. And the multitude of the women cried aloud. And a bear ran upon her, but the lioness went to meet it and tore the bear to pieces. And again a lion that had been trained to fight against men, which belonged to Alexander, ran upon her. And the lioness, encountering the lion, was killed along with it. And the women cried the more since the lioness, her protector, was dead.

Then they sent in many beasts as she was standing and stretching forth her hands and praying. And when she had finished her prayer she turned around and saw a large pit full of water and said, "Now it is time to wash myself." And she threw herself in saying, "In the name of Jesus Christ I baptize myself on my last day." When the women and the multitude saw it they wept and said, "Do not throw yourself into the water!"; even the governor shed tears because the seals were to devour such beauty. She then threw herself into the water in the name of Jesus Christ, but the seals, having seen a flash of lightning, floated dead on the surface. And there was round her a cloud of fire so that the beasts could neither touch her nor could she been seen naked.

But the women lamented when other and fiercer animals were let loose; some threw petals, others nard, others cassia, others amomum, so that there was an abundance of perfumes. And all the wild animals were hypnotized and did not touch her. (*Acts of Paul and Thecla*, 32–35; trans. in Meeks and Fitzgerald 2007, 301–2)

Citizen Alexander then calls for his fiercest bulls to tear Thecla apart, and near the arena Queen Tryphaena faints at the horror. Thinking the city's royal citizen to be dead, the governor halts the games and Alexander begs for forgiveness. In consideration of Queen Tryphaena's powerful family connection to the Roman emperor, the remorseful Alexander prostrates himself at the feet of his imperial governor and cries, "Have mercy upon me and upon the city and set the woman free, lest the city also be destroyed. For if Caesar hear of these things he will possibly destroy the city along with us because his kinswoman, Queen Tryphaena, has died at the theater gate" (*Acts of Paul and Thecla* 36; trans. in Meeks and Fitzgerald 2007, 302). The governor releases Thecla in an official edict declaring her piety and holiness as a "slave of God" (*Acts of Paul and Thecla* 38), evoking Paul's own self-designation (see Chapter 3). Later, the recovered Queen Tryphaena receives the gospel (Greek *euangelion*), rushes to embrace Thecla, and says, "Now I believe that the dead are raised! Now I believe that my child lives" (*Acts of Paul and Thecla* 39; trans. in Meeks and Fitzgerald 2007, 302), and welcomes Thecla into her home. By promoting good citizenship in this world and promising postmortem salvation in the next, the vindication of Thecla refutes the criminal charge on her placard as false. At the story's end, Paul gives Thecla a formal call to evangelize and teach the word of God as her *own* apostle (*Acts of Paul and Thecla* 41). Thecla, the female apostle of Christ, decides that her first mission must be to go home and reconcile with her own mother Theoclia and former fiancé Thamyris.

Historically, *The Acts of Paul and Thecla* defended ascetic Pauline Christianity in the life of the ancient city. The scenes of mothers reuniting with lost daughters (Theoclia and Thecla, Queen Tryphaena and Thecla-as-Falconilla) functioned to support Pauline asceticism as an ultimately pro-citizen *and* pro-family lifestyle. The heroic exploits of the almost martyred and self-baptized Thecla denied the accusations, voiced in the story's opening, that Pauline teachings about a strict sexual renunciation necessarily violated Greco-Roman family values or the welfare of the city. Asserting her own power and freedom from traditionally subordinated women's roles, Thecla belonged to the author's ascetic remaking of Paul. In the story, her strict sexual renunciation proves to be better citizenship for the city and greater piety for the family than the inevitably lewd behavior of horny men, however high ranking their citizenship.

Whether asceticism leads to better citizenship and family life in the Roman Empire was a question that divided the Pauline legacy. Not all followers imagined the apostle's teachings to favor a strict ascetic model of virginity over against marriage. A rival view in second-century Pauline

Christianity directly opposed the teachings that we find in *The Acts of Paul and Thecla*. This opposing view tried to fit Paul's teachings in a decidedly domestic form, to subordinate women with prescriptive codes for household behavior under the *paterfamilias*. The result domesticated the apostle into a traditionally Roman family man.

The "Pauline School": Colossians (ca. 65–75), Ephesians (ca. 80), and the Pastoral Epistles (ca. 95–125)

Scholars today call the New Testament epistles falsely bearing Paul's name the work of the "Pauline School." Set apart as deutero-Pauline ("second" Paul), the writings are called the work of the Pauline School because their theological heritage invoked the apostle as *the* confirmation for its doctrine. But the modern term does not imply an academy of students who actually met or had a strong sense of membership.

Teaching marriage rather than nonmarriage as the Christian ideal, literature of the Pauline School circulated for several centuries in a polemical context of powerful alternatives offered by rival and equally pseudonymous "Pauls" (e.g., *The Acts of Paul and Thecla*). The deutero-Pauline epistles made Paul a family man. The theme participated in ancient household-management literature, which went back to Aristotle's *Politics*. Aristotle wrote that any discussion of the city-state (Greek *polis*) best began with the topic of household management because the family constituted the basic component of the state. His *Politics* compared the household to a body, whose essential members belonged in three naturalized pairings: husband and wife, father and children, master and slave. The trope asserted the male householder's mastery over his wife, children, and slaves as *the* natural hierarchy of the divine moral order. The author of Colossians wrote in the supposed voice of Paul to teach authoritative rules for the household, which Christianized this Aristotelian tradition:

> Wives, be subject to your husbands, as is fitting in the Lord. Husbands, love your wives and never treat them harshly. Children, obey your parents in everything, for this is your acceptable duty in the Lord. Fathers, do not provoke your children, or they may lose heart. Slaves, obey your earthly masters in everything, not only while being watched and in order to please them, but wholeheartedly, fearing the Lord [the same Greek term as previously, "master"]. Whatever your task, put yourselves into it, as done for the Lord and not for your masters, since you know that from the Lord you will receive the inheritance as your reward; you are slaves of the Lord Christ.

> For the wrongdoer will be paid back for whatever wrong has been done, and there is no partiality. Masters, treat your slaves justly and fairly, for you know that you also have a Master in heaven. (Col. 3:18–4:1)

In Colossians, the word of Aristotle thus became the word of Paul. Yet the pseudonymous Paul did not suggest that he was telling his audience something new: he advocated behavior that people (whether Christian or non-Christian) already practiced and took for granted as obviously right. Colossians appealed to common sense, what the reader already "knows" (Col. 3:24), and its logic depended on the supposed obviousness of ordinary (worldly) wisdom. In that wisdom, marriage was not only the Christian ideal but also the norm, which remade Paul into the model of a household manager. The Pauline domestic codes thus turned household mastery into a teachable system, similar to a handbook. The Letter to the Ephesians copies this block of material from Colossians nearly verbatim (Eph. 5:21–6:9), but with a stricter subordination of women and slaves (see Harrill 2006, 85–117).

The domestic codes in the so-called Pastoral Epistles emphasized Paul the family man as *the* model of a Christian, and the ancient household as *the* model of the church. The pseudonymous author of 1 Timothy wrote in the persona of Paul to command, among other things, Christian women to acknowledge their household subordination in their personal appearance:

> I ["Paul"] desire, then, that . . . the women should dress themselves modestly and decently in suitable clothing, not with their hair braided, or with gold, pearls, or expensive cloths, but with good works as is proper for women who profess reverence for God. Let a woman learn in silence and in full submission. I permit no woman to teach or to have authority over a man; she is to keep silent. For Adam was formed first, then Eve; and Adam was not deceived, but the woman was deceived and became a transgressor. Yet she will be saved through childbearing, provided they continue in faith and love and holiness, with modesty. (1 Tim. 2:8–15)

In 1 Timothy, Paul the family man prohibited Christian women from donning expensive clothing, decorative hairdos, and fine jewelry. Such prohibition of noble appearance functioned to prevent women from receiving honor in the public square and so also in the church. Women, in this view, were to remain at home in their female shame as punishment for the fall of man. Traditional (pagan) family values in the wider classical culture thus entered the Christian household in the name of "Paul."

The similarity of the opponents in the Pastorals to the heroes of *The Acts of Paul and Thecla* may be the result of a literary dependence between the two writings. The Pastoral Epistles emphasized patriarchy greater than citizenship, which subordinated Christian women privately to their husbands and away from the public roles of church officers. The Pastorals urged acceptance of this Pauline message over against those of rival Pauline teachers, who apparently preached against marriage and toward a strict asceticism. Those opponents "forbid marriage and demand abstinence from foods, which God created to receive with thanksgiving by those who believe and know the truth" (1 Tim. 4:3). They "make their way into households and captivate silly women" (2 Tim. 3:6) and so violate the naturalness of a domestic hierarchy. They upset "whole families by their teaching" and "must be silenced" (Titus 1:11). The author of the Pastorals applied stock terms of abuse to encourage his audience to stereotype those rivals in terms of their alleged group affiliation with the obvious sort of criminals whom even the pagan world condemned.

The Pastoral Epistles assumed the persona of Paul to affirm the necessity of marriage and its "proper" male domination of women, children, and slaves. A bishop, for example, must prove his managerial skills first at home by maintaining good (hierarchical) order. For the Pastorals, church episcopal office must follow traditionally pagan domestic hierarchy under a *paterfamilias*:

> The saying is sure: whoever aspires to the office of bishop desires a noble task. Now a bishop must be above reproach, married only once, temperate, sensible, respectable, hospitable, an apt teacher, not a drunkard, not violent but gentle, not quarrelsome, and not a lover of money. He must manage his own household well, keeping his children submissive and respectful in every way – for if someone does not know how to manage his own household, how can he take care of God's church? He must not be a recent convert, or he may be puffed up with conceit and fall into the condemnation of the devil. Moreover, he must be well thought of by outsiders, so that he may not fall into disgrace and the snare of the devil. (1 Tim. 3:1–7)

The job description of a bishop used patriarchy as its main family value. The hierarchy of the father in his household served as a natural model for all social organization, including that of the church. This patriarchy required the bishop to be a "real" man, which was defined in classically traditional terms – father, husband, and master.

Paul's literary afterlife on family values thus refashioned the apostle into either the family man (the Pauline School) or the model ascetic (*The Acts of Paul and Thecla*) – two opposing trajectories. Which trajectory has the more legitimate claim on Paul's legacy? To be sure, Paul himself was no family man, and his authentic letters promoted asceticism as the

Christian ideal, which does undermine the legitimacy of the legacy depicted in the strict household codes of the pseudonymous letters of Colossians, Ephesians, and the Pastoral Epistles. But this finding does not mean that *The Acts of Paul and Thecla* has the more legitimate claim to Paul's legacy. As mentioned previously, Paul qualified his sexual ethics to allow weaker members of the church to become married when they proved unable to practice self-control. A strict ascetic position is precisely what Paul opposed in 1 Corinthians. In sum, both *The Acts of Paul and Thecla* and the Pauline School show his presence alive and well in the second century, but neither preserves Paul's own thinking without alteration.

Our thematic analysis thus far has traced the development of multiple and competing strategies by which late ancient Christians turned their hero Paul into a character to embrace, even a divine figure. Yet to focus exclusively on Paul's admirers does not tell the whole of his legacy, of course. We need also to look at his foes.

3. PAUL THE DECEIVER: CONTINUING CRITICISM OF THE APOSTLE

The rise of Paul's fame in late antiquity, in part due to the circulation of Pauline literature into a corpus alongside other "Scriptures" (see Chapter 5), also exposed the figure to various critics. The critics fall into two basic categories. First, certain followers of Messiah Jesus continued to observe the Torah and its obligations for Israel – whom other Christians called Ebionites (second century) and Elchasaites (third century; see Chapter 5 on the Manichaean Paul) – and they condemned Paul as "Satan's apostle." Second, Greco-Roman (pagan) philosophers of the third and fourth centuries attacked Paul in the context of their wider assault on Christianity for its growth among the Roman population. For these various critics, Paul was the Deceiver.

The Apostle of Satan

The Ebionites – a name derived from a Semitic word for "the poor" that evokes a passage in Paul's letters (Gal. 2:10) – were Christians who continued to follow Jewish Law. They apparently venerated the apostles James and Peter exclusively, used Matthew's gospel alone, held the city of Jerusalem in highest esteem, and observed only Jewish ritual customs such as circumcision. The Ebionites rejected Paul as a renegade from Jewish Law and as the apostle of Satan.

The Ebionite Paul had at least three different forms. One form depicted a liar about his past; he was not Jewish but a Greek, born of Gentile parents. The tale exploited commonplace tropes in ancient Jewish literature about Gentiles being a degenerate people exhibiting sexual lust and immoral behavior by their very nature (what we might call ethnic stereotype).

In one story, Paul on an extended visit in Jerusalem falls in love with a beautiful daughter of an important Jewish priest. To get the girl to marry him, Paul accepts circumcision as a Jewish proselyte. When she still refuses his hand in marriage, Paul goes on a violent rampage writing against circumcision and all "the works" of Torah. A second version of the tale also depicts Paul as a raging lunatic. It focuses on a debate between Jewish leaders and the apostles at the Jerusalem temple, in which Paul as the leading prosecutor against the faith slugs James across the head with a metal altar brand. Leaving James for dead on the temple steps, Paul then brutalizes all Christians in Jerusalem and nearby environs. A third account slanders Paul for claiming apostolic authority solely from his vision of the risen Lord, on the argument that, according to the Old Testament, no person can see God and live (see Exod. 33:20). Applying the nickname "Simon" to Paul (after the magician and arch-heretic Simon Magus in Acts 8), this version of the tale holds that any such epiphany more likely came from an evil demon, the "real" source of Paul's gospel.

This literature is not evidence of the historical Paul, because the polemics are flat caricatures or concocted from prefabricated legends. Rather, they testify that Paul's growing legacy even reached congregations that clearly wanted nothing to do with his teachings about uncircumcised Gentiles. The figure of Paul was becoming famous enough to attack. (Readers can find these tales in Meeks and Fitzgerald 2007, 228–35.)

Paul the Contradiction and Mad Magician: Pagans Strike Back

Paul's literary afterlife also gained its pagan foes in late antiquity. In the third and fourth centuries, a period when Christianity had spread to significant percentages of the Roman population, the figure of Paul attracted the ire of Greco-Roman philosophers who condemned the faith as "magic" and *superstitio* for its deviation from legitimate Roman *religio*. The surviving fragments of the first known pagan critic of Christianity, Celsus (ca. 178–180), do not mention Paul explicitly; it is debated whether he read Paul's letters. But the later philosopher Porphyry of Tyre (ca. 234–305), who had studied under the famous Neoplatonist teacher Plotinus in

---

Box 19 Patristic Frankness over Paul's Fight with Peter

Pagan critics like Porphyry forced some Christian theologians in late antiquity to be frank about Paul's fight with Peter (Gal. 2:11–14). In a series of letters, Jerome (347–420) and Augustine (354–430) famously disputed with one another over the interpretation of the passage. Jerome argued that Paul had only *pretended* to rebuke Peter so as not to offend the believing Jewish onlookers; the apostle exercised appropriately compassionate pretense and a tactical device of showpiece oratory. But this line of interpretation horrified Augustine, for Jerome's view introduced the unthinkable – that the divine Scripture could contain lies in some part of its work. Augustine responded with a detailed argument upholding the literal meaning of the passage; Paul did indeed rebuke the sin of the apostle Peter. In his response, Augustine rebuked Jerome for suggesting that lying could be in the Bible:

> Is it the case that those who lie usefully are to be blamed, while those who do so pragmatically necessarily are to be approved? Do those who think this judge that one may lie when one chooses? It is a great question whether a good man may sometimes lie, or whether a Christian may.... But this, as I've said, is a different and important question; those who think that one may lie should choose (the justification) they want, so long as it is unshakably believed and defended that those who wrote sacred Scripture – and most especially the canonical books were completely free from the lie.

Trans. in Griffiths 2004, 150. See also Carriker 1999, and Mitchell 2012.

Rome from 263 to 268, wrote a multivolume work entitled *Against the Christians*. This work condemned Paul as an undignified and contradictory thinker. Porphyry's favorite example was reportedly the well-known passage in Galatians about the conflict between Paul and Peter at Antioch (see Chapters 1 and 2, and Box 19). Porphyry called the description a "childish fight" that exposed Paul's immaturity and lack of poise in comparison with the more mature Peter. For Porphyry, one can see the contradictions in Paul's words as readily as one watches an inept archer shooting himself in the foot.

Porphyry's *Against the Christians* was so widely circulated that it became the likely basis for the longest and most vicious polemic against Paul that survives from antiquity, a tirade by an anonymous fourth-century

Greek known to us only as "The Hellene." The Hellene followed Porphyry's technique of finding contradictions, a device of literary criticism familiar from ancient philosophy's attack on poetry and myths about the gods and goddesses as not being true in a literal sense (see Box 6, Chapter 1). He condemned Paul for the many contradictions that became clearly apparent when reading the apostle's letters side by side and also next to the book of Acts. Paul at one time pretended to be a Jew, and at another time a non-Jew (1 Cor. 9:19–22). Paul preached virginity as the Christian ideal (1 Cor. 7:25–26) yet also warned against false preachers who forbid virgins to marry (1 Tim. 4:1). As well, Paul stood adamantly against circumcision (Phil. 3:2; Gal. 2:3) but later turned at a moment's notice to circumcise his associate Timothy (Acts 16:3). In these inconsistencies, the Hellene argued, Paul was his own worst accuser.

The pagan polemics against Paul show just how central the figure had become in ancient Christian literary culture. Porphyry's writings likely provided the intellectual justification for the conservative religious revival of Roman state cults that we call the Great Persecution of the Church (303–313) under the reign of Diocletian. Afterward, the Roman emperor Julian, who reigned briefly from 361 to 363, repeated several of Porphyry's criticisms of Paul in his book *Against the Galileans*. Nicknamed in Christian culture as the "Apostate" for his adult conversion back to traditional paganism, Julian condemned Paul as nothing more than a lunatic magician whose double-talking led to insane contradictions. Paul, Julian pointed out, kept changing his views about God with shameless adaptability, as sea coral changed its hues to match the color of the rocks upon which it grew – a reference to the apparent tension that ancient readers found in reading Paul's letters as a corpus and alongside the book of Acts (see Chapter 5). Julian's polemics of Paul in *Against the Galileans* had the specific goal of garnering support among the philosophical elite for the emperor's new political project of pagan restoration. Julian tried to restore the traditional cults and sacrifice throughout the Roman Empire – sponsoring the rebuilding of the Jewish temple in Jerusalem, for example – to reverse years of Christianization of Roman culture by his imperial family. Julian's mockery of Paul thus encouraged ancient readers to dismiss the apostle as a mad magician. In Julian's view, Paul's works had bewitched the Romans from their true religious and ancestral tradition of authentic paganism. In the late fourth century, Paul's Roman identity was so obvious in the eyes of Rome's aristocratic elite that it took an emperor like Julian the Apostate to challenge it.

This chapter has surveyed the mixed reception of Paul in late antiquity. I have argued that Paul developed into a key figure in Christian literary culture even though, in the earliest Christianity of his own life-time, he was not the most significant personality. This centrality of Paul in late antiquity arose especially through constructions of his Romanness by later interpreters, which matched what Rome's aristocratic elite saw in themselves. A perennial question in the history of Pauline interpretation is whether the apostle taught a consistent message. Chapter 5 will probe on this question further, by examining how he became a book and the Scriptural Authority, yet another Paul.

5

PAUL THE SCRIPTURAL AUTHORITY
Contradictory Discourses

Late ancient Christians, seeking meaning for Paul, developed contrasting ideas about the nature of the apostle as an oracle of God. In this chapter, I discuss their diverse literary discourses (in the second to the fourth centuries), in which Paul was not so much a story character to embrace or argue with, but really a kind of book to quote from. The survey includes a number of different Christian writers; some number among the celebrated "fathers of the church" (*patristics* is the modern study of these writers), while others have faded into the fog of history as so-called heretics. Yet neither ecclesiastical nor scriptural orthodoxy existed in the pre-Constantinian period, an important point to keep in mind throughout this chapter. All these writers belong to the history of Christianity.

The late ancient writers are, in order of their appearance in our survey, Marcion and Valentinus (mid second century), Irenaeus (late second century), Origen (third century), and John Chrysostom (fourth century). These teachers formulated many different "scriptural Pauls." I begin with a consideration of how Paul's letters, when they became collected into a "book" (Greek *codex*), shaped the content of ancient Christian literary culture.

1. THE PROBLEMS AND POSSIBILITIES OF PAUL'S LETTERS COLLECTED INTO A SINGLE CORPUS

As a direct result of Paul's literary afterlife, the epistle became standard in Christian literary culture to express theological and pastoral thinking (a practice that continues today, in Papal encyclicals, for example). This development marks a departure from literary forms in the Old Testament/ Hebrew Bible, none of whose books are letters, and inspired a host of Pauline imitators – a reason why the epistle is the most common literary form in the New Testament canon. This new scriptural practice developed because Paul's letters circulated beyond their original recipient congregations not as individual works but together in a collection or corpus. Collecting the letters of an important figure into a corpus was a common practice in Greco-Roman culture. Examples range from philosophers like Plato and Epicurus to statesmen like Cicero, Seneca, and Pliny the Younger, each of whom had their letters published (circulated by scribal copies) in a single corpus. A published collection of Paul's letters, in various and sundry versions, circulated early (a few decades after Paul's death, ca. 62) and widely, reaching the hands of many early interpreters and critics, who included the pseudonymous authors of 1 Peter, 2 Peter, the Letter of James, and other apostolic epistles not included in our New Testament (see Appendix 3).

Collecting Paul's letters into a corpus created a problematic legacy, however. Each of his authentic letters was an occasional piece of mail for a particular set of addressees. Paul did not anticipate that his fledgling Thessalonian congregation (to whom he was "gentle among you, like a nurse," 1 Thess. 2:7) might somehow receive also his combative letter to the Galatians; and, conversely, Paul's angry rebuke to the Galatian believers would have been empty if Paul expected them to receive also 1 Thessalonians. Reading Paul's letters side by side made a host of tensions and contradictions apparent to ancient readers, the most infamous being between the combative tone of Galatians and the rhetoric of reconciliation in 1 Corinthians. The question of Paul's consistency was and is a perennial one because Paul himself raised it (see 1 Cor. 9:22). For example, 2 Corinthians preserves the rhetoric of the accusation that Paul exhibited the duplicity of a religious fraud: "For they say, 'His letters are weighty and strong, but his bodily presence is weak, and his speech contemptible'" (2 Cor. 10:10). And, indeed, Paul boasted about his changeability as a good feature of his personality in a famous passage:

> To the Jews I became as a Jew, in order to win Jews. To those under the law I became as one under the law (though I myself am not under the law) so that I might win those under the law. To those outside the law I became as one outside the law (though I am not free from God's law but am under Christ's law) so that I might win those outside the law. To the weak I became weak, so that I might win the weak. I have become all things to all people, that I might by all means save some. (1 Cor. 9:20–22)

Paul claimed that his real self could be found only in the tension of his apparent inconsistencies. A Christian version of Proteus (the Greek sea god capable of assuming many forms, described in Homeric epic), Paul shifts away from grasp just when commentators think they have hold of his meaning: Paul declared that the works of the Law had been abolished, but he also affirmed the Torah's continuing validity; sometimes he pronounced the Law to be impossible to fulfill, but at other times he said that people can and do fulfill the Law; while some of Paul's passages explained the Law to have a positive role in salvation, elsewhere he characterized the Law negatively as the catalyst for sin and death. Such shiftiness in Paul's variable positions on the Jewish Law has bewildered many of his interpreters, both ancient and modern.

The Second Letter of Peter in the New Testament – not by the historical apostle Peter, but an unknown second-century writer under a pseudonym – exemplifies the problem as some ancient Christians saw it. It states: "So also our beloved brother Paul wrote to you according to the wisdom given him, speaking of this as he does in all his letters. There are some things in them hard to understand, which the ignorant and unstable twist to their own destruction, as they do the other scriptures" (2 Pet. 3:16; on this passage, see Harrill 2010). The uncompromising condemnation of rival Christian teachers in 2 Peter bears much in common with Paul's letters: whoever teaches differently must be either "ignorant" or mentally ill ("unstable"). The passage shows that by the early second century, sharp controversies arose over how to interpret a collection of Paul's letters that circulated alongside "the other scriptures" (a likely reference to the Septuagint, which itself was not a full or closed canon at this time).

2. Marcion and Valentinus: Two Pauline Rivals at Rome

In late antiquity, many different Pauline teachers offered their solutions to the problem that the circulation of a Pauline letter corpus posed to believers. In mid-second century Rome, two rival Christian leaders – Marcion and Valentinus – were teaching. Marcion taught a radical Paul that limited the content of a Christian Bible, but Valentinus's esoteric Paul had a more capacious view of Scripture that encouraged the wide reading of texts through the practice of allegory. These two Christian teachers thus read Paul's letters in completely opposite ways.

Let's set the scene. Around the year 150, the Christian subculture in Rome was very small. The odd little groups continued to meet in private homes, without any communal property of their own or public buildings. There was no single or primary leader, much less a unified Church. Because they were so few, the Christians (a term by this time in circulation) had an acute awareness of their differences from each other. The separate house-based congregations featured a great variety of scriptural practices yet also developed shared expressions of religious solidarity. They sent token portions of the Eucharist to each other, exchanged letters and Scripture, often cooperated in charity for the poor, occasionally elected shared officers called "elders" (Greek *presbuteroi*) and "bishops" (*episcopoi*), and sometimes their leaders gathered for occasional citywide meetings. How representative or how much power such citywide meetings of leaders had is unclear. In any case, Christian groups blended well into ordinary city life. They resembled the several voluntary associations (Latin *collegia*) – organized around a patron deity, having a common chest, and meeting in a private household room – that had long been a popular form of neighborhood society. They also had much in common with the city's many philosophical schools (study circles organized around a celebrated teacher), which competed for potential converts by claiming to offer the best moral lifestyle (Josephus described Judaism along similar lines, as "schools of thought," as we saw in Chapter 1). In this urban setting, the early Christian community had both unity and diversity.

Marcion was raised as a Christian in the prosperous Roman colony of Sinope in Asia Minor, on the south shore of the Black Sea (modern Sinop, Turkey). In his late forties or early fifties, he moved his career to Rome (ca. 140). He, therefore, arrived in the imperial capital already a prominent teacher on Scripture and wealthy, from a shipbuilder family. Seeking solidarity with the Roman Christians, Marcion donated a substantial fortune to a common fund shared by local house churches for charity to the poor, showing where he placed his values. The gesture gave Marcion rising fame among Christians in the city, gaining a large following of disciples and house churches of his own.

Yet Marcion became increasingly frustrated that his donation did not offer him greater influence over house churches outside his patronage. He wanted to bring other Christians in line with his reforms, especially on what constituted the authoritative Holy Scriptures. Marcion also advanced a strict asceticism – sexual renunciation and abstinence from meat and wine – that he believed imitated his ultimate hero, Paul, who was to his mind the only true apostle. Baptism into Marcionite churches thus required a vow of celibacy. Soon, his donation was returned, and at least some churches refused to exchange tokens of the Eucharist with his congregations. Finally, in the year 144, Marcion and his fellow Christians mutually withdrew fellowship from each other, with Marcion likely "excommunicating" the other Roman Christians for not accepting his imposition of greater institutional and doctrinal unity. An undeterred Marcion departed Rome and, over the next decades, built his own network of tightly disciplined churches on his vision of the "True Church." Marcion ordained his own bishops, deacons, and presbyters as well as oversaw the building of "proper" Christian sanctuaries and chapels throughout the Roman Empire.

Marcionite Christianity lasted for centuries as perhaps the most radically Pauline church of late antiquity. What was so radical about Marcion? He took Paul's contrast between God's free gift of "grace" and human works of the Jewish "law" (see Rom. 3:30; 5:1–21; Gal. 2:16) to a literal extreme: Paul directly contradicted the Jewish Law, which Marcion took as the entire Old Testament. This literary, bookish contrast attempted to create a coherent reading of the apostle's letters for later Christian communities lacking the intense eschatology that had shaped Paul's apocalyptic hope for Gentiles.

In Marcion's literalism, the only valid way for Gentiles to read the Jewish Scriptures – the Septuagint – was to attend exclusively to the surface meaning and the plain sense of passages. He rejected rival methods of interpretation – allegory, oral tradition, mythmaking – that his fellow Christians (and Paul himself; see Chapter 1, regarding Jewish midrash) applied habitually to read the Septuagint as Christian Scripture, because he rejected the sacredness of the Septuagint for Gentiles. He outlined this fundamental grace-and-law opposition in *The Antitheses*, a work with handbook authority. Marcion's *Antitheses* placed lines from the Septuagint parallel to lines of the Gospels in a series of contradictory propositions, which provided his followers an introduction on how to read scriptures exclusively via Paul's contrast of law and gospel (see Box 20).

The Antitheses listed what Marcion saw as the clear differences between the true God (of Jesus and Paul) and the Jewish deity (of the Old Testament). On a surface reading, Marcion's catalog of contradictions revealed the Creator in the Old Testament to be a merciless, righteous god whose severe realm resembled that of human tyrants: Yahweh thus could not have been the God of Jesus and Paul. In this way, Marcion argued that the God of Jesus and Paul was higher, more loving, and hidden – a Supreme Deity whom Marcion simply called "the Stranger." Marcion therefore affirmed a Christianized polytheism of two deities in a cosmic hierarchy. Marcion's Old Testament God was an overly righteous divinity, appropriate for Jews to worship; it was not an evil figure such as Satan. In Marcion's tiered cosmology, salvific options for Jews would work out in ways different from that of Gentile believers. The Jews would receive their own Christ from their righteous Creator God of the Old Testament (a second, different

---

Box 20 Marcion's *Antitheses*

Moses permits divorce [Deut. 24:1]; but Jesus the Lord forbids it [Luke 16:18; 1 Cor. 7:10].

The God of Moses commands in the Law, "an eye for an eye, a tooth for a tooth" [Exod. 21:24; Deut. 19:21]; but Jesus the Lord says in the Gospel: "If anyone strikes you on the cheek, offer the other as well" [cf. Luke 6:29].

The Old Testament God of Creation, in order to kill as many people as possible in battle, prevented the sun from going down until his prophet had finished annihilating those who made war on his people [Josh. 10:12–14]; but Jesus the Lord says through apostle Paul: "Let not the sun go down on your anger" [Eph. 4:26].

Another prophet of that overly righteous God of Creation commanded killer bears to come from the thicket and devour little children who had harassed him [2 Kings 2:14]; but Jesus the good Lord says: "Let the children come to me and do not forbid them, for of such is the Kingdom of Heaven" [cf. Luke 18:16]. (Marcion, *Antitheses*; trans. adapted from their reconstruction and analysis in Harnack 1990, 53–63; see also Meeks and Fitzgerald 2007, 286–88)

Messiah who had not yet come). Marcion's faith that Jews would eventually receive salvation at their own special moment may have partially retained what many modern scholars today reconstruct as Paul's eschatological hope in the salvation of "all Israel" (Rom 11:26), understood to include both believing Gentiles and unbelieving Jews, but at different times (Marshall 2012). Be that as it may, the circulation of Paul's letters into a corpus thus led Marcion to suggest that Christians should have their own Scripture separate from what Jews already had.

Replacing the rejected Jewish Scripture as irrelevant for Christians, Marcion followed a single written Gospel (apparently a version of the Gospel of Luke). This practice, in itself, is unremarkable because most Christians before the late second century followed a single written Gospel. But Marcion also added his own edited collection of Pauline letters, a so-called "Apostle Book" (Greek *Apostolikon*), which consisted of ten epistles (all but the Pastoral Epistles, which he either rejected or did not know). The book of the "Gospel" (Greek *Euangelion*; that is, Luke) and the book of the "Apostle" made a two-part Christian Bible. For his canon (a prescriptive list of the works to be read in church), Marcion edited out what he saw as confusing ambiguities and interpolations in the received manuscripts to create a new authoritative text. As well, he deleted the Old Testament references quoted in Paul's letters that suggested continuity rather than discontinuity.

Marcion's rival Valentinus was an expert in rhetorical composition and very learned in Paul, the gospels, Jewish Scriptures, and Platonic philosophy. He had moved to Rome in the late 130s from the second city of the Empire, Alexandria in Egypt. Born around 100 in the Egyptian Delta, he was educated in this city whose august academic institutions had long featured the allegorical method of interpretation; the Egyptian Hellenistic capital enjoyed fame throughout the Mediterranean world as home to the greatest intellectual wonders (library, museum, gymnasium, and lighthouse).

In Rome, Valentinus actively encouraged a reputation for bearing "alien" (Eastern) wisdom, packaging his teachings in a highly personal kind of authority that combined visionary experience and scholarly knowledge. He produced an intellectual pedigree of distinguished tutors allegedly in a direct line of successors going back to Christianity's founding apostles – and, ultimately, Jesus. Valentinus had apparently received his theological training from a certain Theudas, a disciple of Paul, thus making Paul the source of his esoteric teachings in an apostolic succession. The direct Pauline line of training reportedly gave him mystical visions and revelations of Jesus Christ, as Paul claimed to have had (cf. 2 Cor. 12:1–4). Valentinus preached, for example, that Jesus Christ had appeared to him as a newborn baby conveying the whole meaning of salvation in a single cosmic myth. That vision became the basis for Valentinus's emphasis on salvation by the personal "knowledge" (Greek *gnōsis*; better translated as "acquaintance") of the divine. For about three decades in Rome, until the 160s (when he fades from our historical record), Valentinus taught mythmaking and an esoteric truth (as opposed to Marcion's plain truth) about Paul and Jesus Christ. He drew a significant following among the tiny groups of believers at Rome into his "school of thought" (Greek *hairesis*), which he founded on the model of the Greco-Roman philosophical school. Enough Roman Christians acknowledged him to be such a gifted teacher that they nearly elected him as a bishop. The production and circulation of Valentinian literature lasted well into late antiquity.

Valentinian scriptural practices sought to help Christian students to discern Paul's esoteric wisdom through a course of study in advanced exegesis and hermeneutics that included the allegorical method. According to Valentinus, Paul chose not to disclose his message openly but, like his master Jesus Christ, taught in parables and other hidden speech. Paul's

---

Box 21 Paul's Vocabulary of Spiritual Hierarchy

Those who are unspiritual do not receive the gifts of God's Spirit, for they are foolishness to them, and they are unable to understand them because they are spiritually discerned. Those who are spiritual discern all things, and they are themselves subject to no one else's scrutiny. "For who has known the mind of the Lord so as to instruct him?" [Isa. 40:13; cf. Wisd. of Sol. 9:13]. But we have the mind of Christ. (1 Cor. 2:14–16)

---

teaching engaged two opposing levels of meaning at once: a surface (plain) meaning for ordinary believers who hear but never understand (whom Valentinus called "the unspiritual ones"), and a deeper (symbolic) level for those personally acquainted with God (whom Valentinus called "the spiritual ones"). Valentinus derived this hierarchy of spiritual over unspiritual kinds of Christians directly from Paul's vocabulary (see Box 21).

Valentinus thus created a new Pauline *mysticism*. He reinforced this mystical theology in specific ritual practices that built community self-definition. The spiritual Elect must first receive initiation into the secret, oral tradition of Paul that Valentinus, in turn, had received from Theudas in order to participate fully in the salvific effect of its mysteries. Valentinus developed, for instance, a new form of baptism employing marriage rites (known as the Bridal Chamber), the meaning of which only initiates using allegorical exegesis could discern.

Through allegory, Valentinus interpreted Paul's letters in an entirely new way. He agreed with other Christians (like Marcion) that Paul's antithesis of works and grace intended a contrast between the incomplete revelation to the Jews and the full salvation effected by Christ to the Gentiles; both Valentinus and Marcion thus divided Gentiles and Jews. But Valentinus disagreed that the contrast functioned only on the level of literal Jews and literal Gentiles. He found a deeper meaning by referencing another passage in Paul's corpus: "For a person is not a Jew who is one outwardly, nor is true circumcision something external and physical. Rather, a person is a Jew who is one inwardly, and real circumcision is a matter of the heart – it is spiritual and not literal" (Rom. 2:28–29). Valentinus took this passage to be an injunction to read the terms allegorically: "Jews" (circumcision) and "Gentiles" (uncircumcision) referred symbolically to the "unspiritual" (ordinary) Christians and the "spiritual" (elite) Christians, respectively. On this view, Paul hid his "real" meaning in metaphors, as the savior Jesus did his in parables, to conceal the divine truth from uninitiated eyes and ears; only an allegorical system of interpretation disclosed the apostle's esoteric meaning. In this way, affirmations of Pauline esotericism functioned to define the Valentinian community as God's Elect. The content of the thinking by "spiritual ones" (Valentinians, who have *gnōsis* of God) was obscure to "unspiritual ones" (other, ordinary Christians), because "the few" always remain unknown to "the many."

Valentinus and his followers certainly had a high regard for the apostle Paul, but it would be misleading to conclude that they considered Paul to be their sole authority or only true apostle (as in Marcion's teachings). To be sure, Valentinians used Paul in liturgical devotions like *The Prayer of the Apostle Paul* (ca. third century), which invoked the divine intercession and enlightenment of the apostle as *the* Evangelist of the Gospel. But, unlike Marcionite Christianity, Valentinian Christianity appealed to an entire range of biblical authorities, including the Old Testament. *The Gospel of Truth* (ca. 150), an important Valentinian sermon on the theme of salvation through a personal acquaintance (*gnōsis*) with God, likely penned by Valentinus himself, contains allusions not just to certain Pauline letters (Romans, 1–2 Corinthians, Colossians, Ephesians) but also to the book of Genesis and to the Gospels of John and Matthew. Valentinians thus venerated a collection of Pauline letters as normative and authoritative Scripture alongside the collections of the already revered works by Moses and by the Gospel authors.

The Gnostics and Valentinus

We know at least one clear influence on Valentinus for such a scriptural Paul – the Gnostics, who derived their name from the Greek *gnōsis*. Valentinus was not a Gnostic – he took pains to separate his views from Gnostic teachers – yet he clearly had contact with Gnostics at Rome and perhaps even had prior acquaintance with their teachings when he studied in Alexandria. Like the Gnostics, Valentinus interpreted the Genesis story of creation in light of Plato's philosophical work *Timaeus*, also a story of the world's creation. Combining these two stories, a scriptural practice we might call mythmaking, led Valentinus to argue that God's rationality worked along the same lines of the complexity of the human mind. God was thus conceived as an expansive reality in manifold divine aspects – or thoughts – emanating from the godhead in the form of multiple aeons, including the Creator (Plato's Demiurge) who appeared in both the Old Testament and a Platonic philosophy. In this Christian theology, human beings understand their true nature, reform their lives, and attain salvation only through the *gnōsis* of God for which they were created.

In their *gnōsis*, the Gnostics had a grim fascination with enumerating the evil rulers (archons) of the lower aeons, associated with the stars and the planets, mentioned in Paul's letters (cf. 1 Cor. 15:24–26; Eph. 2:2). For the Gnostics, Paul warned that such archons threatened human beings (cf. Eph. 6:12). Indeed, entire Gnostic treatises devoted themselves to this mysticism, published pseudonymously or anonymously to heighten their authority as revelatory literature of the past and, apparently, to replace the book of Genesis. In this task, the anonymous author of the Gnostic work *The Reality of the Rulers* (*Hypostasis of the Archons*, ca. third century) claimed inspiration from the "Great Apostle" (Paul) as a divine source of the "Parent of Truth" (*Reality of the Rulers*, 86.20–27; trans. Layton 1987, 68).

Unlike the Gnostics, however, Valentinus and his students published works in their own names, envisioned God to be immanent in Creation (following a model in Paul's theology, cf. Rom. 1:20), made Jesus Christ more central in the *gnōsis* myth of salvation, and reduced the Gnostic antagonism between humanity and its creators. Valentinian writings, in contrast to Gnostic literature, cited from an already circulating corpus of Pauline letters and other holy writings not to replace those scriptures, but in order to bring out their esoteric truth and to provide the hermeneutics for unraveling the enigma of their meaning. We find in Rome around the year 150, then, many different literary venerations of Paul as a book of ancient wisdom.

3. Irenaeus of Lyons: The Rule of Faith and an Unoriginal Paul

If the various and conflicting early Christian venerations of Paul complicated the ideal of unity among Roman believers in Rome, the situation was similar in other parts of the Roman Empire. In Lyons, Gaul (modern France), a young bishop (or presbyter) named Irenaeus (ca. 115–ca. 202), who emigrated from Asia Minor as a missionary to Gaul, tried to shout down any diversity of thought about God, Jesus, and the Apostles. Local persecutions of Christians in 177 increased the urgency of his message, for he blamed the Celtic population's "unjust hatred" of the churches on what he called the "evils" that Valentinians, Marcionites, and other "heretics" performed in the name of Christ. Accusing such teachers and their followers with the stock charges of criminality in Greco-Roman culture – sexual perversion, banditry, and magic – Irenaeus produced a lengthy (five-book) treatise entitled *Against the Heresies (Detection and Overthrow of Gnōsis Falsely So Called)*. One goal of the work was to force consistency onto the collection of Paul's letters, which for Irenaeus was now incorporated into a nascent Christian Bible containing the Old Testament and the Gospels.

To do this, Irenaeus followed a line of argument he learned from an earlier Christian teacher, Justin Martyr (ca. 103–165). Teaching in Rome at the same time as Valentinus and Marcion, Justin denied his competitors the claim even to the name "Christian." Key terms in Paul's letters – "divisions" (Greek *schismata*) and "factions" (Greek *haireseis*) – provided the conceptual framework of Justin's polemic, but with new meanings. Paul had used *haireseis* to describe not heresies but social and economic differences within a single congregation (see 1 Cor. 11:18–19). But Justin took the term to mean "ways of thinking" – thus describing a philosophical school of thought formed around an original teacher and a set of shared doctrines. Accusing Marcion and Valentinus of advancing "original" teachings (a negative term in ancient culture, which valued oldness over newness), Justin denied his co-religionists any link to the Christian ancestral tradition (Jesus, Paul, and the God of Israel). In Justin's new rhetoric of Christianity versus heresy, Irenaeus had found an all-encompassing master narrative for Paul – the so-called Rule of Faith (Latin *regula fidei*).

The Rule of Faith was a dogma declaring that the whole Bible (both the Old and New Testaments) teaches one and the same God throughout, one and the same Christ, and one and the same divine plan of salvation. Asserting unabashedly that "all Scripture is consistent," this Rule blended Paul's letters into a single orthodoxy, unifying the Pauline literary corpus both internally and externally to what the other apostles were recorded to have preached. Irenaeus used his Rule of Faith to condemn Marcion for denying the unity of Scripture, Valentinus for allowing Paul's letters on the surface level to contradict each other, and the Gnostics for falsely claiming the good name of *gnōsis*. Irenaeus declared that because Scripture "plainly declares" its teaching, allegorical myths are not needed to explicate Paul's meaning. On this view, Paul (like Jesus and all the apostles) "clearly points out" apostasy, error, and heresy; "in every epistle," the apostle "plainly testifies" one and the same God taught throughout the Gospels and the whole Bible. Irenaeus thus collapsed the collection of Paul's writings into what we might call sound bites, affirming the consistency of all Scripture. The alleged consistency of all Scripture, properly interpreted through the Rule of Faith, enabled Irenaeus to venerate Paul for being completely unoriginal. In this reading, Paul thus emerged as Every Apostle – a nameless authority needing no introduction except as "the Apostle." The ease of handy dogmatic summaries of the Bible saved Irenaeus the trouble of struggling intellectually with the full text before him. His writings gave the Rule of Faith greater importance than Scripture itself, because the Rule forced the consistency onto Scripture deemed necessary for the authoritative word of God.

4. Origen of Alexandria: The Historical Paul Reappears

In contrast to Irenaeus, the more philosophical Origen (ca. 185–251) struggled intellectually to read Paul's words in their full complexity. Born of devout Christian parents in Alexandria, Egypt, Origen at the age of seventeen saw his father, Leonides, imprisoned and martyred by Roman soldiers (an aristocratic Christian lady took Origen into her household for protection). As members of his church endured martyrdom under Roman rule, Origen grew up to head his own catechetical school. His school, like others in the city, gathered small groups of students at a home for academic reading and interpretation of texts considered important in the Christian community, including the letters of Paul.

In his early writings, Origen lumped all epistles of the apostles together as authoritative but nonetheless inferior to the divinely inspired words of Jesus Christ himself in the gospel literature, but the Pauline literature became more important to Origen when he moved from Alexandria to Palestine (ca. 232). When Origen arrived in Caesarea, Palestine, he discovered it to be a large Jewish center of rabbinic learning. He now lived among large numbers of Hebrews who did not believe in Jesus as the Christ. Encountering this sizeable and flourishing Jewish community at Caesarea pressed Origen to rethink Paul's statements on Israel and the Jews as the chosen people of God. Origen's debates with rabbinic teachers gave him firsthand experience with the hardness of Israel toward Christian acceptance of Jesus as the Messiah. Among the rabbis whom Origen likely engaged was the sage Hoshaya – later called the "father of the Mishnah" – who had established his rabbinic school in Caesarea just two years before Origen arrived in the city. Their two schools were thus active at the same time.

In this social context, Origen directly tackled the question of how Jews and Gentiles relate in God's plan of salvation by writing a commentary on

Paul's Letter to the Romans. Why are Gentiles included in salvation but Jews excluded from it? Origen became less confident that Christians should frame the question of salvation this way, particularly in light of a curious statement in Romans: "So that you may not claim to be wiser than you are, brothers and sisters, I want you to understand this mystery: a hardening has come upon part of Israel, until the full number of Gentiles has come in. And so *all Israel* will be saved" (Rom. 11:25–26, emphasis added). The passage suggests that the Jews have hope, despite apparently negative statements about them in the letter's earlier sections. Origen resolved the letter's tension by realizing its central theme was that salvation comes to the Gentiles only through Israel's unbelief, as Paul writes, "So I ask, have they (the Jews) stumbled so as to fall? By no means! But through their stumbling salvation has come to the Gentiles, so as to make Israel jealous. Now if their stumbling means riches for the world, and if their defeat means riches for Gentiles, how much more will their full inclusion mean!" (Rom. 11:11–12). Israel "stumbles" but does not "fall" from divine grace; Gentiles should praise rather than condemn Israel's unbelief, because Israel's "stumbling" opens a way for Gentile inclusion into God's plan of salvation – the "hardening of Israel" is like God's famous hardening of Pharaoh's heart in the Exodus story (Rom. 9:17–18; cf. Exod. 10:1). This interpretation of Romans holds a very defensible position from the perspective of modern historical criticism. Origen is, therefore, the only ancient interpreter who apparently understood what a consensus of modern critical scholars takes to be Paul's point: to condemn the arrogance of Gentiles who believe their coming to Christ gives them superiority over Israel. By talking with rabbinic teachers, who insisted on a literal reading of the full text, Origen came to see Jewish unbelief in Jesus Christ as modern historians see it described in Paul's writings – as an essential step in God's plan to save "all Israel."

Origen struggled to understand Paul's position not only on the salvation of the Jews but also on Roman imperial authority. On this latter topic, Origen shifted his scriptural practices beyond literal readings of the text. Paul's command to obey government authorities in Romans 13 (see Chapter 3) posed difficulties for Origen to accept on a literal level, given Origen's personal experience of the martyrdom of Christians like his father Leonides by Roman soldiers. "Paul troubles (me) by these words," wrote Origen in his magisterial commentary on the epistle, "that he calls the secular authority and the worldly judgment a minister of God; and that he does this not merely one time, but he even repeats it a second and third time. I would like to endeavor to ascertain the sense in which a worldly judge is a minister of God" (Origen, *Commentary on Romans* 9.28; trans. in Meeks and

Fitzgerald 2007, 543). Seeking to examine what Paul says "more deeply," Origen found "the hidden secrets of Paul's words" by focusing on the key term *conscience* (Rom. 13:5). In this view, Paul teaches the need to follow one's religious conscience, as in dying for Christ through a martyrdom, which means disobeying secular commands of Roman authorities. Just as in the problem of reading Paul's letters side by side in a single corpus, comparing such passages line by line brought Paul's words into an apparent contradiction. But Origen welcomed the contradiction as signaling the necessity of reading the passage beyond its literal level: while the surface meaning addresses the morality of paying taxes and obeying government officers, the deeper spiritual meaning directs the release of one's personal debt of sin. "For on many occasions," Origen explained to his students, "we have repeatedly shown that sin is a debt. So Paul wants every debt of sin to be paid and absolutely no debt of sin to remain among us, but for our debt of love to abide and never to cease; for paying this debt even daily and owing it at all times is beneficial to us" (Origen, *Commentary on Romans* 9.30; trans. in Meeks and Fitzgerald 2007, 545–46). In this allegorical interpretation, Paul commands Christians not literally to pay taxes to the state but spiritually to discharge all their sin as a debt due to God. Anticipating modern attempts to find hidden transcripts (see Chapter 3), Origen's allegorical method enabled the ancient reader to ignore Paul's clear affirmations of Roman imperial authority, yielding a welcome retreat from accepting Rome's persecution of Christians as authorized by God.

5. John Chrysostom: Pauline Inconsistency as the Wise Physician

A similarly curious praise of Paul's literal inconsistency appears in the writings of another commentator, John Chrysostom of Antioch (347–407). With over two hundred fifty sermons on the Pauline letters, covering all of the fourteen epistles in the biblical canon (including Hebrews), as well as seven homilies in praise of the apostle, Chrysostom (the "Golden Mouth") was Paul's most prolific and comprehensive commentator in late antiquity. His extensive works contributed to the rise of a religious cult around the figure of Paul, characterized by such practices as pilgrimage and the veneration of relics (for this martyr cult in Rome, see Chapter 4).

Chrysostom wanted his sermons to inspire church audiences toward a vivid, lively engagement with Paul – to visualize him as a person. For this reason, he presented Paul more as a letter writer and a pastor than the systematic theologian that the collection of his letters into a corpus

---

Box 22 John Chrysostom on Paul's Chains

Oh! those blessed bonds! Oh! those blessed hands, which that chain adorned! Not so worthy were Paul's hands when they lifted up and raised the lame man at Lystra [Acts 14:8–18], as when they were bound around with those chains. Had I been living in those times, how eagerly would I have embraced them, and put them to the very apple of my eyes. Never would I have ceased kissing those hands, which were counted worthy to be bound for my Lord. Do you marvel at Paul, when the viper fastened on his hand, and did him no hurt [Acts 28:4–5]? Marvel not. It reverenced his chain. Yes, and the whole sea reverenced it; for then too was he bound, when he was saved from shipwreck [Acts 27:44]. Were anyone to grant me power to raise the dead at this moment, I would not choose that power, but this chain. Were I free from the cares of the church, had I my body strong and vigorous, I would not shrink from undertaking so long a journey [to Rome], only for the sake of beholding those chains, for the sake of seeing the prison where he was bound. The traces indeed of his miracles are numerous in all parts of the world, yet are they not so dear as those of his scars [Gal. 6:17]. (John Chrysostom, *Homily on Ephesians* 8.1–2; trans. in Schaff 1994, 85–86, altered; see also Mitchell 2002, 181)

---

might suggest. For Chrysostom, every personal detail about Paul – his chains, bed, and mattress, as well as sandals and fingernails – offered an opportunity for a pilgrim's holy edification (see Box 22).

Chrysostom thus connected his sermons to the "real" world of religious icons, cult shrines, reliquaries, liturgical calendars, and martyr tombs, which made present saints like Paul in local sites. Chrysostom urged his congregations, for example, to share in the inspiration that came from visiting the very places of Paul's own preaching and imprisonment, seeing the actual chains that had once bound the apostle, and throwing oneself around the monument of Paul's tomb in Rome "to kiss the very dust of his corpse" (on Paul's tomb, see Conclusion).

In this regard, Chrysostom offered up a commonplace encomium to the city of Rome – praising the Eternal City's immensity, glory, wealth, and imperium over the entire world – only to count those worthy attributes as nothing compared to the fact that Paul wrote to Rome, preached to his beloved Romans, and died there. The divine blessedness of Paul's entombed body, Chrysostom claimed, protected Rome's safety more than all towers or a thousand battlements. All this emphasis on Paul as a body, a person, and a pastor led to the curious veneration of Paul's inconsistency. Chrysostom openly embraced potentially embarrassing questions about Paul's apparent human errors.

Chrysostom dealt with the question of Pauline consistency rhetorically, in order to preach against what he saw as heretical biblical interpretations. He condemned Marcion, for example, for chopping Paul's letters into excerpts, thus taking passages out of their original contexts. Chrysostom rejected Marcion's strategy of making Paul consistent by removing the offending passages as non-Pauline interpolations, because the historical and literary contexts mattered for Chrysostom's understanding of religious truth. Initially, Chrysostom tried a series of rhetorical stratagems from his training in Roman law, which attempted to contain the question of Pauline consistency within exact meanings and connotations of terms. This forensic counterstrategy had insisted that Paul was not variable but uniform and clear, which played on the exact terms describing the legendary but ambiguous figure of Odysseus – "the variable man of many turns" – as well as the mythological monster Proteus. Paul does not say contradictory things about the Law, pleaded Chrysostom, because each of the different passages has its own argumentative context and purpose, all of which aim toward the same apostolic goal. Paul's words may use proper discretion and difference, but not disparity, which should exonerate the apostle from blameworthy inconsistency. Chrysostom insisted on the particularity of each epistle having its place within a larger corpus.

This initial attempt to circumscribe the problem around the exact meanings of terms only begged further the question of Pauline consistency, however. Chrysostom eventually accepted the obviousness of what he had long tried to explain away: Paul's words *are* inconsistent. Chrysostom then used his past oratorical education to embrace Paul's variability to its full extent. Around 390, in homilies honoring Saint Paul on his feast day (for Eastern churches at the time, December 28), he praised the apostle for being a "variable and many-sorted man," language recalling the famous epithets of Odysseus. Chrysostom trumpeted Paul's inconsistency as a noble virtue that Christians everywhere should emulate.

This strategy of praise turned on a famous rhetorical commonplace – that of the doctor. The apostle's "many-faceted identity," preached the Golden Mouth, was not "hypocritical" but imitated how doctors treated their various patients (see Box 23). According to Chrysostom, Paul varied his instructions in the same way that a doctor customarily acted, for a doctor treated patients differently, depending on their illnesses. Like a physician, Paul was "all things to all people" – inconsistent in his various

> ### Box 23 In Praise of Pauline Inconsistency: Paul the Physician
>
> Take the case of a physician. When you see him at one time cauter-
> izing, at another feeding, now using an iron implement, then giving a
> medicinal remedy, once withholding food and drink, and another time
> providing the sick their fill of these things, sometimes completely cover-
> ing up a person with a fever, and at other times ordering him to drink a
> full cup of cold water, you do not condemn his variability, nor his con-
> stant changing. But instead you praise his craft especially when you see
> that it introduces with confidence treatments that seem contradictory
> and harmful to us, and guarantees that they are safe. For this is a man
> who is an expert. If we accept a physician who does these contradictory
> things, how much more should we proclaim the praises of Paul's soul,
> which in the same way attends to the sick? (John Chrysostom, *Homily
> in Praise of Paul* 5.7; trans. in Mitchell 2002, 337)
>
> Therefore Paul should not be condemned if, in imitation of his own
> Lord, at one time he was a Jew, and at another as one not under
> the Law; now was keeping the Law, then despising it; at one time
> was cleaving to the present life, at another condemning it; now was
> demanding money, then rejecting what was offered; sometimes he was
> sacrificing and shaving his head, and at other times anathematizing
> those who did such things; once he circumcised, at another time he
> cast out circumcision. (John Chrysostom, *Homily in Praise of Paul* 5.6;
> trans. in Mitchell 2002, 335)

therapies for the soul. Chrysostom thus addressed the tension that became
apparent by placing a collection of Paul's letters, next to the book of
Acts, into a single corpus. Chrysostom praised the contradictions between
the book of Acts and Paul's letters as reflecting the practices of the wise
physician, who must be inconsistent in dispensing drugs and therapy.

In sum, the late ancient problem of what we might call a "patristic
Paul" centered on the question of its consistency. While Christian writers
like Irenaeus refused to see any contradiction or originality in the apostle,
imposing a Rule of Faith that neutralized difficult passages of Scripture,
others like Chrysostom celebrated the very adaptability and changeability
of Pauline inconsistency as a praiseworthy holiness. Marcion took Paul's
contrast between works and grace – which only appears in Galatians and
Romans, a minor theme in the full context of Paul's corpus – to indicate

the literal rejection the Old Testament and the creation of an exclusively Christian Bible separate from what Jews had. An important insight on this question came from Origen, who more than any other ancient interpreter (with the possible exception of Marcion) understood what a consensus of critical biblical scholars today takes to be Paul's point in Romans – seeing Jewish disbelief as part of God's eschatological plan.

Despite Origen's brilliant insight, early medieval and modern Pauline commentary in the West became obsessed with expelling Jews and Judaism from the apostle's theology. Writers like Augustine (in the late fourth/early fifth century) and Martin Luther (in the late fifteenth/early sixteenth century) warped Paul's contrast between works and grace into an anti-Semitic grand narrative – the ideas of Original Sin and of the introspective conscience. In Chapter 6, I shall explain and challenge this grand narrative as an elaboration upon a cumulative distortion of the writings of the historical figure. That is to say, the West got Paul wrong.

6

HOW THE WEST GOT
PAUL WRONG

The traditional history of Western culture celebrates Paul as the prototypical religious convert. This famous narrative holds that Paul turned his life away from his guilt-filled life as a miserable (read, "Jewish") sinner by examining his conscience introspectively. In a proverbial dark night of the soul, Paul looked deeply into his conscience and discovered that the shortcomings and incapacities for good within his inner self arose from a general condition of evil present in all human nature. His encounter with the risen Jesus brought him the relief of forgiveness of sins and the freedom of divine grace.

I argue that Paul became this key figure most familiar today not for who he was but for who he came to be in the eyes of his later interpreters. The most important interpreter for this legacy in Western culture is Aurelius Augustine, bishop of Hippo in North Africa (354–430). Augustine developed from Paul's letter to the Romans, among other sources, a theory of Original Sin. According to Augustine, all humanity participated in the sin of Adam in the Garden of Eden (cf. Gen. 3); this sin and its punishment are transmitted to subsequent people through sexual intercourse. The invention of Original Sin in the West brought also the idea of the introspective conscience, influencing a host of modern thinkers from Friedrich Nietzsche to Sigmund Freud. To understand the origins of this Pauline master narrative in Western culture, we need to begin with a Christian prophet named Mani in Persian Mesopotamia and his sect known as the Manichaeans.

1. The Apostle of Light: A Manichaean Paul

The Manichaeans received their name from their founder Mani (216–277), from Mesopotamia, then part of the Sassanid Empire. Mani's father belonged to an apocalyptic Messiah Jesus sect known as the Elchasaites, who venerated "true prophets" and the Mosaic Torah. Flourishing in the fertile Tigris-Euphrates valley, the Elchasaites observed repeated baptisms. With its heavy emphasis on repentance, the Elchasaite baptism prepared initiates for an imminent apocalyptic war among godless angels and a final judgment by the Greatest and Highest God. The Elchasaites, like the Ebionites before them (see Chapter 4), rejected the teachings of Paul as antithetical to the Jewish gospel of Jesus Christ and his original disciples.

Starting at the age of twelve – a mere eight years after he received his Elchasaite baptism – Mani had the first of several revelations in which he claimed to see his divine Twin. This celestial double disclosed to Mani the primordial battle between Good and Evil whose effects created the current world. The language of Mani's vision evoked the primeval vision "before the foundation of the world," after the suggestion in the Letter to the Ephesians that Paul saw the world's origins in an apocalyptic flash at his conversion (Eph. 1:4). Reading Ephesians led Mani to lay emphasis on Christianity as "light" (see Eph. 5:9–14). Openly imitating Paul's claim to an apostleship "sent neither by human commission nor from human authorities" (Gal. 1:1), Mani relied on his cosmic revelations to claim a highly ecstatic authority that came from divine, not human, teachers. In subsequent visions, Mani arrived at the understanding that his celestial double commanded him to leave the baptism of the Elchasaites for an independent mission as the Apostle of Light, a title marking Mani as an equal to Paul. Mani thus fully embraced Paul as the central apostle of the Christian faith – likely through the influence of Marcionite circles in the region – and styled himself as Paul had, "the Apostle of Jesus Christ to the nations (Gentiles)." Other titles displaying his divine calling included the "Paraclete" (advocate) promised in John's Gospel to rekindle the Holy Spirit in the place of Jesus Christ after the ascension (cf. John 14:25; 15:26), and the Last or "Seal" of the prophets (anticipating by three centuries the Islamic title of Muhammad).

Mani founded the first self-consciously universal religion in world history. He joined the court of his Sassanid king, Shapur I, to influence the center of the Iranian national religion of Zoroastrianism, and he also traveled as far as India to reform Buddhism. The idea of a world mission received inspiration from Marcionite scriptural practices (see Chapter 5). Following what he believed was Paul's literal rejection of Jewish Scripture, Mani (like Marcion) expunged Old Testament citations from the text of Paul's epistles, condemning them as later interpolations. He repudiated the Old Testament as the "error of the Law" that had misled his former Elchasaite sect from God's new covenant with Gentiles. Rejecting Jewish Law, Mani proclaimed instead the "true Light" required for universal illumination, including the Gentiles. Mani's gospel rebuked worship of the lesser god, Yahweh of the Jewish Bible, and offered Gentiles freedom from the requirements of Torah (circumcision, Sabbath observances, and food taboos). Further Pauline imitations included Mani's writing of letters to his Gentile communities.

Indeed, Mani wrote a great deal. He set down all his teachings systematically in a canon of books that he created for his Manichaean churches. Mani claimed that his books declared the original divine truth that previous religious founders also had announced – Jesus Christ, Zoroaster (Old Iranian *Zarathustra*), and Buddha (Siddahārtha Gautama) – but which their later followers had corrupted. Mani's explicit reason for setting his teachings down in writing, and for overseeing their canonization in his lifetime, was to prevent disputes over doctrine and the corruption of tradition that he claimed had befallen other religious founders who had failed to preserve their doctrines in writings. When he finished his books and his mission to the Mesopotamian heartland, Mani sent disciples west to the Roman Empire and east to India and his native Persia. Centuries later, Manichaean churches could be found as far as the shores of the China Sea.

Mani's books described all reality in terms of light and darkness as the best explanation for the problem of evil. This myth tells his vision of a primordial cosmic battle between the forces of good and the forces of evil – two fundamentally separate realms locked in mortal combat. One realm, the Kingdom of Light, is the residence of God (the "father of greatness") and his wholly good divine attributes of purity, light, power, and wisdom. The second domain, the Kingdom of Darkness, is wholly evil matter that the Devil (the "prince of darkness") rules over with his lesser demonic minions, who fight and devour each other. This Manichaean material dualism offered a powerful alternative to rival solutions for the problem of evil, because it explained evil in the world to come from the separate force of the Devil, whom God did not create.

The Manichaeans taught their esoteric myth by showing what they saw as its concrete evidence in the New Testament. They argued that Paul's use of contrasts – the law and the gospel, light and darkness, grace and "works of the law" – proved the truth of their Christian faith. In his letters, Paul had spoken of a human being's "inner nature" and an "outer nature" (2 Cor. 4:16; cf. Rom. 7:22–23; Eph. 3:16); the Manichaeans took this to mean that the individual human being replicated in miniature the cosmic battle between good and evil. Those inner and outer natures, according to the Manichaeans, were actually two different beings: God created only a person's inner being, while the outer being originated from the Kingdom of Darkness. The specific scriptural proof came from the inner struggle that Paul described in his Letter to the Romans (see Box 24). For Mani

Box 24 Mani's Reading of Paul: The Inner Struggle over Sin

Paul, Romans 7

> For we know that the law is spiritual; but I am of the flesh, sold into slavery under sin. I do not understand my own actions. For I do not do what I want, but I do the very thing I hate. Now if I do what I do not want, I agree that the law is good. But in fact it is no longer I that do it, but sin that dwells within me. For I know that nothing good dwells within me, that is, in my flesh. I can will what is right, but I cannot do it. For I do not do the good I want, but the evil I do not want is what I do. Now if I do what I do not want, it is no longer I that do it, but sin that dwells within me.
>
> So I find it to be a law that when I want to do what is good, evil lies close at hand. For I delight in the law of God in my inmost self, but I see in my members another law at war with the law of my mind, making me captive to the law of sin that dwells in my members. Wretched man that I am! Who will rescue me from this body of death? (Rom. 7:14–24)

Excerpts of Mani, *Letter to Menoch*

> What does Mani say? "Through concupiscence the author of bodies is the devil; through this the devil lies in wait for bodies, not souls; take way," he says, "the root of the malign shoot and you will become spiritual; concerning this the Apostle proclaims to the Romans: *Not the good which I wish, but the evil which I abhor do I perform* [Rom. 7:19]." (Harrison and BeDuhn 2001, 135; sentence in italics indicates verses in the Bible)

> Mani also argued thus. "It is worthwhile," he says, "noting that the first soul which flowed from the God of light received the fabric of the body so that the first soul might rule the fabric with its own reins. *The order came; sin revived* [Rom. 7:9], which seemed captive; the devil found his own limbs, he *seduced* [cf. Rom. 7:11] the matter of concupiscence in the fabric and through the matter of concupiscence he fell. *The law indeed is holy*, but only holy for the holy soul, *and the order is both just and good* [Rom. 7:12], but only for the just and good soul." (Harrison and BeDuhn 2001, 136, altered; sentences in italics indicate verses in the Bible)

and his followers, the first-person speech in Romans 7 represented not just Paul's voice alone; the "I" (Greek *egō*) epitomized each and every individual. The "I" voiced humanity's universal anguish over the inner conflict of the darkness working against the light trapped in every human body. In this way, the Manichaeans in the Roman West made Paul their spokesman.

A passage in Ephesians inspired the Manichaeans to develop a regimen regulating every aspect of daily life to the faith, which promised to separate the inner person from the outer person. The passage reads: "You were taught to put away your former way of life, your old self, corrupt and deluded by lusts, and to be renewed in the spirit of your minds, and to clothe yourself with the new self, created according to the likeness of God in true righteousness and holiness" (Eph. 4:22–24). For the Manichaeans, the old self represented its corruption with darkness, and the new self its restoration back to the Kingdom of Light. The Manichaean church thus promised salvation from Darkness in specific ascetic therapies of self-discipline that cast away the old self (another resonance with Marcionite teachings). The Manichaean church divided its believers into "the Elect" and "the Hearers" (Auditors), a hierarchy. The first group had attained the highest embodiment of a saved soul, and the second had a more moderate – but by no means lax – ascetic regimen for daily life. Paul's Letter to the Ephesians apparently guided Manichaean ethics, community, and cosmology. Among their rituals was the Manichaean Eucharist, the sacramental meal reserved for the Elect, which raised Christ to the level of restoring his scattered light back to the Kingdom of the universal Father. Yet for both categories of Manichaean believers, the Elect and Auditors alike, Pauline literature provided an all-encompassing master narrative about God and the human condition, which served as the authoritative framework of their Christian faith and community self-definition in the West.

This Manichaean Paul returns our attention to Rome in that a former Manichaean, Aurelius Augustine, largely invented his theories of Original Sin and the introspective conscience through a polemical engagement with such a dualistic belief. In this regard, we should view Mani's reading of Paul as one instance of a widespread quest, evident among many Christian teachers of late antiquity, to find an all-encompassing grand narrative of God and salvation, through the act of writing commentaries on the Pauline letters. At Rome, the period between 350 and 450 saw a rise in such Pauline commentaries in Latin due to intense debate and infighting over a host of issues that had long divided Christians, such as the precise nature of Christ and of the human condition in the cosmic scheme of God's salvation. The debate centered on Paul's letters, in part, because their complicated and often disparate affirmations allowed readers to find multiple and conflicting positions that supported each side of a particular dispute. For this reason, Pauline inconsistency at the level of the individual biblical verse made the late ancient quest for the apostle's master narrative all the more urgent.

Because the specific controversies and debates at Rome centered on Paul's words in Latin, the language of the Roman West, the section that follows surveys the first Latin commentators on Paul. As we shall see, much was lost – and gained – in translation, because a Latin misreading of a single line in Paul's letter to the Romans (5:12) helped to lead Augustine to his ideas of Original Sin and the introspective conscience.

2. Lost in Translation: The First Latin Commentaries on Paul

In the late fourth century, Rome saw a rise in the production of Pauline commentaries partly due to conflicts with the Manichaean missionaries. The earliest such Latin commentary comes from an anonymous Roman Christian author to whom the Dutch Renaissance humanist Erasmus (ca. 1466–1536) later gave the moniker *Ambrosiaster* (the Star of Ambrose, that is, Pseudo-Ambrose). Ambrosiaster warns his readers against the door-to-door missions of the Manichaeans, condemning their teachings as the "impure and sordid heresy" predicted by Paul himself (referencing 2 Tim. 3:6–7). Attempting to reclaim Paul from the Manichaeans, Ambrosiaster wrestled with the question of Pauline consistency especially on the level of the individual verse.

Ambrosiaster understood that Greek manuscripts of the Bible often had readings that appeared to support the Manichaean Paul. He thus blamed the divergent readings, apparent evidence for Pauline inconsistency, on the corruption of Greek manuscripts. For example, on Romans 5:14 ("Yet death exercised dominion from Adam to Moses, even over those whose sins were not like the transgression of Adam, who is a type of the one who was to come"), Ambrosiaster commented:

> Some Greek manuscripts say that death reigned even in those who had not sinned in the way that Adam had. If this is true, it is because Satan's jealousy was such that death, that is, dissolution, held sway over even those who did not sin.... Here there is a textual difference between the Latin version and some of the Greek manuscripts. The Latin says that death reigned over those whose sins were like the sin of Adam, but some Greek manuscripts say that death reigned even over those whose sins were *not* like Adam's. Which of the two readings is the correct one?
>
> What has happened is that somebody who could not win his argument altered the words of the text in order to make them say what he wanted

them to say, so that not argument but textual authority would determine the issue. (Ambrosiaster, *Romans*; trans. in Meeks and Fitzgerald 2007, 361–62, emphasis in original)

No verse proved more controversial than Romans 5:12: "Therefore, just as sin came into the world through one man, and death came through sin, and so death spread to all *because all have sinned*" (emphasis added). While the Greek states that all people died "because" (*eph' hō*) they all sinned, both the Old Latin and the Vulgate (Jerome's Latin translation) read that death came to all people "*in quo*" (in whom, or in which) they all sinned. The problem is that the Latin relative pronoun *quo* could be either masculine or neuter. Taking the term as neuter, some ancient Latin interpreters understood *in quo* in a causal sense after its original Greek meaning, to read *in quo* as: "in which (that is, because) all have sinned." But others took *in quo* as a masculine relative pronoun – "*in whom* (that is, Adam) they all sinned" – which gave Paul's terms an entirely new meaning that led to the theory of Original Sin: in Adam all have sinned.

To clarify the ambiguity, Ambrosiaster took *quo* as masculine but gave its phrase a conditional force: "all people *who sin* also die like Adam." He thus carefully limited the consequence of the phrase *in quo* to physical death, not spiritual death and damnation. Ambrosiaster wrote, "The sentence passed on Adam was that the human body would decompose on earth . . . Therefore (spiritual) death did not reign in everyone but only in those who sinned in the same way that Adam had sinned" (Ambrosiaster, *Romans*; trans. in Meeks and Fitzgerald 2007, 361–62, altered). That is to say, all people eventually die because all sinned in Adam "as it were *in a mass*," but spiritual death and damnation happen only to people who sin like Adam. This nuance, however, was lost on later Pauline interpreters.

One Pauline interpreter who apparently understood Ambrosiaster's nuance was the learned Pauline teacher and commentator Pelagius (ca. 350–425). His teachings on Paul sparked a controversy rivaling that of the Manichaeans, one of the most enduring and fiercely contended in the history of Christianity, known as the Pelagian controversy. Augustine was a leading figure in the fifth-century theological debate.

3. The Apostle of Free Will: Pelagius's Paul

A learned rhetorician and Pauline teacher at Rome, Pelagius had emigrated from Britain. Rome in the early fifth century had a Christianized aristocracy of laypeople who exercised more influence in the city than did the bishop and other ordained clergy. Pelagius resided among this new Christianized aristocracy of laypeople. In 410, as King Alaric I (Gothic *Alareiks*) and his Visigoths were sacking Rome, Pelagius fled with other nobles to become refugees in Roman North Africa. It was in North Africa that his teachings came into direct conflict with a local theologian, Aurelius Augustine, who would lead a literary campaign against the Briton and his "Pelagianism."

Pelagius highlighted the importance of human free will. Contesting the rigorous extremes of Manichaeism and its fatalist determinism of material forces in a cosmic dualism, Pelagius stressed personal agency and the capability of people to achieve moral and spiritual perfection through a more moderate ascetic training. He used an expressly adversarial pedagogy of rhetoric to teach Paul's letters much the same way as a Latin orator would teach Cicero's writings. Pelagius attracted many supporters from the wealthiest Roman families, and even some of the clergy.

In this polemical context, Pelagius wrote his own commentary on Paul's Letter to the Romans (ca. 407). This masterpiece of Latin rhetoric explicated Paul's letter at the level of the individual verse, in the tradition of Ambrosiaster's commentary, and asked the provocative question whether a person is saved through predestination or by one's own free will. Pelagius's answer constructed a counter narrative of free will to attack the fatalist determinism of the Manichaean Paul. Against the Manichaean teaching that one's "outer self" (the carnal person) was the alien material of an evil realm, Pelagius asserted the goodness of all creation. Emphasizing the constant role of conscience in human salvation – all people inherit from Adam the innate capacity to choose between good and evil – Pelagius argued that the first (original) sin of Adam affected later generations only in that people habitually imitated it. Following Ambrosiaster, Pelagius qualified Paul's language in Romans 5:12 to allow for the possibility that a person through one's own virtue, moderate asceticism, and scriptural training could successfully overcome the Adamic habituated tendencies to sin and so avoid spiritual death and damnation. Pelagius made his case in a line-by-line commentary of Romans 5:

(Rom. 5:12). *Therefore, just as through one person sin came into the world, and through sin death.* By example or by pattern. Just as through Adam, sin came at a time when it did not yet exist, so in the same way, through Christ, righteousness was recovered at a time when it survived in almost no one. And just as through the former's sin death came in, so also through the latter's righteousness, life was regained. *And so death passed on to all people in that* [in quo] *all sinned.* As long as they sin in the same way, they likewise die. (Pelagius, *Commentary on Romans*; trans. De Bruyn 1993, 92, altered; sentences in italics indicate verses of the Bible in Old Latin)

Pelagius gave the phrase *in quo* a conditional force: Adam's descendants die spiritually if they sin as Adam did. A person's body was, on this view, inherently neither evil nor sinful as the Manichaean missionaries at Rome claimed it to be. From a line in Romans and its single phrase *in quo*, Pelagius thus had support for his Pauline master narrative of free will. As well, throughout his writings, he taught about many other biblical passages that demonstrated free will. Commentary writing was thus not a neutral exercise, but a powerful weapon in the arsenal of Christians to fight each other in a battle over the Bible – between the "determinist Paul" of the Manichaeans and the "free will Paul" of Pelagius.

We see how this master narrative affected daily practice in a letter that Pelagius wrote to a young woman named Demetrias in 413, congratulating the fourteen year old on her sudden announcement to take a vow of celibacy rather than to marry the eligible fiancé her family decided for her. She belonged to one of the wealthiest and most powerful households in Roman aristocratic society, among which Pelagius had cultivated patronage while in Rome. The family had recently fled Italy during Alaric's attacks to resettle on their estate in Roman North Africa.

The letter, a showpiece of Latin rhetoric, provides our most complete and coherent account of Pelagius's thinking. He advised Demetrias that the moral life was not impossible, that free will led to salvation with the aid of God, and that asceticism gained a holy life:

> When I have to discuss the principles of right conduct and the leading of a holy life, I usually begin by showing the strength and characteristics of human nature. By explaining what it can accomplish, I encourage the soul of my hearer to the different virtues. To call a person to something he considers impossible does him no good. Hope must serve as guide and companion if we are to set out the way to virtue; otherwise, despair of success will kill every effort to acquire the impossible. The procedure I have followed in other exhortations should, I believe, be especially observed in this one. Where a more perfect form of life (virginity) is to be established, the explanation of nature's goodness should be correspondingly fuller. With a lower estimation of its capacity, a soul will be less diligent and insistent in pursuing virtue. Not realizing what is within, it will assume that it lacks the capacity. A power that is to be exercised must therefore be brought out into full attention, and the good of which nature is capable must be clearly explained. Once something has been shown possible, it ought to be accomplished. The first foundation to be laid for a pure and spiritual life, therefore, is that a virgin recognize her strengths. She will be able to exercise them well once she realizes she has them. Showing a person that he can actually achieve what he desires provides the most effective incentives for the soul. Even in warfare, the best way to influence and encourage a soldier

is to remind him of his own power. (Pelagius, *Letter to Demetrias* 2; trans. Burns 1981, 40–41, altered)

Pelagius argued for the possibility of humans to do the good and reach salvation with God's help on the logic that God would not have commanded humans to do the unattainable; the moral life was thus fully possible. Because God had given each individual the power to achieve virtue, individuals needed only to recognize their innate potential for morality. Accordingly, this recognition was the first step toward working out one's own salvation in the apostle Paul's spiritual directions that urged one toward the virtuous life. To make this theological point, Pelagius used a famous rhetorical trope in Rome's military culture: a Christian listening to God's orders toward salvation was like a Roman soldier heeding his general's pre-battle harangue, which invariably exhorted troops to remember their own training and own ability, in addition to the directions of their general, from which came the likelihood of victory. Pelagius thus exhorted the believer to attend to the testimony of her good conscience:

> Let us turn now to the secret depths of our souls and each reflect carefully on ourselves. What do our own feelings reveal to us? Let us attend to the testimony of a good conscience and be instructed by the authority within us. Indeed, we should learn its goodness from the mind itself rather than from somewhere else. What do we fear, what makes us ashamed whenever we sin? We give away our guilt by blushing or paleness. Our own conscience torments us even when our anxious mind escapes detection for some little fault. When we do good, in contrast, we are joyful, at ease, and untroubled.... The sinner cannot escape the penalty of his own guilt....
>
> Our souls possess what might be called a sort of natural integrity which presides in the depths of the soul and passes judgments of good and evil.... In writing to the Romans [Rom 2:14–15], the Apostle refers to this law and asserts that it is written in every person, written on the tablet of the heart. (Pelagius, *Letter to Demetrias* 4; trans. Burns 1981, 43–44)

Pelagius's support of Demetrias's decision to abandon marriage and take up the virgin's veil, a lifelong celibacy, specified in detail how she could best be *Roman*. The incentive to virtue, Pelagius claimed, lay in Paul's teachings about the internal judgment of individual conscience. By affirming the scriptural basis of God's goodness in human nature, Pelagius responded to his detractors who caricatured him as an irrational perfectionist:

> We do not defend the goodness of nature by maintaining that it can do no wrong. Certainly we acknowledge that it is capable of both good and evil.

We do, however, refute the charge that nature's inadequacy forces us to do evil. We do either good or evil by our own free will; since we always remain capable of both, we are always free to do either. Why should it be that (at the end of time) some will judge and others be judged unless different choices occur in the same nature, unless we actually do different things when we could all do the same? Again, examples will clarify this point. Adam was driven from paradise; Enoch was delivered from this world. In each case, the Lord showed the freedom of choice: as the sinner could have done well, so the saint could have done ill. Unless each could have done both, neither would the former have deserved to be punished nor the latter to be chosen by a just God....

If even before the Law and long before the coming of our Lord and Savior, some people lived upright and holy lives, as we have said, we should believe all the more that we can do the same after his coming. Christ's grace has taught us and regenerated us as better persons. His blood has purged and cleansed us; his example spurred us to righteousness. We should be better than people who lived before the Law, therefore, and better than people who lived under the law. As the Apostle says [Rom. 6:14], "Sin will no longer rule in you. You are not under the law but under grace." (Pelagius, *Letter to Demetrias* 8; trans. Burns 1981, 49–51, altered)

In such polemical writings, Pelagius revealed his Latin rhetorical training. He affirmed the most cherished insight of classical philosophy: there could be no virtue without the freedom to choose the good. Doing good was difficult, Pelagius admitted, but not impossible; free will remained even when bad habits crushed it down. With abundant examples from the Old Testament patriarchs and from Paul's own words in Romans, Pelagius thus conformed the witness of the Bible to a moral axiom of classical philosophy.

In this way, Pelagius replaced the dualism of Persian Manichaeism with a more Roman ethical teaching. Indeed, the moral imperative to inspect one's conscience loomed large in the moral discourse about being Roman. Roman morality had an extensive philosophy of conscience that had long urged self-knowledge (the critical introspection of one's soul) as a prerequisite for attaining wisdom and the good life. Indeed, few people had stopped to consider the existence of a conscience before the advent of classical philosophy; the term *conscience* does not appear in the Old Testament, for example. The idea began in Greek thinkers like Socrates who exhorted self-knowledge to fulfill the famous maxim inscribed over the entrance to the Greek oracular shrine at Delphi, "Know Thyself." This religious exhortation, traditionally ascribed to Apollo (a central god of prophecy in Greco-Roman culture), urged the seeker of wisdom to inspect his or her conscience to find the reality and truth of divine inspiration. Pelagius found in the Roman philosophy of conscience an interpretative key to access the "real" meaning of God's salvation – free will. His commentary on Romans, therefore, rhetorically "rescues" the apostle Paul from the fatalistic determinism of Manichaean teachers.

Yet Pelagius faced rival Pauline teachers beyond those of the Manichaean missionaries at Rome. Also wanting to rescue Paul from the Persian Manichaeans was a Catholic opponent named Aurelius Augustine.

4. The Apostle of an Introspective Conscience: Augustine's Paul and Its Legacy

Augustine used Paul as a model for how the sinful person feels. The Augustinian model of an *introspective* conscience in Western culture became the basis for much inquiry into the individual self, influencing Thomas Aquinas, Martin Luther, John Calvin, and the Protestant Reformation, as well as Søren Kierkegaard, Carl Jung, and Sigmund Freud (see Box 25).

Box 25 The Freudian Paul

The restoration to the primeval father of his historical rights marked a great progress, but this could not be the end. The other parts of the prehistoric tragedy also clamoured for recognition. How this process was set in motion is not easy to say. It seems that a growing feeling of guiltiness had seized the Jewish people – and perhaps the whole of civilization of that time – as a precursor of the return of the repressed material. This went on until a member of the Jewish people, in the guise of a political-religious agitator, founded a doctrine which – together with another one, the Christian religion – separated from the Jewish one. Paul, a Roman Jew from Tarsus, seized upon this feeling of guilt and correctly traced it back to its primeval source. This he called original sin; it was a crime against God that could be expiated only through death. . . .

Paul, by developing the Jewish religion further, became its destroyer. His success was certainly mainly due to the fact that through the idea of salvation he laid the ghost of the feeling of guilt. (Freud 1939, 109–12; see also Cox 1959. For Paul in the modern Jewish imagination, see Langton 2010)

Yet this Western idea of the introspective conscience – from Mani and Pelagius to Augustine – got the historical Paul wrong. To understand why, we need to trace a brief history of Augustine's career and writings.

Augustine's Career and Writings

A young Manichaean Augustine attended the university at Carthage (370). After his studies, he then relocated to Rome and later received a call to Milan as a Roman professor of rhetoric (384), where he converted to Catholic Christianity (387). Augustine returned to his native North Africa (modern Algeria), where he was forcibly ordained a priest and then made the Catholic bishop of Hippo Regius (395–430). Throughout his long career, Augustine had an intense preoccupation with the figure of Paul.

His interpretation of the Pauline writings is complex because it evolved over this long career, reversing itself on several occasions. In any case, the idea of making Paul the central figure of Christianity likely originated in Augustine's decade-long allegiance to the Manichaeans in Carthage. When the teenaged Augustine joined the Manichaeans as a university student, he would have gone through their formal entrance ritual known as the First Confession. The First Confession required the initiate to release all the encumbrances of guilt accumulated thus far in life by recalling seemingly trivial acts in one's past when internal evil impulses were experienced. A Manichaean teacher would then use a framework of cosmic dualism to give meaning to the memory of those incidents, identifying the inner evil impulses as the alien presences of the Dark Kingdom invading one's body. Augustine in the second book of his spiritual autobiography, *The Confessions*, preserves for us a remnant of this indoctrination process when he recounts the incident when as a youth he was inexplicably moved to steal pears from a tree in someone else's garden. The First Confession ritual of cultivating an introspective conscience, therefore, continued to shape Augustine's thinking on Paul well after he had converted out of the Manichaean ranks.

Augustine's early writings, after his conversion to Catholic Christianity, attempted to rescue Paul from the Manichaeans. Against their separation of law (the evil Kingdom of Darkness) and gospel (the good Kingdom of Light), Augustine defended the holiness of the Old Testament by pointing to Paul's positive use of Jewish Scripture. Following Ambrosiaster's Roman tradition of Pauline commentary in Latin, Augustine sought to discern the meaning of the Bible in the exegesis of individual phrases and clauses. One such clause was, "for the letter kills, but the Spirit gives life" (2 Cor. 3:6), by which Augustine understood Paul telling readers not to take the

Old Testament literally but in a spiritual (figurative) sense through Christ. In this early period, Augustine challenged Manichaean determinism by writing his own commentary on Romans as well as a handbook of specific propositions advising believers how to read Paul's letter to affirm human moral autonomy on a continuum from Adam to the present. Understanding Romans, argued Augustine, meant keeping in mind the letter's main topic of connecting God's law and God's grace. Augustine thus read Paul's connection of *law* (redefined as the Old Testament) and *gospel* (redefined as the New Testament) to affirm the goodness of the Jewish scriptures and the maintenance of human free will against the Manichaeans who saw in Paul a clear condemnation of both.

In later writings, however, Augustine questioned this conclusion and reversed himself. Faith and personal choice could not serve as the basis for one's election, Augustine reasoned, because divine election would then be a reward for merit rather than a free gift of God. He wrote that all human-ity was a "damned mass of sin" as a consequence of Adam's Original Sin and so no human being deserved God's election, but a few sinners became righteous through God's grace. Why some people (the Elect) received this free gift, while the rest of humanity (who were damned) did not, was utterly inscrutable to Augustine, but he found in Paul the model of such a sinner saved despite himself because of God's grace. Having to fit Paul's biography into an idiosyncratic model of conversion was not the only reason Augustine reversed himself on Paul. A historical context of new doctrinal conflicts in fifth-century Italy and Roman North Africa also prompted his new perspective on the apostle. Augustine had to counter the biblical interpretations of Pelagius and his followers, who had, in turn, also attacked the Manichaeans.

In his work *On the Spirit and the Letter* (412), Augustine condemned the Pelagian emphasis on free will as a serious doctrinal error and affirmed in its place the rival concept of predestination:

> But there is an opinion that calls for sharp and vehement resistance – I mean the belief that the power of the human will can of itself, without the help of God, either achieve perfect righteousness or advance steadily towards it. When we press upon those who think this way the presumption of supposing this to happen without divine aid, they stop themselves from daring to say something so irreligious and intolerable. But they say that the reason why it (human goodness) does not happen without divine aid is that God has created human beings in possession of a will that chooses freely, and teaches them by the gift of his commandments the right way of life; so that God's help consists in the removal by instruction of humanity's ignorance, so that people can know what is to be avoided in their actions and what is to be

sought; and thus, by means of the power of free choice belonging to them by nature, people may enter upon the road pointed out to them, and by a way of life of self-control, justice, and piety, they may merit attainment to the life which is both blessed and eternal. (Augustine, *On the Spirit and the Letter*; trans. in Burnaby 1955, 197, altered)

The polemics in this passage gives an inaccurate description of Pelagian belief; Pelagius did not argue that people are without divine aid, but rather that God points the way to salvation through the Scriptures and in Paul's letters especially. In any case, Augustine's attack against Pelagius and the idea of free will was unrelenting:

Our own assertion, on the contrary, is this: that the human will is divinely assisted to do the right in such a way that, besides humanity's creation with freedom to choose, and besides the teaching by which human beings are instructed in how they ought to live, people receive the Holy Spirit, whereby there arises in the human soul the delight in and the love of God, the supreme and changeless Good. This gift belongs to Christians here and now, while they walk by faith, not yet by sight; so that, having this as a down payment of God's free bounty, they may be fired in heart to cleave to their Creator, kindled in mind to come within the shining of the true light; and thus receive from the source of their being the only real well-being. Free choice alone, then, if the way of truth is hidden, avails for nothing but sin; and when the right action and the true aim has begun to appear clearly, there is still no doing, no devotion, no good life, unless it also be delighted in and loved [see Rom. 7:21–22]. And so that it may be loved, the love of God is shed abroad in our hearts, not by the free choice whose spring is in ourselves, but through the Holy Spirit which is given to us. (Augustine, *On the Spirit and the Letter*; trans. in Burnaby 1955, 197–98, altered)

Augustine is saying that humans could not love God without the gift (grace) of the Holy Spirit, given only to God's Elect. People left to decide on their own free will cannot help but choose sin. They may be able to choose to perform individual acts of goodness and to avoid particular sins, but they cannot change the object of their delight; without God's grace, people inevitably delight in things other than God. And, in later works, Augustine's idea of Original Sin evolved to allow some role for free will, in the sense that God inclines certain people's free will in particular directions. Augustine's complex response to Pelagius thus affirmed that humans have both grace and free will. He complained that the Pelagians contradicted the great apostle Paul (Rom. 7, see later discussion). Pelagius had identified *law* to be the external Old Testament rituals and ceremonies that, when read allegorically through Christ, enabled the follower to achieve perfection.

Augustine, in contrast, argued that *law* means the whole system of God's moral commands, which without God's grace do nothing but lead to sin – "the letter" of scriptural teaching thus "kills" the soul.

Augustine shifted the debate with the Pelagians over Law and Grace to an autobiographical reading of Paul's letter to the Romans. In that reading, Augustine pointed to Romans 7, the speech about a tormented conscience (quoted previously, in connection to the Manichaeans), as Paul's soliloquy of his own guilt – Augustine's text proving not only his theory of Original Sin but also that of an introspective conscience. Pelagius had not read this passage autobiographically but as a speech in the character of another, rhetorical persona. To support an autobiographical reading, Augustine referred back to his own personal history as a Catholic convert. In *Confessions* (8.12; trans. Chadwick 2008, 152–54), Augustine tells his story in a scene of dramatic reversal and resolution to a new life as follows. At the age of thirty-three and confronting persistent feelings that he believed to be evil (sexual compulsions and the constant need for praise), Augustine stood in a garden crying over his inability to end his debauched sinning. He searched the hidden depths of his soul and mustered all its pitiful secrets before his conscience ("the eyes of my heart"). During his guilty anguish, he overheard a child in a nearby house singing a refrain that Augustine construed as "take it and read, take it and read," a divine command to open Scripture randomly and to read the first passage his eyes fell upon. Augustine was familiar with this practice of divination (known as bibliomancy), an oracular use of Scripture commonplace in his Roman Christianity. Indeed, this homespun form of Roman divination was especially popular in late antiquity.

Augustine thus took hold of a nearby codex of Paul's letters, opened its pages, and took the first words to catch his eye as an omen of immediate personal relevance. The passage happened to have been from Romans: "Let us live honorably as in the day, not in reveling and drunkenness, not in debauchery and licentiousness, not in quarreling and jealousy; instead, put on the Lord Jesus Christ, and make no provision for the flesh, to gratify its desires" (13:13–14). Augustine later wrote that reading this passage enabled him finally to resolve his internal struggle with what he perceived were evil impulses, with which he had been struggling since his Manichaean days. Unlike the Manichaeans, Augustine owned the sinful feelings inside of him as *his* feelings, not something external to his self. He concluded that only God's gift of grace, and not human free will, bestows on a person the delight in God that mobilizes human feelings toward the removal of sin. In Paul's soliloquy of Romans 7, Augustine thus saw a mirror of his own conscience troubled by the guilt over his own hopelessly impulsive sin inherited from Adam.

Augustine's idea of Original Sin asserts the corporate guilt of all humanity in the fall of Adam and Eve (Gen. 2–3) through a reading of Paul. This reading reimagined Adam's evil act to have been an attempt to do his own will – in other words, *pride* – which was a fall from God's will. This fall resulted not in Adam being under his own control as he had so ardently desired, but in him being at odds with himself (his mind over against his body's lust and desire). Augustine identified this harsh and pitiable existence to be the life of "slavery under sin" that Paul describes in Romans (see Rom. 7:14). In Augustine's reading of Paul, God's punishment fits Adam's crime: "In fact, to put it briefly, in the punishment of that sin the retribution for disobedience is simply disobedience itself. For man's wretchedness is nothing but his own disobedience to himself, so that because he would not do what he could do, he now wills to do what he cannot [see Rom. 7:18–19]" (*City of God* 14.15, trans. Bettenson 1972, 575). The punishment changed human nature for the worse, into animal bodies no longer immortal but subject to decay and physical death. Because all corporate humanity participated in the first transgression of Adam and Eve, every human being shares equally the guilt and its punishment:

> For we were all in that one man, seeing that we all *were* that one man who fell into sin through the woman who was made from him before the first sin. We did not yet possess forms individually created and assigned to us for us to live in them as individuals; but there already existed the seminal nature from which we were to be begotten. And of course, when this was vitiated through sin, and bound with death's fetters in its just condemnation, man could not be born of man in any other condition. Hence from the misuse of free will there started a chain of disasters: mankind is led from that original perversion, a kind of corruption at the root, right up to the disaster of the second death, which has no end [damnation]. Only those who are set free through God's grace escape from this calamitous sequence. (Augustine, *City of God* 13.14; trans. Bettenson 1972, 523, emphasis in original)

Augustine thus took Romans 5:12 to mean that we all were somehow present in Adam's body when he acted against God's will. Even newborn babies share this Original Sin: "even infants have broken the covenant, not in consequence of any particular act in their own life but in consequence of the origin which is common to all mankind, since all have broken God's covenant in that one man in whom [*in quo*] all sinned [Rom. 5:12]"

(Augustine, *City of God* 16.27; trans. Bettenson 1972, 688). All humans are born with the sin of Adam.

Augustine's autobiographical reading of Paul created a foundational model of the introspective self that became normative in Western culture. Augustine portrayed Paul as an anguished convert and miserable sinner, whose spiritual dissatisfaction and tormented introspective conscience led the apostle at his "conversion" to repudiate his past religious self:

> It is not our purpose in this work to expound the Epistle to the Romans, but to use its testimony to prove as surely as we may that the divine aid for the working of righteousness consists not in God's gift of the law, full as it is of good and holy commands, but in that our will itself, without which we cannot do the good, is aided and uplifted by the imparting of the Spirit of grace. Without that aid, the teaching is a letter that kills, since it rather holds people in the guilt of transgression than justifies the ungodly....
>
> The examination and discussion which we have carried out, to the best of that power which the Lord deigns to bestow, has led us to conclude that a person is not justified by the precepts of the good life, but only through the faith of Jesus Christ: that is, not by the law of works but by the law of faith, not by the letter but by the spirit, not by the deserts of our actions but by the grace freely given. (Augustine, *On the Sprit and the Letter* 20–22; trans. in Burnaby 1955, 209–10, 212, altered)

Augustine thus invented from the Pauline distinction between Law and Grace an all-encompassing grand narrative, which few ancient commentators (with the possible exception of Marcion) had noticed as important in Paul's writings.

A Note on Martin Luther's Paul

Over a millennium after Augustine, Martin Luther (1483–1546), a Roman Catholic monk in the Augustinian religious order, developed Augustine's reading of Paul – the guilty sinner troubled by an introspective conscience – but with a greater emphasis on predestination. Luther also read Paul autobiographically, through his own experience as a failed monk, but interpreted the *law* in Paul's writings to mean a general principle of religious legalism. Luther found such legalism in his own German culture, in the medieval system of Catholic penance. A hardline reformer, Luther condemned all Roman Catholic penitential practices (monastic vows, private confessions, the mass, the sale of indulgences) as Pauline "works of the Law" that attempted wrongly to earn the forgiveness of sins.

Against "the law" of the Roman Pope, Luther preached the "gospel" of divine grace that bestowed righteousness (justification) to people by their faith alone, without the Catholic Church's penitential system. Luther's "justification by faith alone" required individual believers to examine their consciences deeply enough to acknowledge each of us as a miserable sinner like Paul:

> Now the true meaning of Christianity is this: that a man first acknowledge, through the Law, that he is a sinner, for whom it is impossible to perform any good work....
>
> What I am saying here on the basis of the words of Paul I learned from my own experience in the monastery about myself and about others. I saw many who tried with great effort and the best of intentions to do everything possible to appease their conscience. They wore hair shirts; they fasted; they prayed; they tormented and wore out their bodies with various exercises so severely that if they had been made of iron, they would have been crushed. And yet the more they labored, the greater their terrors became. Especially when the hour of death was imminent, they became so fearful that I have seen many murderers facing execution die more confidently than these men who had lived such saintly lives.
>
> Thus it is certainly true that those who keep the Law do not keep it. The more men try to satisfy the Law, the more they transgress it [cf. Rom. 7:14–25]. The more someone tries to bring peace to his conscience through his own righteousness, the more disquieted he makes it. When I was a monk, I made a great effort to live according to the requirements of the monastic rule. I made a practice of confessing and reciting all my sins, but always with prior contrition; I went to confession frequently, and I performed the assigned penances faithfully. Nevertheless, my conscience could never achieve certainty but was always in doubt and said, "You have not done this correctly. You were not contrite enough. You omitted this in your confession." Therefore the longer I tried to heal my uncertain, weak, and troubled conscience with human traditions, the more uncertain, weak, and troubled I continually made it. In this way, by observing human traditions, I transgressed them even more; and by following the righteousness of the monastic order, I was never able to reach it. For, as Paul says, it is impossible for the conscience to find peace through the works of the Law, much less through human traditions, without the promise and the Gospel about Christ. (Martin Luther, *Commentary on Gal. 2:16; and on Gal. 5:3*; trans. in Meeks and Fitzgerald 2007, 381, 388)

Luther thus reinvented Augustine's theory of Original Sin and its accompanying idea of the introspective conscience. Consequently, Luther's reading of Augustine's reading of Paul changed the apostle's writings into documents of universal human consciousness.

The Dialectical Paul: A Modern Legend of the Apostle as the "Second Founder of Christianity"

The modern celebration of Paul as the discoverer of the individual conscience is a legend that comes from this Augustinian-Lutheran line of interpretation, a cumulative elaboration upon a distortion of the historical figure. This distortion, in turn, led nineteenth-century scholars to portray Paul as the second founder of Christianity. Two new evolutionary theories shaped this later discussion of Paul: one in philosophy (Hegel's metaphysical dialectic to discern truth) and the other in science (Charles Darwin's empirical observations on the biological development of animal species). The new focus on evolutionary change influenced the emerging field of academic biblical studies in German universities. German biblical scholars used the new, higher criticism to read the Bible less as a treasury of eternal truth and systematic doctrine than as a conflicting assortment of different sources that changed over time. This intellectual culture focused the modern debate over Christian origins on a single question: whether Paul had replaced the teachings of Jesus with Greek philosophical theology; in other words, had Paul "Hellenized" Christianity? The main works in this debate came from such German biblical scholars as Ferdinand Christian Baur (1792–1860) and Adolf von Harnack (1851–1930).

Baur proposed that Paul's conflict with Jewish Christians enabled the liberation of Jesus' core message – a rational universalism – from the particularity of its Palestinian Jewish husk. Von Harnack agreed with, but also modified this basic Judaism and Hellenism model of Christian origins. He remapped Paul's de-Judaizing of Christianity's core teachings in a direct line from Jesus and the Jerusalem church to Paul's Gentile mission. But, according to Harnack, the Hellenization of Christianity came after Paul, in the second century, in the Greek writings of ancient Christian apologists like Justin Martyr. Such research established Paul as the single most important figure in the early church, for it showed that Paul created "Christianity" as a new religion, separate from Judaism (Meeks and Fitzgerald 2007, 398). (As a side note, analogous ideas about Paul had developed also in medieval and early modern Islam, but with negative connotations; see Box 26).

The problem with this dialectical conflict model of Christian origins, however, is that the major evolutionary changes that nineteenth-century scholarship attributed to Paul as the second founder of the religion – worshipping Jesus as God, converting Gentiles, and preaching the Hellenism of Greek philosophy and culture – were already under way in early

---

Box 26 The Muslim Paul

Paul is not mentioned in the Qur'an. But medieval and later Muslim literature portrayed the figure as an evil Roman king of the Jews, with many anachronisms and confusion with the emperor Constantine. This "King Paul" feigned his divine revelation and conversion to Jesus Christ, tricking Jesus' followers into accepting him as a believer. Among Paul's new teachings: the divinity of Jesus, the doctrine of the Trinity, a change in the direction of prayer, the abolition of circumcision and dietary laws, and other pagan (Roman) customs. Paul, it was said, ended his life in suicide, which led directly to all the schisms and heresies of Christianity after him.

The polemics functioned didactically, to warn Muslims of the dangers of schism in their own faith. The moral was that Jesus, a servant and prophet of Allah, brought the same message as Muhammad and the prophets before him did. The "Muslim Paul" thus perverted not only Jesus' teachings but also the perennial truth of Islam. Paul falsified this religious truth by misleading Christians to leave the correct religious practice of Jesus and accept the false religion of the Romans. The tales reflected, in other words, medieval Muslim anxieties about cultural assimilation from contact with Byzantine culture.

See Stern 1968; Koningsveld 1996; Anthony 2009.

Christianity before he became an apostle. The Christ hymn that Paul quotes in Philippians (2:6–11) provides evidence that pre-Pauline believers worshipped Jesus as a divine Lord. And Paul's own letter to the Romans addressed Gentile congregations that he did not found. Paul thus joined a Jesus movement already well developed in the language and religion of Hellenistic and Roman culture. Furthermore, the nineteenth-century approach to Paul is unhelpful because its totalizing interpretative framework sets up "Judaism" and "Hellenism" as code words masquerading as fixed historical entities, which are then said to be capable of interacting with each other. As we saw in Chapter 3, a cultural approach to the life of Paul is more historically useful than is this dialectical one.

Yet the greatest modern proponent of the dialectical Paul is the German philosopher Friedrich Wilhelm Nietzsche (1844–1900), a student of theology at the University of Bonn and the son of a Prussian Lutheran clergyman. Always the original thinker, Nietzsche turned the nineteenth-century question on its head and argued that Paul had Judaized (as opposed to Hellenized) the religion of Jesus. In 1888, Nietzsche gathered together these thoughts on the evolution of Christianity in a polemical essay entitled *The Anti-Christ*. Attacking Protestant (Lutheran) faith and its moral teachings (Original Sin and the introspective conscience), as well as the Jewish religion, Nietzsche applied the dialectics of Hegel's philosophy to elicit the conflict and change of early Christianity. He set up a series of antitheses, a modernized version of Marcion's Pauline project but with exactly the opposite goal. Nietzsche contrasted Jesus' "Gospel" (Greek *euangelion*; "good news") and Paul's "anti-Gospel" (*dusangelion*; "bad news") to highlight their apparent contradictions, with the purpose of exposing Paul as an anti-evangelist (*dus*angelist) and anti-Christ (a figure exactly opposite to that of Jesus). On this model, Paul craved the absolute power of the Jewish priesthood and so adapted the idea of guilt from the expiatory sacrifice at the temple to invent a perverse new religion – Christianity – which directly opposed Jesus' own faith. The Pauline antigospel, according to Nietzsche, wrongly introduced guilt (the introspective conscience) as necessary for salvation, because it denied basic human nature and instincts. Nietzsche described Paul as a Dostoyevskian "Grand Inquisitor" figure who enslaved the gullible masses into blind belief, preaching the lie of an afterlife that threatens eternal damnation for disobedience to the priest. Paul's real motive, Nietzsche explained, was to gain power, to tyrannize over the masses. Nietzsche thus condemned Paul's invention of the introspective conscience as a crime against humanity:

> And from this time an absurd problem [of the cross] rose into prominence: "how *could* God allow it to happen?" To this question the disordered minds of the small community found a reply which in its absurdity was literally terrifying: God gave his son as a *sacrifice* for the forgiveness of sins. Alas! how prompt and sudden was the end of the gospel! Expiatory sacrifice for guilt, and indeed in its most repulsive and barbaric form, – the sacrifice of the *innocent* for the sins of the guilty! What appalling Paganism! – For Jesus himself had done away with the concept "guilt," – he denied any gulf between God and man, he *lived* this unity between God and man, it was this that constituted *his* "glad tidings." . . . St Paul, with that rabbinic impudence which characterizes all his doing, rationalized this conception, this prostitution of a conception, as follows: "if Christ did not rise from the dead, our faith is vain." – And, in a trice, the most contemptible of all unrealisable promises, the *impudent* doctrine of personal immortality, was woven out of the gospel. . . . St Paul even preached this immortality as a reward. (Nietzsche, *The Anti-Christ* 41; trans. in Meeks and Fitzgerald 2007, 412–13, emphasis in original)

Whether or not one agrees with Nietzsche's philosophy, his interpretation of Paul as the first Christian is historically problematic. Not only does its argument depend on the cumulative distortion of Paul in the West (Nietzsche actually condemns the Lutheran Paul), but it also postulates an implausible context for the apostle in his lifetime. Simply put, the argument presumes a Paul *far too important and influential among his contemporaries*. As the first part of this book explained, a consensus of modern critical scholars argues that Paul was neither the first nor the only missionary to the Gentiles. He had competitors (2 Cor. 11:4–5; Gal. 1:6–9; Phil. 3:2–6) who proclaimed different kinds of gospels about the Messiah Jesus to non-Jewish converts. Furthermore, Paul did not work alone but with a circle of his associates. He occasionally even cooperated with independent missionaries, some of whom he names: Apollos (1 Cor. 3:5–9); Junia and Andronicus, who "were in Christ before I was" (Rom. 16:7). Paul openly admitted to be preaching oral traditions about Jesus that he, in turn, received from teachers (1 Cor. 15:3–9).

Moreover, as Origen had realized, Paul considered his gospel to be an integral part of Judaism. Paul's own words make clear that he did not imagine his mission as establishing a separate religion from "Israel" (Rom. 9–11). Paul's letters indicate that he was one of many envoys of Messiah Jesus in the eastern Mediterranean world, operating sometimes in cooperation and at other times in fierce conflict with each other. As we have seen, in his lifetime, the term *Christian* had not yet been invented. How ironic it is that a Jewish envoy became a "second founder" of Christianity in nineteenth-century Western thought.

Moreover, we look in vain for passages where Paul declared himself to have been a sinner. The passages in which he discussed his conscience show it to have been rather robust. That robustness included devotion to Israel and his fellow Jews:

> I am speaking the truth in Christ – I am not lying; my conscience confirms it by the Holy Spirit – I have great sorrow and unceasing anguish in my heart. For I could wish that I myself were accursed and cut off from Christ for the sake of my own people, my kindred according to the flesh. They are Israelites, and to them belong the adoption, the glory, the covenants, the giving of the law, the worship, and the promises; to them belong the patriarchs, and from them, according to the flesh, comes the Messiah, who is over all, God blessed forever. Amen (Rom. 9:1–5)

In this passage, Paul grieved over his fellow Jews who did not believe in Jesus as the Messiah, rather than over any personal guilt or sinning on Paul's part (cf. 1 Tim. 1:15, a deutero-Pauline work of the second century that remade Paul into "the foremost" sinner). Indeed, also as Origen brilliantly saw, Paul's whole discussion in Romans 9–11 praised Israel as God's chosen people and rationalized Jewish unbelief in Messiah Jesus as part of God's plan for the salvation of "all Israel." The apostle certainly did not tell Jews to repent of their sins and to end the anguish of their plagued consciences, although he certainly wanted them to accept Jesus as the Messiah.

Paul's boasting of his robust conscience appears also in his claims about his personal integrity to the Corinthians: "Indeed, this is our boast, the testimony of our conscience; we have behaved in the world with frankness and godly sincerity, not by earthly wisdom but by the grace of God – and all the more toward you" (2 Cor. 1:12). We find Paul boasting further about his clear conscience in a remarkable statement imagining himself before the Final Judgment. As he insisted, "I am not aware of anything against myself, but I am not thereby acquitted. It is the Lord who judges me" (1 Cor. 4:4). In another place, he wrote:

> So we are always confident; even though we know that while we are at home in the body we are away from the Lord – for we walk by faith, not by sight. Yes, we do have confidence, and we would rather be away from the body and at home with the Lord. So whether we are at home or away, we make it our aim to please him. For all of us must appear before the judgment seat of Christ, so that each may receive recompense for what has been done in the body, whether good or evil. (2 Cor. 5:6–10)

Paul's autobiographical reflections expressed pride over his whole life in Judaism. He insisted, "I, too, have reason for confidence in the flesh. If anyone else has reason to be confident in the flesh, I have more: circumcised on the eighth day, a member of the people of Israel, of the tribe of Benjamin, a Hebrew born of Hebrew; as to the law, a Pharisee; as to zeal, a persecutors of the church; as to righteousness under the law, blameless" (Phil. 3:4–6). Paul thus bragged about his ability to fulfill the Jewish Law; indeed, he was "blameless" (flawless) as to the "righteousness" that the Law required. To be sure, the apostle Paul wrote that he chose to let go of all the former gains achieved from his Pharisaic past, throwing them away like "rubbish" (Phil. 3:7–8), but this was yet another way to boast about them. He claimed to throw away achievements in Judaism that lesser apostles, his opponents, wished they could have for themselves. That is to say, Paul gained *auctoritas* by refusing to keep the official honors of his youth.

Paul showed few signs of sufferings in his conscience or of any shortcomings in fulfilling the Torah. On the one hand, he wrote that he regretted his past persecution of the church (see 1 Cor. 15:9, "For I am the least of the apostles, unfit to be called an apostle, because I persecuted the church of God"). On the other hand, he boasted of it as proof of his great religious zeal (Phil. 3:6). Given the history of interpretation surveyed previously, we would expect to find more evidence that Paul considered himself a miserable sinner. The only possible passage would be Romans 7, but this rhetorical speech personified a character other Paul himself (see Stendahl 1976, 78–96). Other passages are more directly autobiographical, which I explained in Part I.

In short, Paul did not stop being Jewish when he became an apostle. Rather, he rejected his Pharisaic community and his past synagogue leadership. As an apostle of Messiah Jesus, Paul spoke of his new form of being Jewish with pride and expressions of *auctoritas*. Paul's Jewishness was thus not fixed or bounded, but a *plural* cultural identity that shared a Roman discourse of authority. Despite long-lasting claims in the history of Pauline interpretation, Paul preached neither the necessity of guilt nor the need to discover an introspective conscience. Such interpretations result from the ways in which post-biblical thinkers projected themselves into their reinventions of Paul, as they still do today.

CONCLUSION: GOING BEYOND THE EPITAPH

A traditional biography would end with an account of the subject's death, which might also describe the gravesite or quote the tombstone's epitaph to find closure. But such a conventional conclusion poses several problems. First, it implies a false ordering of events, namely, that the biographical text is somehow coterminous with the life. A biography is not the same as the subject's actual life. Second, contemporary historians do not know where or how Paul died, nor whether his remains survive (see Chapter 2). How do we tackle these problems? As the Introduction explained, my historical solution has been to take up the form of antibiography and study many different Pauls. In that goal, let's find not one but several epitaphs.

The traditional epitaph of Paul is located at the ancient (and modern) pilgrimage site of the apostle's legendary tomb. On June 29, 2009, in Rome and broadcast live on Italian television, an emotional Pope Benedict XVI announced that carbon dating of the bones inside the marble sarcophagus under Rome's second largest basilica, Saint Paul Outside-the-Walls (Italian *Basilica Papale di San Paolo fuori le mura*), "seems to confirm the unanimous and uncontested tradition that they are the mortal remains of the Apostle Paul." The announcement was a bombshell, and a carefully orchestrated papal performance – it came in a homily on the successful closure of a pastoral effort to celebrate the "Year of St. Paul" worldwide for Roman Catholics in the name of all Christians. Six years previously, Vatican archaeologists had, under the pavement of the basilica, unearthed the sarcophagus, which dates from the reign of the fourth-century emperor Theodosius I and bears the epitaph "Apostle Paul, Martyr" (Latin *Paulo apostolo mart*). Vatican authorities had declared, "At last, today pilgrims visiting the basilica can see the side of the sarcophagus through a small window we left open under the papal altar." The epitaph points to an important theme that I have explained in the second part of this book – that Christians in late antiquity mostly viewed Paul as a martyr, not as the paradigmatic "sinner."

In any case, the papal-ordered radiocarbon dating indicates that the bone fragments apparently come from the first or second centuries C.E. The scientific test itself does not, however, prove that the bones necessarily belong to Paul's body, only that their age calculates to be within a historical range of years that *might* include Paul's lifetime. Likewise, the sarcophagus's epitaph bearing Paul's name also does not prove the mortal remains to be Paul's; the inscription dates only to the fourth century. As Chapter 4 has shown, artifacts of the martyr cult do not constitute primary evidence for reconstructing the historical Paul. The site of the basilica, near the Tiber River, became Paul's tomb based on legends.

The historical significance of Pope Benedict's announcement lies in its updated reaffirmation of the same legal claim made by a papal predecessor, the fourth-century bishop Damasus, which declares Paul's body infallibly to be Roman property. The papal claim objectifies a particular body, the bone fragments venerated by the city's martyr cult, as "the" Paul, and rejects all other "Pauls" (whom other Christians might venerate) as imposters. The invention of a Pauline martyr cult continues to reshape Roman identity and public memory even today. A *Roman* Paul dies hard.

The approach to Paul advocated in this book has led us to Rome many times over. But we should move beyond the "Apostle Paul, Martyr" epitaph because it gives us the false impression that the Paul of both history and faith can be fixed at a place (Rome) and an identity (martyr). Even in the martyr cult, this entombed body (or, rather, bone fragments) is not all of Paul; his severed head still rests according to popular tradition in another papal basilica, Saint John Lateran, the cathedral church of the Diocese of Rome. At any rate, many different Pauls remain alive today in the memory of modern Western culture, whose popular and academic conceptions I have challenged in this book.

Contesting popular conceptions, I have made the historical argument that Paul did not consider himself "Christian" (a term not yet coined in his lifetime) but always Jewish. He expressed pride in being a "member of the people of Israel" and a "Hebrew born of Hebrews" even when he noted his past persecution of the church, and in all his actions he claimed to have been "blameless" as to righteousness under the Torah (Phil. 3:5–6). The primary evidence thus does not support the modern, highly psychoanalytical portrait of Paul as a prototypical sinner who converted from a past life because of personal introspection of his tormented conscience. I agree with a consensus of biblical scholarship that has exploded the entire edifice of the introspective conscience as an ideology of modern Western culture. Paul was not the converted sinner whom Martin Luther reinvented in his Protestant theology of "Justification by Faith Alone," based upon Augustine's theology.

In addition to popular conceptions, I have contested also the historical Pauls that some of my fellow academic biblical scholars have constructed. Against an allegedly anti-imperial Paul who subverted the fundamental (pagan) culture of ancient Rome, I have advocated an alternative reading of the primary sources precisely within Roman cultural identities. Paul's writings advanced a particularly Roman discourse of "clout" (*auctoritas*) over subordinates and colleagues, an unofficial authority that provoked the challenge of rivals. Furthermore, such language participated in Roman ideas of conquest and mapping, which expressed a unity of different provincials (Greek *ethnē*, "Gentiles") under a single *imperium*. Roman identities are an overlooked facet of the historical figure, which bring a continuity between the Jewish "Saul" and the Christian "Paul." It is historically inaccurate to imagine that *being Jewish* and *being Roman* were bounded entities, necessarily separated in Paul's day. Roman identities were how Paul experienced his Jewishness.

I have also tried to survey another part of Paul's "life story" – his legend. How did Paul's character and teaching live after he died? To answer this question, I have described the various stories that reinvented him in late antiquity, which show the character of Paul's life in the thinking and sensibilities of people who used him as an imperial hero, family man, ascetic role model, or object of derision. Often hilarious in their retelling, this material is nonetheless important for our historical knowledge of the ancient church (but not the life of Paul), because it testifies to Paul's influence on and signficance in diverse kinds of developing Christianity.

Examining these lively stories has led us, in turn, to the contradictory discourses of interpreters for whom Paul was less a character to embrace or argue with, but really more a kind of book to quote from. Such discourses have enormous importance for the history of the biblical canon, increasing our understanding of how Paul became a scriptural authority. From Marcion and Valentinus at Rome to Irenaeus, Origen, and John Chrysostom, we encountered a wide diversity of rival Pauls. Paul as *book* even received veneration when the circulation of Pauline letters into a single corpus made some ancient readers see the apparent inconsistency of the apostle's words.

How do we sum up all the lives of these many different Pauls? To express the sharp interpretative battles in late antiquity that led to the demise of most of them, especially when Augustine got his hands on Paul (literally, by grabbing a book of his letters), an alternative epitaph might quote from 2 Peter: "his letters contain some things that are hard to understand" (2 Pet. 3:16). That is to say, interpreting Paul is more complicated than simply reading the Bible for an alleged "plain sense"; its meaning is not obvious. Serious students, as my first religious studies professor (John Howard Schütz) wisely informed me as a college freshman, need to study the New Testament in its literary and historical contexts. These contexts include other early Christian literature, ancient Mediterranean religions, early Judaism, and Roman history – professional academic fields not normally combined.

Yet it is important to go beyond the idea of an epitaph, because an antibiography is best left open ended. Finishing this book does not bring closure to Paul. Just when an interpreter believes to have grasped the "real" Paul, new information in the process of research invariably causes the figure, like the shape-shifting Proteus of Homeric epic, to slip away unrecognizable. The very act of examining the evidence, as in the Heisenberg uncertainty principle, changes the figure into multiple Pauls and meanings. Critical biblical scholars, myself included, recognize that our incomplete evidence can never support certainty. On each point of evidence presented in this book, my goal has been to provoke further study. There is no end to Paul.

APPENDIX 1: EXTANT WRITINGS ATTRIBUTED TO SAINT PAUL IN ROUGH CHRONOLOGICAL ORDER

AUTHENTIC

1. The First Epistle to the Thessalonians, in the New Testament, ca. 51.
2. The First Epistle to the Corinthians, in the New Testament, ca. 53/54.
3. The Epistle to the Galatians, in the New Testament, ca. 54.
4. The Second Epistle to the Corinthians (a collection of letter fragments), in the New Testament, ca. 54–56.
5. The Epistle to the Philippians, in the New Testament, ca. 56.
6. The Epistle to Philemon, in the New Testament, ca. 56.
7. The Epistle to the Romans, in the New Testament, ca. 57.

PSEUDONYMOUS

8. The Epistle to the Colossians, in the New Testament, ca. 65–75.
9. The Epistle to the Ephesians, in the New Testament, ca. 80. The letter was originally addressed to all Christians generally ("to the saints"), but later scribes inserted the phrase "who are in Ephesus" to make the address more specific. The earliest and best Greek manuscripts lack any references to the Ephesians.
10. The Epistle to the Hebrews, in the New Testament, ca. 60–90. Although frequently cited in late antiquity as a letter of Paul, and admitted into the New Testament canon on that basis, the work does not bear Paul's name and important patristic authors denied that Paul wrote it. Yet hints at the end (Heb. 13:22–25) seem to suggest that the anonymous author does want the reader to think that he is Paul.
11. The Second Epistle to the Thessalonians, in the New Testament, ca. 70–95.
12. The First Epistle to Timothy, in the New Testament, ca. 95–125.
13. The Second Epistle to Timothy, in the New Testament, ca. 95–125.
14. The Epistle to Titus, in the New Testament, ca. 95–125.

15. *The Correspondence of Paul with the Corinthians*, a section of which is also known as *3 Corinthians*, second century, included within the apocryphal *Acts of Paul*. Translated in Elliott 1993, 380–82.
16. *The Coptic Apocalypse of Paul*, also known as *The Gnostic Apocalypse of Paul*, second century. Translated in Robinson 1988, 256–59.
17. *The Epistle to the Laodiceans*, ca. second to fourth century. Translated in Elliott 1993, 546. Marcion included a letter by this title among the Pauline epistles, but the earlier "Laodiceans" was likely our letter to the Ephesians – see Tertullian, *Against Marcion* 5.17; trans. Evans 1972, 613.
18. *The Apocalypse of Paul*, also known as *Visio Pauli*, ca. third century. Translated in Elliott 1993, 616–44.
19. *The Correspondence of Paul and Seneca*, fourth century. Translated in Elliott 1993, 547–53.

APPENDIX 2:
RECONSTRUCTING
PAUL'S CORINTHIAN
CORRESPONDENCE: A PUZZLE

Because Paul must have written more than just two letters to Corinth (see 1 Cor. 5:9), biblical scholars have proposed various theories to reconstruct the complex history of the Corinthian correspondence. Although a few scholars still maintain the literary unity of 2 Corinthians (which is also a hypothesis), a current consensus agrees that 2 Corinthians 10–13 comes originally from a different letter. The identification of the other pieces of the jigsaw puzzle is an open question, however. Indeed, some scholars prefer to remain agnostic on the rest of the pieces rather than presume that we know what Paul wrote. To be sure, all the scholarly proposals are tenuous.

In order to provide readers with some kind of guide through the quagmire, I have decided to adopt as a working hypothesis a recent proposal (Mitchell 2005), which I and other scholars (Roetzel 2007 and 2009) find suggestive. Admittedly, it is little more than a series of hypotheses laden with guesses, without any more independent verification than any other theory. Yet it at least attempts to explain all the evidence. I outline this hypothesis next.

Letter 1 (not extant), mentioned in 1 Corinthians 5:9, ca. 52. Paul writes concerning some ethical matters.

Letter 2 (entire), our 1 Corinthians, ca. 53/54. Dealing with escalating internal conflicts over status in the congregation, Paul urges his believers to reconcile with each other as one body in Christ.

Letter 3 (extant only as a fragment), preserved in 2 Corinthians 8, ca. 54/55. Paul writes to raise funds for the Jerusalem churches.

Letter 4 (extant only as a fragment), preserved in 2 Corinthians 2:14–7:4 (excluding 6:14–7:1), ca. 55. Paul defends himself against charges of religious fraud. The excluded fragment likely comes from a separate letter, by rival missionaries to Corinth, attacking Paul (see Betz 1994).

Letter 5 (extant only as a fragment), the "letter of tears," preserved in 2
Corinthians 10:1–13:10, ca. 55. Paul rebukes his congregation angrily for
accepting the leadership of rival Christian missionaries (the "super apostles").

Letter 6 (extant only as a fragment), preserved in 2 Corinthians 1:1–2:13; 7:5–
16; and 13:11–13. The congregation has apparently turned to accept Paul's
leadership, and so Paul writes for reconciliation while also underscoring his
honesty and goodwill, ca. 55/56.

Letter 7 (extant only as a fragment), preserved in 2 Corinthians 9. His fight
with the congregation now in the past, Paul administers the final stages of
the collection for Jerusalem, ca. 56.

APPENDIX 3: ANCIENT CHRISTIAN WORKS CONTAINING PAULINE TRADITIONS AND LEGENDS

1. The Acts of the Apostles, in the New Testament (8–28), ca. 95–115. From the same author of the Gospel of Luke, this highly theological narrative presents Paul as the greatest hero of a "unified" Church, who brings the gospel from its origins in Jerusalem to the imperial capital of Rome, with powerful orations, great miracles, and dramatic travels as God's "chosen instrument" (Acts 9:15), the historical reliability of which is disputed among modern scholars. Historical claims about Paul (and Christian origins) should, therefore, be drawn from Acts only with great caution.

2. The Epistle of James (2:14–26), in the New Testament, ca. late first century. The pseudonymous letter's particular contrast of faith and works, which echoes Paul's own terminology, points to a literary relationship with a corpus of Paul's letters. Discussed in Mitchell 2007.

3. Clement of Rome, *First Letter of Clement to the Corinthians* (5.1–7; 47), ca. 96. Written by Clement, a Christian leader in Rome, to the church at Corinth, this letter is the earliest attestation of Paul's epistles outside of the New Testament writings. It rebukes certain youthful factions for refusing to give respect to church elders (bishops and deacons), suggesting that conflicts within the Corinthian congregation continued well after Paul's death. It venerates the apostle as a "herald of both East and West," a reference to Paul's plan in Romans for a Spanish mission. Translated in Ehrman 2003, vol. 2, 43–45, 119–20.

4. The First Epistle of Peter, in the New Testament, ca. 80–100. The pseudonymous letter's language of subordination, in particular the household duty codes (1 Pet. 2:18–3:7), parallels the contemporaneous deutero-Pauline epistles, suggesting that the work comes from or at least is influenced by Paulinist circles.

5. The Second Epistle of Peter, in the New Testament, ca. early second century. This pseudonymous work, by an author different from that of 1 Peter, mentions the apostle Paul as a scriptural authority (2 Pet. 3:15–16)

in its response to scoffers who dispute, among other things, the author's interpretation of Paul's letters. Another early source showing that Paul's letters circulated in a corpus.

6. *The Letters of Ignatius of Antioch* (ca. 100–118). An early Christian leader (a bishop of Antioch), Ignatius wrote these seven letters (*To the Ephesians, To the Magnesians, To the Trallians, To the Romans, To the Philadelphians, To the Smyrnaeans,* and *To Polycarp*) while traveling through Asia Minor, under Roman guard, to his martyrdom in Rome. He imitates Paul's writing style, cites passages from a Pauline letter corpus, and emphasizes an episcopal authority similar to that in the Pastoral Epistles. Translated in Ehrman 2003, vol. 1, 201–363.

7. *The Letter of Polycarp to the Philippians,* ca. 110. This letter by an early bishop (elder) of Smyrna, known also from a letter to him by Ignatius and from *The Martyrdom of Polycarp* (ca. 155), reflects knowledge of a collection of Pauline writings. Its vision of church authority parallels that in the Pastoral Epistles. Translated in Ehrman 2003, vol. 1, 323–53.

8. Irenaeus of Lyons, *Against the Heresies* (3.1; 3.14), ca. 180. The main source of the legend that "Luke, the beloved physician" (mentioned in Col. 4:14) was Paul's traveling companion who carefully recorded Paul's preaching in a "book" (the canonical book of Acts). Anthologized in Meeks and Fitzgerald 2007, 186–87.

9. *The Acts of the Scillitan Martyrs,* ca. 180. In the midst of a persecution in North Africa, these Christians carried with them a corpus of Pauline writings ("books and letters of a just man named Paul") in a carrying case. This early source mentions the circulation and veneration of Paul's letters as Scripture. Translated and discussed in Eastman 2011, 157–58.

10. *The Epistle of the Apostles,* also known as *Epistula Apostolorum,* (31), ca. 180. This anonymous source, which apparently had limited geographical and chronological circulation, invents whole new dialogues of the risen Jesus at the resurrection, which includes Jesus telling the original disciples about Paul's future conversion and mission. Anthologized in Meeks and Fitzgerald 2007, 212.

11. *The Martyrdom of Paul,* ca. 190, included within the apocryphal *Acts of Paul.* Describes Paul's beheading and subsequent return appearance before Nero. Paul's main converts in the narrative are high-ranking Roman magistrates in Nero's court. Anthologized in Meeks and Fitzgerald 2007, 225–27.

12. *The Acts of Paul and Thecla,* ca. 190, included within the apocryphal *Acts of Paul.* The adventures of a female convert named Thecla, who at the narrative's end gets a call from Paul to be an apostle in her own right. Highly popular in late antiquity, the work generated the cult of Saint Thecla, which was widespread and with many veneration sites throughout

the Mediterranean world, and offers the only surviving description of what ancient Christians imagined Paul looked like: short, bald, bowlegged, having knit eyebrows and a crooked nose. Anthologized in Meeks and Fitzgerald 2007, 296–303.

13. "Paul and the Baptized Lion," ca. 190, an anonymous fable included within the apocryphal *Acts of Paul*. Paul encounters a friendly, talking lion that requests to be baptized. Later the plot circles back to the baptized lion, which is among the fierce beasts set loose on the condemned Paul but facilitates the apostle's escape. Loosely based on Paul's statement about fighting "wild beasts at Ephesus" (1 Cor. 15:32), this charming tale is a Christianized version of the famous Greco-Roman fable "Androclus and the lion" (see Aulus Gellius, *Attic Nights* 5.14), which circulated widely in classical antiquity for the amusement and instruction of children. Anthologized in Meeks and Fitzgerald 2007, 214–15.

14. *The Acts of Peter* (1–3), late second century. Describes Paul's departure from Rome for his missionary journey to Spain, which "fills in the gaps" of Paul's career (see Rom. 15:24, 28). Several of Paul's converts in the narrative are magistrates in Nero's court and high-ranking Roman women. Translated in Elliott 1993, 399–401.

15. *The Preachings of Peter*, also known as *Kerygmata Petrou*, second century, fragments of which are included within the later Pseudo-Clementine homilies (novel-like literature falsely ascribed to Saint Clement of Rome). This apocryphal work, produced by Jewish-Christian circles hostile to Pauline followers, denies that Peter preached the abandonment of the Jewish Law. Peter in the text debates with and condemns "Simon Magus" (the arch-heretic from Acts 8:9–24), but the particular substance of the polemic makes it clear that Paul is the figure being attacked – as the "apostle of Satan." Anthologized in Meeks and Fitzgerald 2007, 230–34.

16. *Recognitions of Clement* (1.70–71), of uncertain date (ca. late second century?), included within the Pseudo-Clementine homilies. This work preserves another fragmentary source that critiques Paul as the "persecutor of the faith," in ways similar to *The Preachings of Peter* and the "The Ascents of James." The source apparently stemmed from a Jerusalemite Christian community observant of Torah and hostile to Paul, which resettled in Pella, Macedonia, as refugees of the Jewish War against Rome in 68 C.E. Anthologized in Meeks and Fitzgerald 2007, 234–35.

17. "The Ascents of James," also known as *Anabathmoi Iakobou*, third century, extant only in paraphrase within the *Panarion* (*Haereses*) by the heresiologist Epiphanius of Salamis. This is an apocryphal account of the martyrdom of James (the brother of Jesus) by communities called Ebionites, which slanders Paul as born Gentile – an ethnic Greek passing as a believing Jew but in actuality "the enemy." Anthologized in Meeks and Fitzgerald 2007, 229–30.

18. Tertullian, *Against Marcion* (5.1), ca. 212. Tertullian imagines the patriarch Jacob prophesying in his last words to his sons (Gen. 49:27) that the "ravenous wolf" Paul will spring from the tribe of Benjamin to "educate Christ's sheep as a teacher of the nations." A fanciful attempt to find the two phases of Paul's life foretold in the Old Testament. Anthologized in Meeks and Fitzgerald 2007, 211–12.

19. Clement of Alexandria, *Stromata*, also known as *Miscellanies*, (3.53), ca. 215. A source that mentions Paul's "consort" (wife), who stayed at home while Paul went on his missionary journeys so as not to be "an inconvenience for his ministry." Clement concocts the legend from a misreading of Paul's reference to "my true companion" in Philippians 4:3. Anthologized in Meeks and Fitzgerald 2007, 213.

20. Clement of Alexandria, *Stromata*, also known as *Miscellanies*, (6.5), ca. 215. A source purporting to quote Paul saying that even pagan prophetic books, such as the *Sibylline Oracles*, support the truth of the Christian gospel. An attempt to trace this tradition of early Christian apologetics back to Paul himself. Anthologized in Meeks and Fitzgerald 2007, 216.

21. *The Acts of Xanthippe and Polyxena*, third century. An early Christian romance about a pair of female converts, the premise of whose adventures is that Paul had visited Spain. Translated in Craigie 1990.

22. Eusebius of Caesarea, *Ecclesiastical History* (2.25), early fourth century. Excerpts a tradition claiming to come from a Roman presbyter named Gaius (ca. 200), which tells pilgrims that the site of Paul's burial place, the "trophy" (memorial) of Paul, is just outside Rome on the road known as the Ostian Way. Translated in Williamson 1989, 63.

23. Jerome, *Commentary on Philemon* (on vv. 23–24) and *De viris illustribus* (5), 387–393. Jerome claims that Paul's family came from Palestine but had to emigrate from Gischala (modern Gush Halav) in the Upper Galilee when "the town was captured by the Romans" (ca. 6 c.e.?) to Tarsus in Cilicia. The church father also writes that Paul in his final days had not one but two trials before the emperor Nero: Paul's "first defense" was "dismissed by Nero," enabling Paul to preach the gospel in the West (an awkward attempt to harmonize the disparate sources of Acts 28:11–31; Rom. 15:24, 28; and 2 Tim. 4:16–17). At his "second defense," Paul was martyred (beheaded) in Rome "in the fourteenth year of Nero" (ca. 67/68) and buried "in the Ostian Road," the "twenty-seventh year after our Lord's passion." Translated with commentary in Murphy-O'Connor 1996, 37–39.

24. The Latin *Passion of Saint Paul the Apostle*, fourth century. Presents an apocryphal legend of Paul borrowing a scarf (veil) from a woman named Plautilla to use as a blindfold for his beheading and miraculously returning it to her. An obvious parallel to the apocryphal Jesus legend of Veronica's Veil. Discussed in Eastman 2011, 58–59, 65.

25. Ambrosiaster, *Commentary on Second Corinthians* (on 11:23), late fourth century. Imagines Paul's daily schedule: Paul spent his mornings ("from dawn to about eleven o'clock") doing manual labor in a local workshop, and his afternoons ("until four o'clock") preaching in public so energetically that he usually persuaded "those who spoke in opposition to him." Anthologized in Meeks and Fitzgerald 2007, 213.

26. Damasus of Rome, *Epigram* (20), 366–384. Placed on a marble plaque at the Roman Catacombs on the Appian Way, this poem by a Roman bishop commemorates the burials of Paul (and Peter) "here," which either means *at this site* or in the city of Rome *as a whole*. The latter may more likely be the original meaning, but the former is the more traditional one. Translated and discussed in Eastman 2011, 97–107.

27. Archaeological Works. In 390/91, the Roman emperor Theodosius I dedicated a new basilica on the Ostian Way to venerate the martyr cult site of Paul's tomb (replacing the emperor Constantine I's basilica on the site, built in the early fourth century), which stood largely intact until a devastating fire in 1823; the current church, Rome's second largest basilica and commonly called the church of Saint Paul Outside-the-Walls, was dedicated in 1854. In December 2006, Vatican archaeologists announced the discovery of a sarcophagus, or stone coffin, buried underneath the basilica's main altar, with a marble slab bearing the phrase "Apostle Paul, Martyr" (Latin *Paulo apostolo mart*) embedded in the floor above the tomb. In June 2009, Pope Benedict XVI declared that bone fragments found inside the sarcophagus are the mortal remains of the Apostle Paul, after scientific tests (carbon dating) dated them to the first or second century – "confirming the unanimous and uncontested tradition" of Saint Paul's tomb at the site. (A rival cult site for Paul's "tomb" is the double memorial to both the apostles Peter and Paul in the cemetery beneath the church of Saint Sebastian on the Appian Way).

28. The Latin *Passion of the Holy Apostles Peter and Paul*, sixth century. Locates the site of Paul's martyrdom on the Ostian Way, which leads to Rome's seaport of Ostia Antica at the mouth of the Tiber River. Also contains a legend that Greek Christians attempted to steal the bodies of Paul and Peter away to the East but were intercepted by Roman Christians, who buried the bodies temporarily "in a place called the Catacombs" on the Appian Way and later translated the relics to their permanent locations on the Ostian Way (for Paul) and at the Vatican (for Peter). Translated and discussed in Eastman 2011, 62–69, 110–11.

29. The Greek *Acts of the Holy Apostles Peter and Paul*, sixth century. In a close literary relationship with both of the Latin *Passions* mentioned previously, this work presents nonetheless an alternative tradition that locates the site of Paul's death on an estate called Aquae Salvias, which was on the Laurentinian Way (Via Laurentina), not the Ostian Way. It also repeats several other apocryphal legends. From the fourth-century

Latin *Passion*: the legend of the bloody scarf/veil but with the woman's name changed to Perpetua and an additional healing miracle (her blind eye is restored when she places the bloody scarf/veil back over her face). From the sixth-century Latin *Passion*: the legend of the bodies of Paul and Peter being taken from Rome, intercepted, and finally reburied in their permanent cult locations. Translated and discussed in Eastman 2011, 58–59, 62–69, 110–11.

NOTES AND FURTHER READING

Preface and Introduction

Biography: Jopling 1992; O'Brien 1991 (also antibiography); Weitzman 2011, ix–xxvi. Doing history: Tosh 2010, 88–146. Ancient letters as historical sources: White 2010, 63–64. Excellent introductions to Paul's life and letters, the Pauline pseudepigrapha, and the problem of using the Acts of the Apostles as history: Collins 1988; Ehrman 2012, 306–434; Knox 1987; Meeks and Fitzgerald 2007, xiv–xix; Roetzel 1998 and 2009. Ancient forgery: Ehrman 2011 and forthcoming. Paul and Gentile Christianity: Mitchell 2006.

Chapter 1

Paul's birth and education: Baumgarten 2000; Donfried 2006; Engberg-Pedersen 2001; Hays 1989; Hock 2003; Jaffee 2001, 39–64; Mason 2009, 185–215; Saldarini 1992; Stowers 1994. The event at Damascus and Paul's apocalyptic hope for Gentiles: Betz 1992; Eisenbaum 2009; Fredriksen 2002 and 2008, 20–39; Fredriksen 2012, 22–49; Riesner 1998, 14–15; Stendahl 1976, 7–23. Diaspora synagogues: Rajak 2006. From persecutor to apostle: Gager 1981; Hultgren 1976. Epiphanies and confessors: Lane Fox 1986, 376–81; Winkler 1985, 233–34, 238–41. Flight from Damascus: Campbell 2002; Welborn 1999. Jerusalem and Antioch: Fredriksen 2008, 16–40; Murphy-O'Connor 1996, 130–57; Sanders 1990.

Chapter 2

Ancient travel: Casson 1974; Lintott 2008, 257–58. Ancient workshops: Kehoe 2007. The workshop context of Paul's ministry: Hock 1980; Meeks

2003, 51–73. The social psychology of Paul's new converts: Harrill 2002; Malherbe 1987 and 2000, 105–33. Paul, Torah, and the challenge of another gospel: Fredriksen 2010; Gager 2000, 77–99; Gaston 1987; Hays 2002; Martyn 1997, 117–26, 302–6; Sanders 1977 and 1983. Paul's quarrelsome converts: Martin 1995; Meeks 2003; Meeks and Fitzgerald 2007, 21–23; Mitchell 2005. The crowning achievement of Paul's Aegean mission: cf. Sanders 1991, 18–22.

CHAPTER 3

Excellent survey of Roman history: Wells 1995. Paul and empire: Crossan and Reed 2004; Georgi 1991; Oakes 2005; Wengst 1987; cf. Brodd and Reed 2011. Roman cultural identities: Dench 2005; Jones 2004; Revell 2009; Wallace-Hadrill 2008. Roman provincial administration: Garnsey and Saller 1987, 20–40. Interpreting classical texts: Heath 2002, esp. 51–53. *Auctoritas*: Galinsky 1996 and 2012. Paul's discourse of authority: Harrill 2006, 22–26; Meeks 2002, 201; Meeks forthcoming. Valerius Maximus: Shackleton Bailey 2000, 75–83. Hidden transcripts: Scott 1990. Roman peace: Woolf 1993. Paul living within Roman authority: Engberg-Pedersen 2006; cf. Jewett 2007, 780–803. Paul and angels: Martin 2010, esp. 674.

CHAPTER 4

Paul the Roman hero: Eastman 2011; Klauck 2008; Pervo 2010, esp. 149–85; Trout 2005; see also Alexander 2005, 183–206; and Sterling 2007. The Roman religious context: Beard, North, and Price 1998, ix–x, 20–21, 132–34; Luck 2006, 210; MacMullen 2010. Constantine the Great: Cameron 2006; Drake 2000. Paul the sexual role model: Balch 1981 and 1988; Dunning 2011; Ehrman 2012, 421–34; Harrill 2006, 35–36; MacDonald 1983; Martin 2006, 65–76; Meeks 1993. Paul the Deceiver: Berchman 2004; Crook 2002; Klijn and Reinink 1973; Meeks and Fitzgerald 2007, 228–35, 265–71.

CHAPTER 5

Paul becomes a book: Pervo 2010, 23–61; see also Dassmann 1979; Lindemann 1979; and Rensberger 1981. Marcion and Valentinus: Barton 1997, 35–62; Brakke 2010 and 2012; Dahl 2000; Gamble 2006; Harnack 1990; Marshall 2012. Irenaeus of Lyons: Grant 1997; Minns 2006; Norris 1990;

Osborn 2001. Origen of Alexandria: Heine 2010, 144–218. John Chrysostom: Mitchell 2002.

Chapter 6

The Manichaean Paul: Bammel 1993; BeDuhn 2010; Betz 1986; Gardner and Lieu 2004; Lieu 1992. First Latin commentaries on Paul: Lunn-Rockliffe 2007; Wiles 1967. Pelagius's Paul: De Bruyn 1993; Rees 1991. Augustine's Paul and its legacy: Bammel 1992; Beatrice forthcoming; Fredriksen 1986, 2008, 2009, and 2012; Gamble 1995, 239–40; Martin 2000; Mattox 2009; Meeks and Fitzgerald 2007, 355–433, 689–94; Stendahl 1976, 78–96; Westerholm 2004. Paul the second founder of Christianity: Baur 1875, 3–4; Baur 1878, 44–66, 75–77; Harnack 1957, 176–89; Meeks and Fitzgerald 2007, 395–433.

Conclusion

Archaeological discoveries at Paul's tomb site: Eastman 2011, 36–42; Valsecchi 2006. Papal verification of Paul's bones: Fournier 2009; *New York Times* 2009.

BIBLIOGRAPHY

Alexander, Loveday C. A. 2005. *Acts in Its Ancient Literary Context: A Classicist Looks at the Acts of the Apostles*. London: T. and T. Clark International.

Anthony, Sean W. 2009. "The Composition of Sayf b. 'Umar's Account of King Paul and His Corruption of Ancient Christianity." *Der Islam* 85: 164–202.

Balch, David L. 1981. *Let Wives Be Submissive: The Domestic Code of 1 Peter*. Chico, Calif.: Scholars Press.

———. 1988. "Household Codes." Pages 25–50 in *Greco-Roman Literature and the New Testament*. Edited by David E. Aune. Atlanta: Scholars Press.

Bammel, Caroline P. 1992. "Augustine, Origen and the Exegesis of St. Paul." *Augustianum* 32: 341–68.

———. 1993. "Pauline Exegesis, Manichaeism and Philosophy in the Early Augustine." Pages 1–25 in *Christian Faith and Greek Philosophy in Late Antiquity: Essays in Tribute to George Christopher Stead*. Edited by Lionel R. Wickham and Caroline P. Bammel. Leiden: E. J. Brill.

Barton, John. 1997. *Holy Writings, Sacred Text: The Canon in Early Christianity*. Louisville, Ky.: Westminster John Knox Press.

Baumgarten, Albert I. 2000. "Seekers after Smooth Things." Pages 857–59 in vol. 2 of Schiffman and VanderKam 2000.

Baur, Ferdinand Christian. 1875. *Paul, the Apostle of Jesus Christ: His Life and Work, His Epistles and His Doctrine: A Contribution to a Critical History of Primitive Christianity*. Vol. 1. 1845. Edited by Eduard Zeller. Translated by Allan Menzies. London: Williams and Norgate.

———. 1878. *The Church History of the First Three Centuries*. 3d ed. Vol. 1. 1860. Translated by Allan Menzies. London: Williams and Norgate. Excerpts anthologized in Meeks and Fitzgerald 2007, 399–408.

Beard, Mary, John North, and Simon Price. 1998. *Religions of Rome. Volume 1: A History*. Cambridge: Cambridge University Press.

Beatrice, Pier Franco. Forthcoming. *The Transmission of Sin: Augustine and His Sources*. 1978. Translated by Adam Kamesar. New York: Oxford University Press.

BeDuhn, Jason David. 2010. *Augustine's Manichaean Dilemma. Volume 1: Conversion and Apostasy, 373–388 C.E.* Philadelphia: University of Pennsylvania Press.

Berchman, Robert M. 2004. *Porphyry against the Christians.* Leiden: E. J. Brill.

Bettenson, Henry, trans. 1972. *Concerning the City of God against the Pagans / Augustine.* New York: Penguin Books.

Betz, Hans Dieter. 1986. "Paul in the Mani Biography (Codex Manichaicus Coloniensis)." Pages 215–34 in *Codex Manichaicus Coloniensis: Atti del simposio internazionale.* Edited by Luigi Cirillo. Cosenza: Marra Editore.

———. 1992. "Paul." Pages 186–201 in vol. 5 of Freedman 1992.

———. 1994. "2 Cor 6:14–7:1: An Anti-Pauline Fragment?" 1973. Reprint. Pages 20–45 in idem, *Paulinische Studien: Gesammelte Aufsatze III.* Tübingen: Mohr Siebeck.

Brakke, David. 2010. *The Gnostics: Myth, Ritual, and Diversity in Early Christianity.* Cambridge, Mass.: Harvard University Press.

———. 2012. "Scriptural Practices in Early Christianity: Towards a New History of the New Testament Canon." Pages 263–80 in *Invention, Rewriting, Usurpation: Discursive Fights over Religious Traditions in Antiquity.* Edited by Jörg Ulrich, Anders-Christian Jacobsen, and David Brakke. Frankfurt: Peter Lang.

Brisson, Luc. 2004. *How Philosophers Saved Myths: Allegorical Interpretation and Classical Mythology.* 1996. Translated by Catherine Tihanyi. Chicago: University of Chicago Press.

Brodd, Jeffrey, and Jonathan L. Reed, eds. 2011. *Rome and Religion: A Cross-Disciplinary Dialogue on the Imperial Cult.* Atlanta: Society of Biblical Literature.

Brooke, George J. 2000. "Florilegium." Pages 297–98 in vol. 1 of Schiffman and VanderKam 2000.

Brunt, P. A., and J. M. Moore, eds. 1967. *Res Gestae Divi Augusti: The Achievements of the Divine Augustus.* New York: Oxford University Press.

Burchard, C. 1985. "Joseph and Aseneth." Pages 177–247 in *The Old Testament Pseudepigrapha. Volume 2: Expansions of the "Old Testament" and Legends, Wisdom and Philosophical Literature, Prayers, Psalms, and Odes, Fragments of Lost Judeo-Hellenistic Works.* Edited by James H. Charlesworth. Garden City, N.Y.: Doubleday.

Burnaby, John, trans. 1955. *Augustine: Later Works.* Philadelphia: Westminster Press.

Burns, J. Patout. 1981. *Theological Anthropology.* Philadelphia: Fortress Press.

Cameron, Averil. 2006. "Constantine and the 'Peace of the Church.'" Pages 538–51 in Mitchell and Young 2006.

Campbell, Douglas A. 2002. "An Anchor for Pauline Chronology: Paul's Flight from 'the Ethnarch of King Aretas' (2 Corinthians 11:32–33)." *Journal of Biblical Literature* 121: 279–302.

Carriker, Anne P. 1999. "Augustine's Frankness in his Dispute with Jerome over the Interpretation of Galatians 2:11–14." Pages 121–38 in *Nova*

Doctrina Vetusque: Essays on Early Christianity in Honor of Fredric W. Schlatter, S.J. Edited by Douglas Kries and Catherine Brown Tkacz. New York: Peter Lang.

Casson, Lionel. 1974. *Travel in the Ancient World*. Toronto: Hakkert.

Chadwick, Henry, trans. 2008. *Confessions / Saint Augustine*. Oxford: Oxford University Press.

Collins, Raymond F. 1988. *Letters That Paul Did Not Write: The Epistle to the Hebrews and the Pauline Pseudepigrapha*. Wilmington, Del.: Michael Glazier.

Colson, F. H., trans. 1939. *On the Special Laws, Book 4. On the Virtues. On Rewards and Punishments / Philo*. Vol. 8. Loeb Classical Library. Cambridge, Mass.: Harvard University Press.

———, trans. 1962. *On the Embassy to Gaius / Philo*. Vol. 10. Loeb Classical Library. Cambridge, Mass.: Harvard University Press.

Cooley, Alison. 2009. *Res Gestae Divi Augusti: Text, Translation, and Commentary*. Cambridge: Cambridge University Press.

Cox, David. 1959. *Jung and St Paul: A Study of the Doctrine of Justification by Faith and its Relation to the Concept of Individuation*. New York: Association Press.

Craigie, W. A., trans. 1990. "The Acts of Xanthippe and Polyxena." Pages 203–17 in *The Ante-Nicene Fathers: Translations of the Writings of the Fathers down to A.D. 325*. Vol. 10, Original Supplement to the American Edition. Edited by Allan Menzies. 1885. Reprint. Grand Rapids, Mich.: William B. Eerdmans.

Crook, John Granger. 2002. *The Interpretation of the Old Testament in Greco-Roman Paganism*. Peabody, Mass.: Hendrickson.

Crossan, John Dominic, and Jonathan L. Reed. 2004. *In Search of Paul: How Jesus's Apostle Opposed Rome's Empire with God's Kingdom*. San Francisco: HarperSanFrancisco.

Dahl, Nils Alstrup. 2000. "The Particularity of the Pauline Epistles as a Problem in the Ancient Church." 1962. Reprint. Pages 165–78 in idem, *Studies in Ephesians: Introductory Questions, Text- & Edition-Critical Issues, Interpretation of Texts and Themes*. Edited by David Hellholm, Vemund Blomkvist, and Tord Fornberg. Tübingen: Mohr Siebeck.

Dassmann, Ernst. 1979. *Der Stachel im Fleisch: Paulus in der frühchristlichen Literatur bis Irenäus*. Münster: Aschendorff.

Davis, Stephen J. 2001. *The Cult of Saint Thecla: A Tradition of Women's Piety in Late Antiquity*. Oxford: Oxford University Press.

De Bruyn, Theodore. 1993. *Pelagius' Commentary on St Paul's Epistle to the Romans: Translated with Introduction and Notes*. Oxford: Clarendon.

Dench, Emma. 2005. *Romulus' Asylum: Roman Identities from the Age of Alexander to the Age of Hadrian*. Oxford: Oxford University Press.

Donfried, Karl P. 2006. "Rethinking Paul: On the Way Toward a Revised Paradigm." *Biblica* 87: 582–94.

Drake, H. A. 2000. *Constantine and the Bishops: The Politics of Intolerance*. Baltimore, Md.: Johns Hopkins University Press.

Dunning, Benjamin H. 2011. *Specters of Paul: Sexual Difference in Early Christian Thought*. Philadelphia: University of Pennsylvania Press.

Eastman, David L. 2011. *Paul the Martyr: The Cult of the Apostle in the Latin West*. Atlanta: Society of Biblical Literature.

Ehrman, Bart D. 2003. *The Apostolic Fathers*. 2 vols. Loeb Classical Library. Cambridge, Mass.: Harvard University Press.

———. 2011. *Forged: Writing in the Name of God. Why the Bible's Authors Are Not Who We Think They Are*. New York: HarperOne.

———. 2012. *The New Testament: A Historical Introduction to the Early Christian Writings*. 5th ed. New York: Oxford University Press.

———. Forthcoming. *Forgery and Counterforgery: The Use of Literary Deceit in Early Christian Polemics*. New York: Oxford University Press.

Eisenbaum, Pamela. 2009. *Paul Was Not a Christian: The Original Message of a Misunderstood Apostle*. New York: HarperCollins.

Elliott, J. K. 1993. *The Apocryphal New Testament: A Collection of Apocryphal Christian Literature in an English Translation*. Oxford: Clarendon Press.

Engberg-Pedersen, Troels. 2006. "Paul's Stoicizing Politics in Romans 12–13: The Role of 13.1–10 in the Argument." *Journal for the Study of the New Testament* 29: 163–72.

Engberg-Pedersen, Troels, ed. 2001. *Paul Beyond the Judaism / Hellenism Divide*. Louisville, Ky.: Westminster John Knox Press.

Evans, Ernest, ed. and trans. 1972. *Adversus Marcionem / Tertullian*. Vol. 2. Oxford: Clarendon Press.

Feldman, Louis H., trans. 1965. *Jewish Antiquities: Book 20 / Josephus*. Vol. 9. Loeb Classical Library. Cambridge, Mass.: Harvard University Press.

Fournier, Keith. 2009. "Pope: Bones of the Apostle Paul Scientifically Verified." *Catholic Online*. 30 June. www.Catholic.org.

Fredriksen, Paula. 1986. "Paul and Augustine: Conversion Narratives, Orthodox Traditions, and the Retrospective Self." *Journal of Theological Studies*, n.s. 37: 3–34.

———. 2002. "Judaism, the Circumcision of Gentiles, and Apocalyptic Hope: Another Look at Galatians 1 and 2." 1991. Reprint. Pages 235–60 in *The Galatians Debate: Contemporary Issues in Rhetorical and Historical Interpretation*. Edited by Mark D. Nanos. Peabody, Mass.: Hendrickson.

———. 2008. *Augustine and the Jews*. New York: Doubleday.

———. 2009. "Paul." Pages 621–28 in *Augustine through the Ages: An Encyclopedia*. Edited by Allan D. Fitzgerald. Grand Rapids, Mich.: William B. Eerdmans.

———. 2010. "Judaizing the Nations: The Ritual Demands of Paul's Gospel." *New Testament Studies* 56: 232–52.

———. 2012. *Sin: An Early History of an Idea*. Princeton: Princeton University Press.

———. Forthcoming. "Retrospect is the Mother of Anachronism, or How Later Contexts Affect Pauline Content." *Jews and Christians in the First and Second*

Centuries: How to Write Their History. Edited by Peter J. Tomson and Joshua Schwartz. Leiden: E. J. Brill.

Freedman, David Noel, ed. 1992. *The Anchor Bible Dictionary*. 6 vols. New York: Doubleday.

Freud, Sigmund. 1939. *Moses and Monotheism*. Translated by Katherine Jones. New York: Vintage Books.

Friesen, Steven J. 2010. "The Wrong Erastus: Ideology, Archaeology, and Exegesis." Pages 231–56 in *Corinth in Context: Comparative Studies on Religion and Society*. Edited by Steven J. Friesen, Daniel N. Schowalter, and James C. Walters. Leiden: E. J. Brill.

Gager, John G. 1981. "Some Notes on Paul's Conversion." *New Testament Studies* 27: 697–704.

_____. 2000. *Reinventing Paul*. New York: Oxford University Press.

Galinsky, Karl. 1996. *Augustan Culture: An Interpretive Introduction*. Princeton: Princeton University Press.

_____. 2012. *Augustus: Introduction to the Life of an Emperor*. Cambridge: Cambridge University Press.

Gamble, Harry Y. 1995. *Books and Readers in the Early Church: A History of Early Christian Texts*. New Haven: Yale University Press.

_____. 2006. "Marcion and the 'Canon.'" Pages 195–213 in Mitchell and Young 2006.

Gardner, Iain, and Samuel N. C. Lieu, eds. 2004. *Manichaean Texts from the Roman Empire*. Cambridge: Cambridge University Press.

Garnsey, Peter, and Richard Saller. 1987. *The Roman Empire: Economy, Society and Culture*. Berkeley and Los Angeles: University of California Press.

Gaston, Lloyd. 1987. *Paul and the Torah*. Vancouver: University of British Columbia Press.

Georgi, Dieter. 1991. *Theocracy in Paul's Praxis and Theology*. 1987. Translated by David E. Green. Minneapolis: Fortress Press.

Gilbert, Gary. 1991. "The Making of a Jew: 'God-fearer' or Convert in the Story of Izates." *Union Seminary Quarterly Review* 44: 299–313.

Gillman, Florence Morgan. 1992. "Erastus." Page 571 in vol. 2 of Freedman 1992.

Goldman, Arthur (Steven). 2011. *Four Square and the Politics of Sixth Grade Lunch*. Westerville, Ohio: National Middle School Association.

Grant, Robert M. 1997. *Irenaeus of Lyons*. London: Routledge.

Griffiths, Paul J. 2004. *Lying: An Augustinian Theology of Duplicity*. Grand Rapids, Mich.: Brazos Press.

Harnack, Adolf von. 1957. *What is Christianity?* 1900. Translated by Thomas Bailey Saunders. New York: Harper. Excerpts anthologized in Meeks and Fitzgerald 2007, 419–24.

_____. 1990. *Marcion: The Gospel of the Alien God*. 1924. Translated by John E. Steely and Lyle D. Bierma. Durham, N.C.: Labyrinth Press.

Harrill, J. Albert. 2002. "Coming of Age and Putting on Christ: The *Toga Virilis* Ceremony, Its Paraenesis, and Paul's Language of Baptism in Galatians." *Novum Testamentum* 44: 251–77.

———. 2003. "Paul and Slavery." Pages 575–607 in Sampley 2003.

———. 2006. *Slaves in the New Testament: Literary, Social, and Moral Dimensions*. Minneapolis: Fortress Press.

———. 2010. "Stoic Physics, the Universal Conflagration, and the Eschatological Destruction of 'the Ignorant and Unstable' in 2 Peter." Pages 115–40 in *Stoicism in Early Christianity*. Edited by Tuomas Rasimus, Troels Engberg-Pedersen, and Ismo Dunderberg. Grand Rapids, Mich.: Baker Academic.

———. 2011. "Paul and Empire: Studying Roman Identity after the Cultural Turn." *Early Christianity* 2: 281–311.

Harrison, Geoffrey, and Jason BeDuhn. 2001. "The Authenticity and Doctrine of (Ps.?) Mani's *Letter to Menoch*." Pages 128–72 in *The Light and the Darkness: Studies in Manichaeism and its World*. Edited by Paul Mirecki and Jason BeDuhn. Leiden: E. J. Brill.

Hays, Richard B. 1989. *Echoes of Scripture in the Letters of Paul*. New Haven: Yale University Press.

———. 2002. *The Faith of Jesus Christ: The Narrative Substructure of Galatians 3:1–4:11*. 2d ed. Grand Rapids, Mich.: William B. Eerdmans.

Heath, Malcom. 2002. *Interpreting Classical Texts*. London: Duckworth.

Heine, Ronald E. 2010. *Origen: Scholarship in the Service of the Church*. New York: Oxford University Press.

Hemingway, Ernest. 1929. *A Farewell to Arms*. New York: Charles Scribner's Sons.

Hock, Ronald F. 1980. *The Social Context of Paul's Ministry: Tentmaking and Apostleship*. Philadelphia: Fortress Press.

———. 2003. "Paul and Greco-Roman Education." Pages 198–227 in Sampley 2003.

Hultgren, Arland J. 1976. "Paul's Pre-Christian Persecutions of the Church: Their Purpose, Locale, and Nature." *Journal of Biblical Literature* 95: 97–111.

Jaffee, Martin S. 2001. *Torah in the Mouth: Writing and Oral Tradition in Palestinian Judaism, 200 BCE–400 CE*. New York: Oxford University Press.

Jewett, Robert. 2007. *Romans: A Commentary*. Hermeneia. Minneapolis: Fortress Press.

Jones, Christopher P. 2004. "Multiple Identities in the Age of the Second Sophistic." Pages 13–21 in *Paideia: The World of the Second Sophistic*. Edited by Barbara E. Borg. Berlin: Walter de Gruyter.

Jones, Horace Leonard, trans. 1929. *Geography / Strabo*. Vol. 6. Loeb Classical Library. Cambridge, Mass.: Harvard University Press.

Jopling, David A. 1992. "At the Limits of Biographical Knowledge: Sartre and Levinas." Pages 79–101 in *Shaping Lives: Reflections on Biography*. Edited by Ian Donaldson, Peter Read, and James Walter. Canberra: The Humanities Research Centre of the Australian National University.

Kehoe, Dennis P. 2007. "The Early Roman Empire: Production." Pages 543–69 in *The Cambridge Economic History of the Greco-Roman World*. Edited by Walter Scheidel, Ian Morris, and Richard Saller. Cambridge: Cambridge University Press.

Kent, John Harvey. 1966. *Corinth: Results of Excavations Conducted by the American School of Classical Studies at Athens. Volume 8, Part 3: The Inscriptions, 1926–1950*. Princeton: American School of Classical Studies at Athens.

Klauck, Hans-Josef. 2008. *The Apocryphal Acts of the Apostles: An Introduction*. Waco, Tex.: Baylor University Press.

Klijn, A. F. J., and G. J. Reinink. 1973. *Patristic Evidence for Jewish Christian Sects*. Leiden: E. J. Brill.

Knox, John. 1987. *Chapters in a Life of Paul*. Rev. ed. Macon, Ga.: Mercer University Press.

Koningsveld, P. S. van. 1996. "The Islamic Image of Paul and the Origin of the Gospel of Barnabas." *Jerusalem Studies in Arabic and Islam* 20: 200–228.

Lane Fox, Robin. 1986. *Pagans and Christians*. New York: Alfred A. Knopf.

Langton, Daniel R. 2010. *The Apostle Paul in the Jewish Imagination: A Study in Modern Jewish-Christian Relations*. Cambridge: Cambridge University Press.

Layton, Bentley, trans. 1987. "The Reality of the Rulers." Pages 69–79 in idem, *The Gnostic Scriptures: A New Translation with Annotations and Introductions*. New York: Doubleday.

Lieu, Samuel N. C. 1992. *Manichaeism in the Later Roman Empire and Medieval China*. Tübingen: Mohr Siebeck.

Lim, Timothy H. 2002. *Pesharim*. London: Sheffield Academic Press.

Lindemann, Andreas. 1979. *Paulus im ältesten Christentum: Das Bild des Apostels und die Rezeption der paulinischen Theologie in der frühchristlichen Literatur bis Marcion*. Tübingen: Mohr Siebeck.

Lintott, Andrew. 2008. *Cicero as Evidence: A Historian's Companion*. New York: Oxford University Press.

Lipsett, B. Diane. 2011. *Desiring Conversion: Hermas, Thecla, Aseneth*. New York: Oxford University Press.

Luck, Georg. 2006. *Arcana Mundi: Magic and the Occult in the Greek and Roman Worlds: A Collection of Ancient Texts*. 2d ed. Baltimore: Johns Hopkins University Press.

Lunn-Rockliffe, Sophie. 2007. *Ambrosiaster's Political Theology*. New York: Oxford University Press.

MacDonald, Dennis Ronald. 1983. *The Legend of the Apostle: The Battle for Paul in Story and Canon*. Philadelphia: Westminster Press.

MacMullen, Ramsay. 2010. "Christian Ancestor Worship in Rome." *Journal of Biblical Literature* 129: 597–613.

Malherbe, Abraham J. 1987. *Paul and the Thessalonians: The Philosophical Tradition of Pastoral Care*. Minneapolis: Fortress Press.

———. 1998. "Conversion to Paul's Gospel." Pages 231–44 in *The Early Church and Its Context: Essays in Honor of Everett Ferguson*. Edited by

Abraham J. Malherbe, Frederick W. Norris, and James W. Thompson. Leiden: E. J. Brill.

———. 2000. *The Letters to the Thessalonians: A New Translation with Introduction and Commentary*. Anchor Bible 32b. New York: Doubleday.

Marshall, John W. 2012. "Misunderstanding the New Paul: Marcion's Transformation of the *Sonderzeit* Paul." *Journal of Early Christian Studies* 20: 1–29.

Martin, Dale B. 1990. *Slavery as Salvation: The Metaphor of Slavery in Pauline Christianity*. New Haven: Yale University Press.

———. 1995. *The Corinthian Body*. New Haven: Yale University Press.

———. 2006. *Sex and the Single Savior: Gender and Sexuality in Biblical Interpretation*. Louisville, Ky.: Westminster John Knox Press.

———. 2010. "When Did Angels Become Demons?" *Journal of Biblical Literature* 129: 657–77.

Martin, Thomas F. 2000. "*Vox Pauli*: Augustine and the Claims to Speak for Paul, an Exploration of Rhetoric at the Service of Exegesis." *Journal of Early Christian Studies* 8: 237–72.

Martyn, J. Louis. 1997. *Galatians: A New Translation and Commentary*. Anchor Bible 33a. New York: Doubleday.

Mason, Steve. 1991. *Flavius Josephus on the Pharisees: A Comparative-Critical Study*. Leiden: E. J. Brill.

———. 2009. *Josephus, Judea, and Christian Origins: Methods and Categories*. Peabody, Mass.: Hendrickson.

Mattox, Micky L. 2009. "Martin Luther's Reception of Paul." Pages 93–128 in *A Companion to Paul in the Reformation*. Edited by R. Ward Holder. Leiden: E. J. Brill.

Meeks, Wayne A. 1993. "'To Walk Worthily of the Lord': Moral Formation in the Pauline School as Exemplified by the Letter to Colossians." Pages 37–58 in *Hermes and Athena: Biblical Exegesis and Philosophical Authority*. Edited by Eleonore Stump and Thomas P. Flint. Notre Dame, Ind.: University of Notre Dame Press.

———. 2002. *In Search of the Early Christians: Selected Essays*. Edited by Allen R. Hilton and H. Gregory Snyder. New Haven: Yale University Press.

———. 2003. *The First Urban Christians: The Social World of the Apostle Paul*. 2d ed. New Haven: Yale University Press.

———. Forthcoming. "From Jerusalem to Illyricum, Rome to Spain: The World of Paul's Missionary Imagination." *The Rise and Expansion of Christianity in the First Three Centuries C.E.* Edited by Clare E. Rothschild and Jens Schröter. Tübingen: Mohr Siebeck.

Meeks, Wayne A., and John T. Fitzgerald, eds. 2007. *The Writings of St. Paul: Annotated Texts, Reception and Criticism*. 2d ed. Norton Critical Editions. New York: W. W. Norton.

Minns, Denis. 2006. "Truth and Tradition: Irenaeus." Pages 261–273 in Mitchell and Young 2006.

Mitchell, Margaret M. 2002. *The Heavenly Trumpet: John Chrysostom and the Art of Biblical Interpretation.* Louisville, Ky.: Westminster John Knox Press.

———. 2005. "Paul's Letter to Corinth: The Interpretive Intertwining of Literary and Historical Reconstruction." Pages 307–38 in *Urban Religion in Roman Corinth: Interdisciplinary Approaches.* Edited by Daniel N. Showalter and Steven J. Friesen. Cambridge, Mass.: Harvard University Press.

———. 2006. "Gentile Christianity." Pages 103–24 in Mitchell and Young 2006.

———. 2007. "The Letter of James as a Document of Paulinism?" Pages 75–98 in *Reading James with New Eyes: Methodological Reassessments of the Letter of James.* Edited by Robert L. Webb and John S. Kloppenborg. London: T. and T. Clark International.

———. 2012. "Peter's 'Hypocrisy' and Paul's: Two 'Hypocrites' at the Foundation of Earliest Christianity." *New Testament Studies* 58: 213–34.

Mitchell, Margaret M., and Frances M. Young, eds. 2006. *The Cambridge History of Christianity. Volume 1: Origins to Constantine.* Cambridge: Cambridge University Press.

Murphy-O'Connor, Jerome. 1996. *Paul: A Critical Life.* Oxford: Clarendon.

New York Times. 2009. "Pope Says Tests 'Seem to Conclude' Bones Are the Apostle Paul's." By the Associated Press. June 29, the New York edition, A5.

Norris, Richard A., Jr. 1990. "Irenaeus' Use of Paul in His Polemic against the Gnostics." Pages 79–98 in *Paul and the Legacies of Paul.* Edited by William S. Babcock. Dallas: Southern Methodist University Press.

Oakes, Peter. 2005. "Re-mapping the Universe: Paul and the Emperor in 1 Thessalonians and Philippians." *Journal for the Study of the New Testament* 27: 301–22.

O'Brien, Sharon. 1991. "Feminist Theory and Literary Biography." Pages 123–33 in *Contesting the Subject: Essays in the Postmodern Theory and Practice of Biography and Biographical Criticism.* Edited by William H. Epstein. West Lafayette, Ind.: Purdue University Press.

Osborn, Eric. 2001. *Irenaeus of Lyons.* Cambridge: Cambridge University Press.

Pervo, Richard I. 2010. *The Making of Paul: Constructions of the Apostle in Early Christianity.* Minneapolis: Fortress Press.

Rajak, Tessa. 2006. "The Jewish Diaspora." Pages 53–68 in Mitchell and Young 2006.

Rees, B. R. 1991. *The Letters of Pelagius and His Followers.* Woodbridge: Boydell.

Rensberger, David K. 1981. "As the Apostle Teaches: The Development of the Use of Paul's Letters in Second-Century Christianity." Ph.D. diss., Yale University.

Revell, Louise. 2009. *Roman Imperialism and Local Roman Identities.* Cambridge: Cambridge University Press.

Riesner, Rainer. 1998. *Paul's Early Period: Chronology, Mission Strategy, Theology.* 1994. Translated by Doug Stott. Grand Rapids, Mich.: William B. Eerdmans.

Robinson, James M. 1988. *The Nag Hammadi Library in English.* 3d ed. San Francisco: Harper and Row.

Roetzel, Calvin J. 1998. *Paul: The Man and the Myth*. Columbia: University of South Carolina Press.

———. 2007. *2 Corinthians*. Nashville, Tenn.: Abingdon Press.

———. 2009. *The Letters of Paul: Conversations in Context*. 5th ed. Louisville, Ky.: Westminster John Knox Press.

Saldarini, Anthony J. 1992. "Pharisees." Pages 289–303 in vol. 5 of Freedman 1992.

Sampley, J. Paul, ed. 2003. *Paul in the Greco-Roman World: A Handbook*. Harrisburg, Pa.: Trinity Press International.

Sanders, E. P. 1977. *Paul and Palestinian Judaism*. Minneapolis: Fortress Press.

———. 1983. *Paul, the Law, and the Jewish People*. Minneapolis: Fortress Press.

———. 1990. "Jewish Associations with Gentiles and Galatians 2:11–14." Pages 170–88 in *The Conversation Continues: Studies in Paul and John in Honor of J. Louis Martyn*. Edited by Robert T. Fortna and Beverly R. Gaventa. Nashville, Tenn.: Abingdon Press.

———. 1991. *Paul: A Very Short Introduction*. New York: Oxford University Press.

Sartre, Jean-Paul. 1977. "On *The Idiot of the Family*." Pages 109–32 in idem, *Life/Situations: Essays Written and Spoken*. 1975. Translated by Paul Auster and Lydia Davis. New York: Pantheon Books.

———. 1981–1993. *The Family Idiot: Gustave Flaubert, 1821–1857*. 1971–1972. Translated by Carol Cosman. 5 vols. Chicago: University of Chicago Press.

Schaff, Philip, ed. 1994. *A Select Library of the Nicene and Post-Nicene Fathers of the Christian Church: First Series. Volume 13: Saint Chrysostom: Homilies on Galatians, Ephesians, Philippians, Colossians, Thessalonians, Timothy, Titus, and Philemon*. 1886. Reprint. Grand Rapids, Mich.: William B. Eerdmans.

Schiffman, Lawrence H., and James C. VanderKam, eds. 2000. *Encyclopedia of the Dead Sea Scrolls*. 2 vols. New York: Oxford University Press.

Scott, James C. 1990. *Domination and the Arts of Resistance: Hidden Transcripts*. New Haven: Yale University Press.

Shackleton Bailey, D. R., trans. 2000. *Memorial Doings and Sayings / Valerius Maximus*. Vol. 2. Loeb Classical Library. Cambridge, Mass.: Harvard University Press.

Stendahl, Krister. 1976. *Paul Among Jews and Gentiles*. Philadelphia: Fortress Press.

Sterling, Gregory E. 2007. "From Apostle to the Gentiles to Apostle of the Church: Images of Paul at the End of the First Century." *Zeitschrift für die neutestamentliche Wissenschaft* 98: 74–98.

Stern, S. M. 1968. "'Abd al-Jabbār's Account of How Christ's Religion Was Falsified by the Adoption of Roman Customs." *Journal of Theological Studies*, n.s. 19: 128–85.

Stowers, Stanley K. 1994. *A Rereading of Romans: Justice, Jews, and Gentiles*. New Haven: Yale University Press.

Thackeray, H. St. J., trans. 1989. *The Jewish War / Josephus*. Vol. 2. Loeb Classical Library. Cambridge, Mass.: Harvard University Press.

Tosh, John. 2010. *The Pursuit of History: Aims, Methods and New Directions in the Study of Modern History*. 5th ed. Harlow: Pearson Education Limited.

Trout, Dennis E. 2005. "Damasus and the Invention of Early Christian Rome." Pages 298–315 in *The Cultural Turn in Late Ancient Studies: Gender, Asceticism, and Historiography*. Edited by Dale B. Martin and Patricia Cox Miller. Durham, N.C.: Duke University Press.

Valsecchi, Maria Cristina. 2006. "St. Paul's Tomb Unearthed in Rome." *National Geographic News*. 11 December. news.nationalgeographic.com

Vermes, Geza. 2004. *The Complete Dead Sea Scrolls in English*. Rev. ed. New York: Penguin Books.

Wallace-Hadrill, Andrew. 2008. *Rome's Cultural Revolution*. Cambridge: Cambridge University Press.

Weitzman, Steven. 2011. *Solomon: The Lure of Wisdom*. New Haven: Yale University Press.

Welborn, Laurence L. 1999. "The Runaway Paul." *Harvard Theological Review*. 92: 115–63.

Wells, Colin. 1995. *The Roman Empire*. 2d ed. Cambridge: Mass.: Harvard University Press.

Wengst, Klaus. 1987. *Pax Romana and the Peace of Jesus Christ*. 1986. Translated by John Bowden. Philadelphia: Fortress Press.

Westerholm, Stephen. 2004. *Perspectives Old and New on Paul: The "Lutheran" Paul and His Critics*. Grand Rapids, Mich.: William B. Eerdmans.

White, Peter. 2010. *Cicero in Letters: Epistolary Relations of the Late Republic*. New York: Oxford University Press.

Wiles, Maurice F. 1967. *The Divine Apostle: The Interpretation of St Paul's Epistles in the Early Church*. Cambridge: Cambridge University Press.

Williamson, G. A., trans. 1989. *The History of the Church from Christ to Constantine / Eusebius*. 1965. Revised and edited by Andrew Louth. London: Penguin Books.

Wills, Lawrence M. 1991. "The Depiction of the Jews in Acts." *Journal of Biblical Literature* 110: 631–54.

Winkler, John J. 1985. *Auctor & Actor: A Narratological Reading of Apuleius's "The Golden Ass."* Berkeley and Los Angeles: University of California Press.

Woolf, Greg. 1993. "Roman Peace." Pages 171–94 in *War and Society in the Roman World*. Edited by John Rich and Graham Shipley. London: Routledge.

INDEX OF BIBLICAL CITATIONS

INDEX